A YEAR IN THE LIFE OF
MEDIEVAL
ENGLAND

Toni Mount has been a history teacher for twenty years. She has an MA for her research on medieval medical manuscripts from the University of Kent. Her previous books include *Everyday Life in Medieval London*, *The Medieval Housewife* and *Dragon's Blood & Willow Bark*, all published by Amberley.

A YEAR IN THE LIFE OF
MEDIEVAL
ENGLAND

TONI MOUNT

AMBERLEY

To Bethan Lily, Owen Thomas and Isaac Albert – the new generation of Mounts

This edition published 2019

Amberley Publishing
The Hill, Stroud
Gloucestershire, GL5 4EP

www.amberley-books.com

British Library Cataloguing in Publication Data.
A catalogue record for this book is available from the British Library.

ISBN 978 1 4456 9444 3 (paperback)
ISBN 978 1 4456 5240 5 (ebook)

Typesetting and Origination by Amberley Publishing.
Printed in the UK.

CONTENTS

INTRODUCTION

A Year in the Life of Medieval England was conceived as a diary with entries covering events from AD 1066 to 1500, one for each day of the year, including 29 February. I tried to select a wide range of subject matter: from local news and weather reports to events of national significance; from poetry to health and gardening tips, songs and cookery recipes – a mixture of items like those we might see today in newspapers and magazines. My aim has been to give the reader a taste of the lives and interests of the people in medieval England.

Court rolls, coroners' rolls and wills give insights into the lives of the common folk and, usually being dated, were important sources for this book. Unfortunately, a few excellent stories were undated, so these haven't made it into the diary. Occasionally, even big celebrity events, such as the death of King John, are given various dates in different sources, in which case I have made that clear.

As with any diary, there were dates when more than one event occurred; on other days nothing happened – or at least nothing was recorded, insofar as I could discover – in which case I took the opportunity to put in recipes or medical remedies appropriate to the season, instructions for bathing, comments on medieval sleep patterns or similar insights into everyday life.

One possible problem for readers, with this day-by-day format, is that although the days are chronological, the years are not, so entries may leap from the eleventh century to the fifteenth, back to the twelfth and then forward again to the fourteenth. This was unavoidable and meant that a monarch might have died in April, been crowned in September and was born in November, so his story is told backwards. To aid the reader,

I have included a timeline of English kings to provide a chronological framework against which other events can be set.

Most important to medieval folk, at a time when the great majority of the population was tied to the land, was the agricultural round of tasks through the seasons, as set down in this late fifteenth-century carol from a manuscript in the Bodleian Library, Oxford:

> January – By this fire I warm my hands,
> February – And by my spade I delve my lands.
> March – Here I set my things to spring,
> April – And here I hear the birds sing.
> May – I am light as bird on bough,
> June – And I weed my corn well enow.
> July – With my scythe my mead I mow,
> August – And here I shear my corn full low.
> September – With my flail I earn my bread,
> October – And here I sow my wheat so red.
> November – At Martinmas I kill my swine,
> December – And at Christmas I drink red wine.

J. L. Forgeng, *Daily Life in Chaucer's England*

Also of significant importance in this historical period was the Roman Catholic Church, with its calendar of feasts and saints' days, some of which I have included. Church laws controlled everyone's lives. For example, you couldn't marry during Lent and on almost half the days in the year meat was supposed to be off the menu, although it is impossible to be certain just how strictly the rule was observed. For example, when Christmas Day fell on a Friday – as it does in 2015 and did so in 1304, 1388, 1467 and 1472, for instance – which took priority: the Chrismas boar or Friday's fast? I don't know the answer to that but I have tried to reflect some of these issues in my choice of material.

I had great fun compiling the entries and hope readers will enjoy this journey through the year, either as a dip-into book or as a trip back in time to meet our ancestors.

Toni Mount
December 2015

MEDIEVAL KINGS OF ENGLAND TIMELINE

Timeline for medieval Kings of England

Kings of England Timeline

Name	Nickname/Other Title	Date of Birth	Came to Throne	Coronation	Died/Abdicated	Events of Interest
Harold II	Godwinson/Earl of Wessex	1022	6 Jan 1066	c. same day	d. 14 Oct 1066	won at Stamford Bridge then died at battle of Hastings
William I	the Conqueror/Duke of Normandy	1028	14 Oct 1066	25 Dec 1066	d. 9 Sep 1087	commissioned the Domesday Book 1086
William II	Rufus	1056	9 Sep 1087	26 Sep 1087	k. 2 Aug 1100	killed in a hunting accident in New Forest
Henry I	Beauclerc	1068	2 Aug 1100	5 Aug 1100	d. 1 Dec 1135	his only legitimate heir was a daughter
Stephen	Count of Blois	c. 1092/97	1 Dec 1135	22 Dec 1135	d. 25 Oct 1154	a troubled reign when 'Christ and his saints slept'
Henry II	Plantagenet/FitzEmpress/ Curtmantle	5 Mar 1133	25 Oct 1154	19 Dec 1154	d. 6 July 1189	blamed for the murder of Thomas Becket
Richard I	the Lionheart	8 Sep 1157	6 July 1189	3 Sep 1189	d. 6 Apr 1199	went on Crusade, taken prisoner in Austria
John	Lackland	24 Dec 1166	6 Apr 1199	Ascension Day 1199	d. 19 Oct 1216	sealed Magna Carta 15 June 1215

Timeline for medieval Kings of England

Kings of England Timeline

Name	Nickname/Other Title	Date of Birth	Came to Throne	Coronation	Died/Abdicated	Events of Interest
Henry III	of Winchester	1 Oct 1207	19 Oct 1216	28 Oct 1216	d. 16 Nov 1272	Simon de Montfort led Barons' War 1263–65
Edward I	Longshanks/Hammer of the Scots	17 Jun 1239	20 Nov 1272	19 Aug 1274	d. 7 July 1307	built castles, fought the Welsh and the Scots
Edward II	of Caernarfon	25 Apr 1284	8 July 1307	25 Feb 1308	ab. 20 Jan 1327	first English Prince of Wales 1301
Edward III	of Windsor	13 Nov 1312	25 Jan 1327	1 Feb 1327	d. 21 Jun 1377	ruled during the time of the Black Death
Richard II	of Bordeaux	6 Jan 1367	22 Jun 1377	16 July 1377	ab. 29 Sep 1399	the Peasants' Revolt 1381
Henry IV	Bolingbroke/Duke of Lancaster	15 Apr 1367	30 Sep 1399	13 Oct 1399	d. 20 Mar 1413	usurped the throne from his cousin, Richard
Henry V	of Monmouth	9 Aug 1387	21 Mar 1413	9 Apr 1413	d. 31 Aug 1422	victor at Agincourt 1415
Henry VI	of Windsor	6 Dec 1421	1 Sep 1422	6 Nov 1429	removed 4 Mar 1461	his spells of madness caused Wars of the Roses
Edward IV	Duke of York/Earl of March	28 Apr 1442	4 Mar 1461	28 Jun 1461	d. 9 Apr 1483	took the throne for the House of York
Edward V	Prince of Wales	4 Nov 1470	9 Apr 1483	none	uncertain	one of the 'Princes in the Tower'
Richard III	Duke of Gloucester	2 Oct 1452	26 Jun 1483	6 July 1483	k. 22 Aug 1485	Last English king to die in battle
Henry VII	Tudor/Earl of Richmond	28 Jan 1457	21 Aug 1485	30 Oct 1485	d. 21 Apr 1509	dated his reign to the day before Bosworth

JANUARY

1st – A Day for Gifts

In medieval England, the day for giving and receiving gifts was 1 January rather than Christmas. *The Ryalle Book*, a manual for royal practices which dates to Edward IV's reign, explains how the king was to receive his New Year presents:

On New Year's Day in the morning, the King, when he cometh to his foot-sheet, an usher of the chamber to be ready at the chamber door; and say: 'Sire, here is a year's gift coming from the Queen.' And then he shall say: 'Let it come in, Sire.' And then the usher shall let in the messenger with the gift and then after that the greatest estates' servant as is come, each after other as they be estates ; and after that done, all other lords and ladies after the estates that they be of. And all this while the King must sit at his foot-sheet. This done, the chamberlain shall send for the treasurer of the chamber and charge the treasurer to give the messenger that bringeth the queen's gift, and he be a knight, the sum of ten marks, and he be a squire, eight marks, or at the least 100 shillings, and the king's mother 100 shillings, and those that come from the king's brethren and sisters, each of them six marks, and to every duke and duchess, each of them five marks, and every earl and countess 40 shillings. This being the rewards of them that bringeth the year's gifts. For I report me unto the king's highness, whether he will do more or less: for this I know hath been done. And this done, the

King to go make him ready, and go to his service in what array that him liketh.

On New Year's Day 1464/65, Sir John Howard gave a gift of horses to King Edward IV and his queen, Elizabeth Woodville. The horses are even named in the Howard accounts: Lyard Duras (Lyard means 'grey') was a fine courser, costing £40; Lyard Lewes for the queen was worth only £8.

> J. Ashdown-Hill, *Richard III's 'Beloved Cousyn':*
> *John Howard and the House of York*

New Year's Day (and Christmas and May Day too) was a time for medieval Mummers' plays. These were free street theatre entertainments, although the players would pass around hats, pots and even ladles, hoping the audience would put in a few coins. A favourite play was that of St George in which the not-so-saintly knight fought and slew an assortment of enemies, from dragons and evil knights to Beelzebub. New Year was a popular opportunity for George to do his worst. Costumes were often very basic but the players either blackened their faces or wore masks – it was a tradition since pagan times that they shouldn't be recognised, except as the character they played. The script was always in verse. Here is a brief excerpt from one of many versions, though no originals are extant:

> [Saint George]:
> Show me the man that dare before me stand
> I neither care for thee, nor thy bright sword in hand
> Pray what bold art thou?
>
> [Bulgard]:
> I am the Turkish champion,
> From Turkeyland I came
> I come to fight the daring Saint,
> George they call his name
> And if he calls himself the champion,
> I think myself as good
> And before I would surrender
> I would lose my precious blood

[Saint George]:
Stir up the fire and make a light
And see Saint George and the Turkey fight
The hour is gone
The clock's struck one
Tip, tap, bodge

[They fight and Bulgard falls.]

[This text was noted down at
a modern re-enactment]

2nd – The Epiphany Rising

The Epiphany Rising, also known as the Rebellion of the Three Earls, was a failed attempt to assassinate the Lancastrian usurper, Henry IV, in early January 1400. The deposed king, Richard II, had rewarded his supporters with a wealth of new titles but, upon seizing the throne in the autumn of 1399, Henry Bolingbroke, Duke of Lancaster, had stripped his opponents of their highest ranks. Dukes were now reduced to earls and, not surprisingly, were unimpressed by the replacement king. Their aim was to remove him permanently and replace King Richard II on his rightful throne.

The conspirators had first met to discuss their plans on 17 December 1399 at Westminster. The plot involved capturing the new king while he was at Windsor for a tournament during the feast of Epiphany, killing him and restoring Richard to the throne. The ringleaders were John Montagu, 3rd Earl of Salisbury, John Holland, 1st Earl of Huntingdon (formerly Duke of Exeter) and his brother, Thomas Holland, 3rd Earl of Kent (formerly Duke of Surrey; the Hollands were half-brothers to Richard II), and Thomas Despenser, 4th Baron Despencer (formerly Earl of Gloucester). Other conspirators included Ralph, Lord Lumley, Sir Thomas Blount, Sir Bernard Brocas and possibly Edward of Norwich, 1st Earl of Rutland (formerly Duke of Aumale). Whether he was fully in their confidence, Rutland certainly knew of the plot because it was he who betrayed them to Henry.

So that their scheming came to nothing, a forewarned Henry did not come to Windsor as planned but began to raise an army in London. The

Earls of Kent and Salisbury arrived at the castle with a force of about 400 men-at-arms and archers; but, learning that the king wasn't coming, they left in haste, fleeing into the West Country.

There they tried to raise a rebellion but few supported their cause. In their attempts to gather men and seize Cirencester in King Richard's name, Lumley was beheaded in a violent skirmish by the townsfolk, and Salisbury, Kent and Brocas were captured. Held briefly in custody, the two earls were beheaded without trial on 7 January 1400; Brocas was taken to London and beheaded at Tyburn. Blount escaped to Oxford, only to be hanged, drawn and quartered on 12 January, and Despencer was captured at Bristol by a mob and was also summarily beheaded on 13 January. Huntingdon was captured at Pleshey and dealt with in the same way on 16 January. The executed rebels were subsequently attainted (stripped of all titles and estates and their heirs disinherited) in March; the sons of Kent, Salisbury and Huntingdon were later restored to their fathers' titles but the attainders were not formally reversed until 1461 by the first Yorkist parliament of Edward IV.

As for Henry IV, the rebellion convinced him that a deposed king in imprisonment was a dangerous threat to the new Lancastrian regime. By 17 February 1400, King Richard would be dead in Pontefract Castle 'by means unknown'.

3rd – A Polite Request

On this day, Edward Plumpton, a lawyer and secretary to Lord Strange at Latham Hall, Lancashire, wrote to his affluent relative, Sir Robert Plumpton. Edward asks him to take care of his servant, also named Robert, who has become too fat to ride most horses, such that Edward has given him a mount that had previously carried the fellow into battle – presumably in full armour. This is an excerpt from the letter:

To the right honourable my especyall good master, Sir Robart Plompton, kt.

After the most humble and due recommendation, please yt your mastership ... Sir, Robart my servant is a true servant to me, nevertheless he is large to ryde and over weyghty for my horse; wherefore he hartely desireth me to wryte to your mastership for him. He is a true man of tongue and hands, and a kind and good man. If yt please your mastership to take him to your service, I beseech you to be his good master … Sir, I have given to him the blacke horse that bar [bore] him from the field and if ther be any service that ye will command me, I am redy and wilbe to my lives end at your commandement.

Wrytten at Lathum. Your most humble servant, Ed. Plompton, sectory to my lord Straung.

T. Stapleton (ed.), *The Plumpton Correspondence*

To modern readers, this sounds like a grovelling letter, fit to have been penned by Dickens' Uriah Heap, but this is the usual tone of medieval correspondence and was simply a polite and well-mannered request. Historians are fortunate that 'the Plumpton correspondence', a treasure trove of about 250 letters and papers dated from 1461 to 1552, has survived as a fascinating source of information, revealing the lives of a family of knightly status with estates mostly in the Knaresborough area of Yorkshire.

4th – A Perennial Complaint

In winter weather in a time before central heating, with draughty castles and houses, colds and chills must have been common complaints. A fifteenth-century leechbook contains medicinal remedies for just about every ailment, although some are difficult to identify, as are some of the ingredients. Here is a sample of treatments for headaches caused by colds:

For the headache that cometh of cold. Seethe [boil] betony in wine and wash thine head therein.

Another. Take incense and pigeon's dung and wheat flour, an ounce of each, and temper [mix] them with the white of an egg; and whereso the head acheth, bind it, and it shall vanish anon.

Another. Make a garland for the headache. Take ammi [a plant from Spain] that spicers have and beat it well in a brazen mortar and take camomile dried and make a powder of it; and then take these powders by even portions and put them in a long narrow pocket that it may be full of powder and that it may go about the patient's head, and look to it that the powders be evenly distributed. Then seethe it in a pottle [four pints] of white wine and when it is well sodden, squeeze out the juice from the pocket and swathe it about his head as hot as he may suffer it and do so each night when he goest to bed as long as the wine will last. – Proved.

W. R. Dawson, *A Leechbook of the Fifteenth Century*

The first remedy, using betony, may well have benefitted the sufferer as this plant is a source of compounds still used in the treatment of headaches and migraine today. The second remedy sounds less likely to work; although the incense might have helped clear the sinuses I'm sure the pigeon dung would have been better omitted from the recipe. The doctor had most faith in the third treatment which he has 'proved' to work. Ammi, in the third treatment, was a Mediterranean plant, also known as 'Spanish toothpick'. A spicer would have it, we are told. A spicer was a grocer or wholesale importer of exotic goods, such as pepper, nutmeg and crimson dye, who might also be an apothecary – a medieval pharmacist. One person could be all these things at once as the trades overlapped so much. In this recipe, the soothing camomile may have helped the patient to relax and sleep.

5th – Twelfth Night

Twelfth Night has been celebrated as the end of the Christmas season since the Middle Ages. One of the most important days in the Christian calendar, Twelfth Night marked the eve of the feast of Epiphany, when the three wise men, or Magi, came to see the Christ child.

A special Twelfth Night Cake was the centrepiece of the celebration. A slice was given to all members of the household. Traditionally, the cake contained a dried bean and a dried pea. The man whose slice contained the bean was elected king for the night; whoever got the pea was his queen. If a woman found the bean, she chose the king, while a man who found the pea in his slice of cake could choose the queen. The royal pair then directed the rest of the company for a crazy evening of fun, giving the revellers ridiculous tasks to perform or ordering them to behave in ways they never would otherwise. Even if the pair were lowly servants, their temporary lordly status was recognised by the whole household, including their masters.

In England, the Twelfth Night cake was a rich, heavy fruitcake that contained honey, flour, ginger, pepper and lots of raisins. The cake could be a huge work of art and was cut into slices: one portion was reserved for God, another for the Virgin Mary and three more slices for the Magi. These portions were given to the poor who came begging alms that day.

6th – A New King

On this day in 1066, a Thursday, Harold Godwinson, Earl of Wessex, was crowned King of England as Harold II, following the death of his brother-in-law, Edward the Confessor.

In 1367, in Bordeaux in south-western France, the Black Prince's wife, Princess Joan of Kent, gave birth on this day to the couple's second son, Richard of Bordeaux. The royal couple already had a firstborn son and heir, Edward of Angoulême. Joan also had children from a previous marriage to Thomas Holland. When Richard was still a baby his elder brother died, so Richard became second in line to the throne of his grandfather, King Edward III. However, his father, the Black Prince, died a year before his grandfather, so it was ten-year-old Richard who became king in 1377.

In the Christian calendar, 6 January sees the end of the twelve days of Christmas. Known as the Feast of Epiphany, this day is also called the Adoration of the Magi or the Feast of the Three Kings (or wise men/ magi): Caspar, Melchior and Balthasar. The Bible tells that these three kings saw a bright star appear in the heavens on the night when Christ was born. They followed it and found the Christ Child, presenting him with gifts of gold, frankincense and myrrh. So in medieval times, Epiphany was the time for gift-giving – as it still is in some European countries – and also a day for English kings to wear their full regalia, reminding their subjects that they were equal with their biblical royal antecedents. This church ceremony, known as 'crown-wearing', dates back to the Norman Conquest, when William I thought it might be as well to remind the defeated Saxons that he was now their undisputed monarch. It continued as a tradition into the fifteenth century, and the sovereign always attended the ceremony in person, making an offering of gold at the high altar.

7th – St Distaff's Day

This day was, in theory, the first day back to normal after the Twelve Days of Christmas for women. Undoubtedly, they had been cooking and caring for the family throughout the holiday but 7 January was known as St Distaff's Day because today they had to return to their dutiful spinning. The day has no connection to any spinning saint but the process was vital, as the only means of turning raw wool or flax into thread for weaving into cloth. The day refers to the distaff and drop spindle, the apparatus familiar to every woman before the invention of the spinning wheel.

Spinning with a distaff and spindle was a slow process, taking a week to spin a pound-weight of wool into yarn. The spinning wheel was quicker and more efficient but women complained that they preferred the distaff. There was a good reason for this: the first spinning wheels were huge contraptions, whereas a distaff was carried under the arm, the spindle left dangling and turning in the fingers, winding on the thread as it was formed. The wheel kept a woman in one position to work at it, at home – a lonely occupation. With a distaff, she could move around, go outside, meet her neighbours and spin together while they chatted, making the task more pleasurable and sociable. Every woman, whether lady or lowly housewife, was expected to spend time spinning, and for those who, for whatever reason, remained unmarried, made a full-time occupation of being a 'spinster'.

http://www.tellinghistory.co.uk/resources/distaff.htm

8th – The Great Frost

Extreme weather was not unusual in the first decades of the fourteenth century. There was snow and ice on the ground from 15 December

1305 to 27 January 1306, and when it finally melted, more snow fell on 13 February that didn't disappear until 13 April 1306:

And the fish died in the ponds, and the birds in the woods, and the cattle in the fields. And many of the birds of heaven were so wasted away that they were caught without any net or snare by the hand of man.

C. D. Yonge (ed.), *The Flowers of History*

The *Chroniques de London* noted that during the winter of 1307/1308: 'There was such great ice on the Thames that many people went by foot on the ice to Southwark, and back to London.' During the winter of 1309/10 the weather was again bitterly cold. In London, the period was called the Great Frost; the writer of the *Chroniques de London* had this to say:

There was such cold and such masses and piles of ice on the Thames and everywhere else that the poor were overcome by excessive cold ... The river froze so solidly, bonfires could be lit on it.

All the winters between 1312 and 1317 were also bitterly cold with much snow and hard frosts.

9th – A Well-Amended King

On this day in 1455, Edmund Clere wrote from Greenwich Palace to the Paston family in Norfolk. Edmund was an esquire in King Henry VI's household and sent good news. The king had been suffering from some kind of long-term and debilitating mental collapse, during which period his wife, Queen Margaret, had given birth to his son and heir; but around Christmas 1454, the king suddenly recovered his sanity, as Edmund reports in this letter:

Right well beloved cousin, I recommend me to you, letting you know such tidings as we have. Blessed be God, the King is well amended and has been since Christmas ...
    And on Monday afternoon the Queen came to him and brought my Lord Prince, her son, with her. And then he [the king] asked

what the Prince's name was and the Queen told him 'Edward'; and then he held up his hands and thanked God therefore. And he said he never knew till that time nor understood what was said to him, nor knew where he had been while he was sick until now. And he asked who were the godfathers and the Queen told him and he was well pleased ... And he says that he is in charity with all the world, and he would that all the lords were so. And now he says Matins of Our Lady and evensong and hears his Mass devoutly; and Richard [the bearer of the letter] shall tell you more tidings by mouth.

By your cousin, Edmund Clere.

R. Virgoe, *Illustrated Letters of the Paston Family*

The Lancastrian king's mental problems in the early 1450s were the spark that ignited the Wars of the Roses. To contemporaries, they were known as the 'Cousins' Wars' and were fought between the royal houses of York and Lancaster, each with their own supporters.

Initially, the up-and-coming Norfolk gentry, the Paston family, took the Lancastrian side, but they made their peace with the victorious Yorkists in 1461. Luckily for historians, much of the family's correspondence, from 1419 to the first decade of the 1500s, has survived, giving us some valuable insights into the lives of fifteenth-century gentry folk and the world in which they lived.

10th – A Clerk's Will

On this day in 1484, the will of John Hardheede, MA, a clerk at Trinity Hall, Cambridge University, was granted probate by the Archbishop of Canterbury at his palace at Knole, in Kent. As a scholar at the university, John left some books to his fellows: Master John Breton, a Doctor of Divinity, was to have John's best 'porteose' – a portable breviary or church service book – who was forbidden to sell it but had to donate it 'after his conscience'. Master John Campe, a fellow at Pembroke Hall, was to have a volume entitled *Saint Thomas Upon the fourt of the Sentence,* a book on logic and philosophy, the second-best porteose and a bible, as well as a piece of silver.

John also bequeaths his clothes, giving John Halowe of Trinity Hall a gown with a hood; Aleyn Seymper, the university beadle, gets the best doublet, the best bedcover and 6s 8d; his wife Joan is to have money to buy a lambskin; and John Crosse, his servant, is to have a doublet and hose and 3s 4d. John Bernard, a Cambridge barber-surgeon, does very well from the bequests, receiving a russet gown and hood, a fustian doublet, a shirt, a cap and a selection of bedding and linen. John Smyth, a London stockfishmonger – a seller of dried fish – is to have the remaining bedding and bed-hangings, sharing them with his daughters, Joan and Isolde.

The will goes on to bequeath various other properties – but I wonder most of all at the possible confusions of John Hardheede's social life: apart from Aleyn the beadle, all his friends are called John!

L. Boatwright, et al. (eds), *The Logge Register,* vol. I

11th – Plough Monday

Plough Monday was the name given to the first Monday after 6 January, marking the return to agricultural work after the Christmas festivities. In some areas of England it was common for the farm labourers to tour the villages with their plough, raising money, perhaps with singing, mummers' plays and dancing. The participants sometimes disguised themselves, blacking their faces so they couldn't be recognised if they ploughed up the gardens of householders unwilling to make contributions. The earliest record of Plough Monday was in Durham, held on 11 January 1378, and it's thought that the tradition went on throughout England in medieval times; today, the celebrations are still enjoyed in parts of the East Midlands and East Anglia. There was also a church ceremony involving blessing the plough, either on Plough Monday or the Sunday immediately before.

12th – Table Manners for Children

Good manners were vital for anyone hoping to improve their standing in society. By the fifteenth century, when people were increasingly able to read and young apprentices were often expected to be literate, books on manners and etiquette became popular – so popular that when William Caxton introduced the first printing press into England, setting it up at the Almonry beside Westminster Abbey, one of the earliest books he printed was *Table Manners for Children* by the poet John Lydgate. Here are stanzas numbers two and eight (of fourteen) to give you an idea of the good manners of the day:

> Do not keep looking round, don't be engrossed
> In all the bustle of your master's hall.
> Don't slouch and lean your back against a post,
> Or look, as in a mirror, at the wall.
> Picking your nose is nasty for us all.
> Your master wants you quiet and alert,
> Not scratching at some imaginary hurt ...

> In courtesy again, do not emit
> Unpleasant noises – they are an offence;
> Nor, with old escapades, your fellow twit[annoy].
> Be mindful of your master – that shows sense.
> Don't play with knives – please heed my arguments;
> Sit still and decorously when you eat,
> And do not tap or shuffle with your feet.

J. Lydgate, *Table Manners for Children*

13th – A Complaint Against the Chief Justice

King Edward I ordered that anyone who had a complaint against his justiciars, judges, ministers or bailiffs should come, in person, to present it before parliament, which he had summoned to meet in London on the feast of St Hilary in 1290.

As a result, evidence came to light that Thomas de Weyland, Chief Justice of the Common Bench, was guilty of causing two of his squires to commit murder at a village fair on 20 July 1289, killing William Carwel, a servant of the Earl of Norfolk. Whether Thomas had encouraged the terrible deed or not, after his squires returned to his house and reported what had occurred, he made no move to have them arrested, thus becoming an accessory after the fact, at the very least. The Earl of Norfolk ordered a court of enquiry on 4 September and the men were executed ten days later.

Meanwhile, the Chief Justice was indicted for harbouring the killers and his arrest was ordered. Although taken into custody by an officer of the Sheriff of Suffolk, Thomas managed to escape under cover of darkness and sought sanctuary at a friary near Bury St Edmunds. The claim of sanctuary meant he had forty days grace; he even wore the habit of a Franciscan friar in the hope of escaping justice, but King Edward sent Robert Malet to starve him out, along with the friars harbouring the felon. Thomas surrendered to Malet and was escorted back to the Tower of London. There he was arraigned and given three choices: he could stand trial and take his chances on the verdict – which might mean a death sentence; or he could submit to life imprisonment without trial; or he could agree to 'abjure the king's dominions for evermore' – to go into exile, in other words. Thomas chose exile. He took an oath not to return to any English territory and was allowed nine days to reach Dover, travelling barefoot, bareheaded and carrying a cross to his allotted port of departure.

By 1292, Thomas was living in Paris. Exile had been a good choice because the king granted him a pardon in 1297 and he was able to return to England, dying at home the following year.

G. J. Aungier (ed.), *Chroniques de London*

*

Also on this date in 1397, John of Gaunt married Katherine Swynford, his long-time mistress, taking her as his third wife.

14th – Called to Witness

In York, Christopher Bell had been in trouble on a few counts, including arguments concerning the construction of and payment for a scaffold. This was not necessarily a scaffold for the hangman but could have been scaffolding as used in roof repairs, since Christopher was a tiler by trade. Now he needed a good character witness to get him out of a tight spot:

Memorandum. On this date William Wiseman, a tailor, came in person before the mayor, John Fereby, and there swore upon the holy evangelists [the Gospels] that he knew neither treason nor felony [committed] by one Christofor Bell, tyler, nor unfitting words said about the said Christofor Bell within this city nor elsewhere and that he is ready and will be ready to prove that at time [when required].

L. C. Attreed, *York House Books*

(See also 9 September).

15th – John the Gardener's Horticulture Handbook

This was the time of year to graft your fruit trees, according to John the Gardener of Kent, writing his fourteenth-century handbook on horticulture:

> In the calendars of Januar'
> Thou shalt trees both set and rear
> To graft therein apple and pear.

Grafting the scions of new varieties of fruit onto stout young native trees was a process well known to English gardeners since Anglo-Saxon times. King Edward I was especially keen on fruit, paying 1s 6d for 100 cherry trees, four quince trees costing 2s, two peach trees costing 1s and an unspecified number of gooseberry bushes costing just 3d – all to be planted in the royal gardens at the Tower of London in 1275.

T. McLean, *Medieval English Gardens*

16th – Reimbursement for a Dead Horse

A party of civic dignitaries from York, including the Lord Mayor and 'a cook', had taken a gift – perhaps a Christmas or New Year's present – to Middleham Castle in North Yorkshire, for Edward of Middleham, the nine-year-old

Prince of Wales, son of Richard III. Sadly, the little boy died unexpectedly in April that year, a terrible shock for the king and queen. On the journey to Middleham, the cook's horse had died and he asked the city to reimburse him. I have modernised the rather eccentric Middle English spelling:

Item: the cook's horse. This day it was agreed that for as much as when my lord the mayor and my masters, his brethren [the aldermen of York] rode to my lord the prince, to Middleham with a present, their cook rode upon a horse, the which horse died on the journey, that the said cook, towards the loss of the said horse, shall have from the commons gudes [funds] of this city 13s 4d.

L. C. Attreed. *York House Books*

17th – Royal Cherry Pottage

Bearing in mind all those cherry trees Edward I had planted at the Tower of London (see 15 January), here is a royal recipe to use the fruit. The wine, white bread, sugar, cloves and gold leaf would have made this dish very expensive and fit for a king:

Cherry pottage. Take cherries & do out the stones & grind them well & draw them through a strainer into a pot & do thereto [add] sweet butter [unsalted] & myed wastel bread [white breadcrumbs] & cast thereto good wine & sugar. Salt it and stir it well together. Dress it in a dish and set therein gilded cloves & strew sugar above.

M. Black, *The Medieval Cookbook*

I have modernised the spelling but, as was usual with medieval recipes, no amounts of ingredients or cooking times were given. Instead of grinding and straining the cherries, a blender could now do the job.

18th – Henry VII's Oath

On this day in 1486, King Henry VII married Elizabeth of York, the eldest daughter of the Yorkist king, Edward IV (died 1483; see

9 April). Henry was twenty-nine, his bride ten years younger. The marriage of Henry Tudor and Elizabeth was no love match but had been arranged by their mothers during the reign of King Richard III. Margaret Beaufort Edward IV's and queen Elizabeth Woodville came up with a treasonous scheme: Margaret's only child, Henry, should take the throne of England, to which he had a slight and dubious claim. Once he had taken it by force from Richard III, he would marry Elizabeth of York, uniting the two rival houses of Lancaster and York.

In December 1483, in the cathedral in Rennes in France, Henry Tudor swore an oath promising to marry Elizabeth, and thereafter began to plan his invasion. He was victorious eighteen months later at the battle of Bosworth (see 22 August). Five months later, after having been crowned as king by right of conquest, Henry VII fulfilled his oath and married Elizabeth of York. That the coronation of Henry VII took place months before his marriage to Elizabeth was a way to distance himself from his wife's own claim to the throne. It was also necessary for him to summon Parliament in order that the assembly could overturn an act of Richard III's which had declared Elizabeth and her siblings to be illegitimate as their parents' marriage was supposedly bigamous – the king couldn't marry a bastard. The wedding went ahead and Elizabeth was soon pregnant, but the reversal of Richard III's act would open up a whole new problem that came to haunt Henry until the end of the century (see 23 January).

http://nerdalicious.com.au/history/
elizabeth-of-york-and-her-kings-henry-vii/

19th – Sumptuary Laws

In fourteenth-century England, the king and Parliament began to introduce Sumptuary Laws to restrict what people ate, but particularly, what people wore. After the Black Death had caused a shortage of labourers, the lower classes began to charge more for their services, despite legislation to prevent this. Becoming a little more affluent, with a few coins to spare for luxuries for the first time in history, townsfolk and merchants could now afford to dress like their social superiors. The upper classes could not allow the lower orders to dress above their station: it was an affront to God not to keep to your correct place in society. It was said that many a merchant's wife plunged him into debt trying to keep abreast of courtly fashions. Hence, the Sumptuary Laws.

In 1363, King Edward III did a thorough job on the matter, bringing in a swathe of new restrictions on what people of different social backgrounds could wear:

Lords with lands worth £1,000 annually and their families: no restrictions.

Knights with land worth 400 marks [£266 13s 4d] annually and their families may dress at their will, except they may wear no weasel fur, ermine or clothing of precious stones other than the jewels in women's hair.

Knights with lands worth 300 marks [£200] annually and their families may wear fabric worth no more than 6 marks [£4] for the whole cloth: no cloth of gold, nor a cloak, mantle or gown lined with pure miniver, sleeves of ermine or any material embroidered with precious stones; women may not wear ermine or weasel-fur, or jewels except those worn in their hair.

Esquires with land worth 200 marks per year [£133 6s 8d] and merchants with goods to the value of £1,000 and their families may wear fabric worth no more than 5 marks [£3 6s 8d] for the whole cloth; they may wear cloth of silk and silver, or anything decorated with silver; women may wear miniver but not ermine or weasel-fur, or jewels except those worn in the hair.

Esquires, gentlemen with £100 per year, and merchants with goods to the value of £500 and their families may wear fabric worth no more than 4½ marks [£3] for the whole cloth; no cloth of gold, silk, or silver, no embroidery, no precious stones or fur.

Yeoman and their families may wear fabric worth no more than 40s [£2] for the whole cloth, no jewels, no gold, silver, embroidery, enamelware or silk; no fur except lamb, rabbit, cat or fox; women not to wear a silk veil.

Servants and their families may wear fabric worth not more than 2 marks [£1 6s 8d] for the whole cloth; no gold, silver, embroidery, enamel or silk; women not to wear a veil worth more than 12d.

Carters, ploughmen, drivers of ploughs, oxherds, cowherds, swineherds, dairymaids and everyone else working on the land who does not have 40 shillings of goods: no cloth except blanket and russet at 12d per ell, belts of linen.

http://rosaliegilbert.com/sumptuarylaws.html

Despite the government's best efforts, it seems to have been the case that most folk ignored the laws, as and when it suited them. One blatant miscreant of the early fifteenth century was Margery Kempe of Lynn in Norfolk. Later in life, she became a mystic and renounced her love of fine fashion, confessing this and her many other sins to a local priest, requiring him to write everything down in a kind of memoir. She was only a merchant's wife but admits her pride in her affluent wardrobe, describing the ornate costume in which she would promenade through Lynn 'wearing gold pipes on her head, and her hoods with the tippets were fashionably slashed, her cloaks modishly slashed and underlaid with various colours between the slashes'.

This was the ultimate in haute couture, having an underdress of expensive textile showing through the purposed slashes of an over garment. The gold wires [pipes] set off by streamers [tippets] in a headdress was the pinnacle of fashion and imported from Europe at great expense. Margery says, 'She was enormously envious of her neighbours if they were dressed as well as she was. Her whole desire was to be respected by people.'

Margery even went into business for herself, so that she had her own income and her husband wouldn't know how much money she spent; she was determined to be better dressed than any other woman in church every Sunday, whatever the Sumptuary Laws dictated.

http://college.holycross.edu/projects/
kempe/town/whiteclo.htm

20th – Parliament's First Commons Sitting

This day in 1265 saw the first sitting of a Parliament which involved people other than the nobility in discussing politics. Previously, these Great Council meetings had only been attended by bishops, abbots and the nobility – what we now term the House of Lords – but in December 1264, knights of the shires and a few of the more important citizens had been summoned as well. These less exalted folk – commoners – would come to form the House of Commons.

The writs of summons for those required to attend Parliament had been issued by Simon de Montfort, Earl of Leicester, the leader of the baronial rebellion against King Henry III. This was the first time in English history that Parliament had been called by someone other than the king. Simon had defeated Henry III at the battle of Lewes in May 1264 and was now governing the country, though ruling in the name of the king, who was in his custody. But Simon's power was still contested. Some of the most powerful nobles remained in arms against him, controlling strategic castles, and Henry's queen, Eleanor of Provence, was active in her husband's support just across the Channel, in France.

Hoping to ward off any rebellion, Simon called a Parliament to show that he was governing with the guidance and support of representatives from across the realm – the more, the better. The writs sent out to summon people still exist to prove that Simon cast the net wide in order to have plenty of supporters in the assembly. If the meeting lacked a number of noblemen, lords who refused to answer the summons of an earl of no greater significance than themselves, the attendance was increased by the presence of the commons: knights of the shires and burgesses of the towns. It wasn't the first time that knights had been present in Parliament, but the assembly of January 1265 was different in that both they and the townspeople were there to discuss and advise on some of the most important issues facing English government at the time. This precedent led to the establishment of the two Houses of Parliament – the Lords and the Commons – a significant step towards modern democracy.

https://history.blog.gov.uk/2015/01/20/
simon-de-montforts-1265-parliament/

21st – Pears in Confection

Here is a fourteenth-century recipe for 'Pears in Confection', taken from a cookery book thought to have been used at the court of King Richard II:

Take pears and trim them clean. Take good red wine and mulberries or sandalwood and boil the pears in it. And when they are cooked, take them out. Make a syrup of Greek wine with white sugar and powdered ginger and put the pears in it. Boil it a little and serve it forth.

L. J. Sass, *To the King's Taste*

As with most medieval recipes, amounts of ingredients and cooking times aren't included. Presumably, the cook was expected to taste the dish as he went, to ensure it was well flavoured, and to know how long things took to cook, which would depend on how hot the fire burned, so a fair bit of guesswork and testing would have been involved.

There were dozens of varieties of pears available to the medieval cook, more than we have nowadays, but the best pears to keep their shape when cooked were Wardens and these are still available to us today.

The mulberries or sandalwood were used here as food colouring, to dye the pears a deep red. Today, we think of sandalwood as a perfume. Medieval folk loved to colour and perfume their food – a meal was a treat for all the senses – and sandalwood also gives an unusual but very pleasant flavour.

22nd – Medieval Forensics

A coroner's inquest was held on 22 January 1368 into the death of an unborn child in Chesterfield, Derbyshire. There was an argument between Joanna, wife of John, and Agnes Spicer. During the squabble, Agnes struck Joanna in the stomach with her fist. Joanna was pregnant and said that Agnes's blow killed the child in her womb – presumably, the pregnancy was at a stage when the mother could feel the baby moving and this movement ceased. Six days after the assault, Joanna gave birth to a stillborn daughter. Agnes was arrested and imprisoned, awaiting trial.

S. Butler, *Forensic Medicine in Medieval England*

23rd – *Titulus Regis*

On this day in 1484, King Richard III's only parliament of his two-year reign was opened with a speech from Chancellor Russell on the theme of peace. 'A good lawmaker for the ease and solace of the common people,' was how a later Lord Chancellor described Richard III. Many of the acts passed by his Parliament show that he tried to improve conditions for the ordinary people, but the most important matter to be dealt with was the confirmation of Richard's entitlement to be king, set out in the act known as the *Titulus Regis*.

The main points of the act were that the children of his brother, Edward IV, were illegitimate and, because the children of his other deceased elder brother, George, Duke of Clarence (see 18 February), were barred from inheriting the throne by their father's attainder for treason, Richard was the next lawful heir. There were two reasons for declaring Edward's children to have been born out of wedlock. Firstly, prior to becoming king, Edward already had a contract of marriage with Lady Eleanor Butler, before he married Elizabeth Woodville in May 1464. A perfectly valid contract would have consisted of vows exchanged between the couple, not necessarily in the presence of a priest or any witnesses, followed by sexual intercourse, which sealed the deal in the case of ordinary folk – but not for kings. Secondly, once Edward became king, his marriage to Elizabeth, even if it hadn't been bigamous, was clandestine, conducted privately without the banns being called or the assent of the nobility – all things that were vital in the case of a king's marriage.

The existence of the pre-contract cannot now be proved – thanks to Henry VII destroying all the evidence – but it seems to have been acknowledged by many people in 1483. On the other hand, there is no doubt that Edward's marriage to Elizabeth was conducted in secret. Sadly, Eleanor Butler wasn't available to confirm the pre-contract, having died in 1468. In the summer of 1483, England needed a strong and able king if peace was to be maintained.

Few people relished the thought of having Edward's son, Edward V, a child of twelve, on the throne. Knowing Edward IV's delight in amorous liaisons, it was easy to believe that he had seduced Lady Eleanor, and his furtive marriage to Elizabeth Woodville compounded the issue.

In the event, Richard's accession to the throne was stage-managed as a 'request' from the lords and commons that he accept the Crown, there being no closer legitimate heir. Reluctantly, so it's said, he agreed after much deliberation, on the condition that, when Parliament met, his right should be enacted in law. Once Parliament had accepted Richard's claim and the *Titulus Regius* was enrolled, his title was as legal and acceptable as those of any other medieval king.

http://www.richardiii.net/2_5_0_riii_controversy.php#precontract

24th – Murder of a Justice of the Peace

Sir Roger Belers, a Justice of the Peace described as 'very old', was murdered by Eustace de Folville and his brothers near Reresby, close by Leicester, at some time before the feast of the conversion of St Paul (25 January) on 24 January 1326.

G. J. Aungier (ed.), *Chroniques de London*

25th – Edward II Deposed

In 1327, Edward II was deposed by his wife, Queen Isabella, whom he called the She-Wolf of France, and her lover, Roger Mortimer of Wigmore. They put Edward and Isabella's son on the throne in place of his father, hurrying to have the coronation on 1 February. The new king, Edward III, was just fourteen and Isabella and Roger hoped to rule as regents in his name. But they had underestimated the teenager. Although not yet eighteen, in 1330, now with a queen, Philippa of Hainault, and a son and heir of his own, Edward took action against his mother and her lover: he caught Mortimer by surprise at Nottingham Castle on 19 October 1330. Mortimer was executed and Edward III's personal reign began. He was far more lenient with his mother, treating her with the respect due to a dowager queen.

26th – An English King of France

On this day in 1340 (although some sources say 25 January), while in Ghent in Flanders (modern Belgium), King Edward III of England declared himself to be the true King of France. This may sound outrageous but Edward had good reason at the time – future English kings less so, although they maintained the fiction of being kings of France until 1801! This is how it came about.

Since October 1337, relations between England and France had been deteriorating. King Philippe VI of France had sent ships to assist the Scots in attacking English merchant shipping and ports. In 1339, the French attacked Gorey Castle on the island of Jersey, but without success as the garrison held out and fought them off. Philippe then planned to invade England with a force of around 20,000 to 25,000 men. A French fleet attacked Dover, Folkestone and Sandwich but was driven back to France.

In revenge, the English attacked Boulogne. King Edward badly needed allies in his fight with the French. Through the wool trade England had close ties with Flanders and the Low Countries, strengthened by Edward's marriage to Philippa of Hainault, his beloved queen, and it was here he hoped for support. With little liking for or trust in their powerful neighbour and overlord, the King of France, the counts of Hainault and Namur promised help if Edward took his army into northern France – which he did. However, having thought the matter through more deeply, the counts changed their minds, realising the perilous situation they would be in if they made an outright enemy of Philippe, the king to whom they'd sworn oaths of fealty for their lands and titles. Edward continued without their support, confronting the French at La Fremengerie. But the French refused to fight and the English, short of supplies, were forced to give up. The threat that the French would invade England remained and Edward desperately needed those allies. In Ghent, he took the most daring risk, claiming that *he*, not Philippe de Valois, was rightful King of France. That being the case, the reluctant counts could swear fealty to Edward with clear consciences and become his allies without endangering their rights and titles.

Edward's claim was not just a convenient fiction. It centred on the fact that Isabella, his mother, was the daughter of King Philippe IV, who had died in 1314. Since then, each of Philippe IV's three sons – John I, Philippe V and Charles IV – had ruled briefly in turn and died without a son to take the throne. On his deathbed in 1328, the last of the sons, Charles IV, designated Philippe de Valois, his first cousin, as regent. Charles' wife was pregnant and it was hoped the child would be a boy: it was a girl and Philippe de Valois claimed the throne himself. Edward claimed the throne as Isabella's son and Philippe IV's grandson. Under English law that was a right and lawful claim but French Salic law stated that the line of succession could not pass through the female line.

In response to Edward's temerity, Philippe VI declared that all the English-held lands in France were now forfeit. Edward would have to fight not only to keep England safe from invasion but to reclaim his lands in Gascony in south-west France, which he held as Duke of Aquitaine and liegeman to the King of France. These were complicated issues and so began the conflict between England and France that would last, on and off, for over one hundred years – known to us as the Hundred Years War.

http://www.timeref.com/episodes/
edward_iii__the_hundred_years_war.htm

27th – The Vicar of Hertlepe

Probate was granted on the will of Sir William Bulbet, the vicar of Hertlepe (Hartlip) in Kent, on this day in 1432. This is what he had written earlier in the month on 1 January:

Seeing before me the imminent danger of death, I wish to be buried at the entrance of the church of Hertlepe. I leave to Alice my sister a best gown with hood of scarlette. To Agnes daughter of the said Alice, 6s 8d. To Elizabeth her sister, 3s 4d. To Alice my sister seven silver spoons. To John Makett guardian of my body, 6s 8d. To the same John a lined gown and a shirt with one pair of breeches and one pair of shoes and all the usual garments of my body not otherwise left.

I leave to the amending of a window in honour of the Blessed Virgin Mary in the said church of Hertlepe, 40s. I leave to painting The Holy Cross in memory of the Passion of Our Lord Jesus Christ and in remission of my sins as honourably as it can be done [no amount stated]. I leave to seven poor men of the parish of Rawnston seven pair of shoes.

Residue to my executors *viz* John Nicholl of Rowchestr [Rochester], John Gibbe of Vpchirche [Upchurch] and John Atter Water of Hertlepe to dispose for me as they shall answer in the day of Judgment before the High Judge.

Medieval & Tudor Kent Wills at Lambeth – Book 22

28th – A Death in the Family

On 28 January 1483, the London widow, Agnes Cely, matriarch of the Cely family, wool merchants and great letter writers, drew up her will.

Agnes wanted to be buried beside her husband, Richard, beneath his tomb in their parish church of St Olave by the Tower of London. Her eldest son Robert hadn't gone into the family business – he was to receive ten marks annually for the next ten years. Otherwise, after a few bequests to her nephew studying at Oxford and to William Marion, a close family friend who is often mentioned in the Celys' correspondence, the remainder of her possessions are to be shared between her second son, Richard, and youngest son, George, who now run the wool business together.

L. Boatwright, et al. (eds), *The Logge Register,* vol. 1

When old Richard Cely had died in 1482, the family commemorated him in a series of feasts, making sure their position in London society was properly recognised. For the funeral feast, a cook and two spit-boys were hired at a cost of 12*d*, but in order that the guests should be suitably impressed, the Celys also hired Thomas Lyn, a professional butler, for 16*d*. At the year's mind feast, twelve months later, which ended the period of mourning, a cook, named Wylchyr, or Wylshyre, was paid the considerable sum of 13*s* 4*d* for his services, but he must have been worth it because the family hired him again the following year, when Richard's widow, Agnes, died. The family's good friend, William Marion, was paid to take care of the arrangements for her funeral feast. Having calculated the quantities needed, he ordered wild fowl from Collett the poulterer, various meats from Croke the butcher and spices from William Dygon the grocer. To impress the guests, the Celys also hired sixteen sets of pewter dishes for the occasion.

B. Henisch, *The Medieval Cook*

29th – School Grammar

A late fifteenth-century school book has come down to us, preserved as a manuscript in the library of the seventeenth-century diarist, Samuel Pepys. Among the exercises a pupil was required to learn by heart was a long list of collective nouns e.g. a pride of lions. Apart from this familiar example of nouns applied to animals, there are numerous others for people, some quite amusing, running to seven pages. Here is a selection:

A charge of courtiers
A discretion of priests
An abominable sight of monks
A superfluity of nuns
A sentence of judges
A damning of jurors
An execution of officers
A faith of merchants
A great science of mariners
A blast of soldiers
A laughter of ostlers [who tend horses]
A glossing of taverners
An evil smartness of pedlars
A misbelief of painters
A melody of harpers
A rascal of boys
A disworship of Scots [apologies to any Scottish readers!]

G. A. J. Hodgett, *Stere htt Well*

Whoever wrote this – possibly a merchant who sailed abroad, judging from the gracious nouns for merchants and mariners – had a low opinion of monks, nuns, the judiciary, itinerant salesmen, children and especially our neighbours north of the border. He evidently liked stable hands, pub landlords and musicians but didn't trust artists.

30th – Marital Disputes

On this date in 1394 and subsequent other dates, the Church court in York heard numerous depositions regarding the marriage of Margery Spuret and Thomas de Hornby. Here is an excerpt from the deposition of Isabel Spuret who was a witness:

Isabel Spuret of York, mother of Margery, forty years of age and more, of free status and good standing as she says, admitted and diligently examined … She says she was present in the house of Roger del Grene in Castlegate, York five years ago around the feast of the Blessed Virgin Mary in the autumn when the said Thomas said to the said Margery, taking her by the hand, 'Are you willing to allow me to look for a wife wherever I will?' and she replied, 'I am willing'. The said Thomas immediately said, 'I want to have you for my wife' and she replied, 'And I want to have you for my husband'. Present were this witness [Isabel], Juliana del Grene, her fellow witness, and the contracting parties. Asked about sexual intercourse, she says that he knew her [Margery] carnally afterwards.

P. J. P. Goldberg, *Women in England, c. 1275–1525*

With both parties having given their consent and having sealed the contract by the act of consummation, this would be recognised by the Church as a legal and binding marriage. Clearly, Thomas was trying to get out of the contract, so Margery brought witnesses to court in support of her claim. Thomas brought a countersuit, producing witnesses willing to swear that he wasn't even in York on that day, but miles away, dealing with some business regarding a will.

The case was still dragging through the court in August, with both parties producing yet more witnesses. Sadly, as happens so often with such proceedings, the court's verdict isn't recorded, so we don't know whether Thomas had to remain wed to Margery or not.

31st – A Novel Cure

For those unfortunate enough to have a wound that became infected, here is a weird medieval cure, supposedly, but not one I'd recommend, especially for the wildlife required:

A powder for fester, right good. Take a toad or an adder and a weasel or a mole and a cock-raven and burn them in a pot that is new, all to powder, and put it in the fester.

W. R. Dawson, *A Leechbook of the Fifteenth Century*

FEBRUARY

1st – Edward III and Isabella

On 1 February 1327, aged only fourteen, Edward III was crowned King of England by Archbishop Reynolds in Westminster Abbey, following the forced abdication of his father, Edward II.

This came about because in 1325 the French king, Charles IV, had demanded that Edward II pay him homage for the English duchy of Aquitaine. Edward was reluctant to go abroad because his barons in England were threatening revolt, particularly over his relationship with his favourite, Hugh Despenser the Younger. To solve the difficulty – as he thought – he created his son Edward of Windsor as Duke of Aquitaine in his place and sent him to France to perform the homage. Young Edward was accompanied by his mother Isabella, sister of King Charles of France. She was supposed to negotiate a peace treaty with the French but seemed to have preferred having an affair with an exiled English baron, Roger Mortimer of Wigmore. While in France, the lovers conspired together, planning to depose King Edward. The King of France was so disgusted by his sister's adulterous liaison that he had her escorted out of the country.

Now in the Low Countries to win allies and build up diplomatic aid for the venture Isabella arranged for Prince Edward to be betrothed to twelve-year-old Philippa of Hainault, gaining the military support of her father William, Count of Hainault and Holland. They launched invasion of England and Edward II's forces either deserted him or joined Isabella and Mortimer. The king was forced to give up his throne to his son on 25 January 1327. For three years, his mother and her lover ruled England in the young king's name but, in 1330 Edward overthrew their regime, confined his mother under virtual house arrest, had Mortimer executed and began to rule in his own right.

(See also 13 November).

2nd – Candlemas

In the medieval Church, this day was celebrated as the feast of the Purification of the Blessed Virgin Mary, being forty days after Christmas. Jewish law required that a mother had to be 'cleansed' after giving birth before she could return to society. The Roman Catholic Church similarly demanded that a woman be 'churched' about six weeks after having a baby – only then could she attend church regularly once more and be socially acceptable again. In England, the day was also known as Candlemas, when it was customary to carry candles in procession to Mass before blessing them and distributing them among the congregation. Cowie and Gummer (p. 40) suggest Candelmas may have replaced a pagan festival in which torches were carried in honour of the Mother-Earth goddess to ensure a fruitful year to come.

Despite the religious aspects of the day, war made no concessions. In 1141, King Stephen was fighting at the battle of Lincoln, trying to defeat Robert, Earl of Gloucester's army during the civil war. Robert was the illegitimate half-brother of the Empress Maud (aka Matilda), wife of Geoffrey Plantagenet and heiress to King Henry I. Stephen fought valiantly but was captured and imprisoned. However, his queen – also named Matilda – led an army that captured Earl Robert, so the two royal women exchanged their prisoners and the war began again.

In 1461, during another civil war – known today as the Wars of the Roses – the future King Edward IV fought the battle of Mortimer's Cross on this day, defeating the Lancastrian army and claiming the throne of England for himself and the House of York.

3rd – The Death of John of Gaunt

On 3 February 1399, John of Gaunt, Duke of Lancaster and the fourth son of Edward III and Queen Philippa, died. He had been born at Ghent (or Gaunt) in Flanders in March 1340. In his infancy, he was created Earl of Richmond and admitted into the Order of the Garter. In 1359, he married Blanche, co-heir of Henry, Duke of Lancaster; when his father-in-law died in 1361, John was given the title. He was also the Earl of Derby, Lincoln and Leicester, and held the high office of Steward of England. Three wives later, at the age of fifty-eight, the brother of the Black Prince, uncle of Richard II, father of the future king, Henry IV, and the grandfather of Henry V, also held a legitimate claim to the throne of Castile. John of Gaunt was the richest nobleman and the greatest subject in England, the owner of huge estates and thirty castles. From his duchy, he could raise 1,000 men-at-arms and 3,000 archers. He loved hunting and is said to have killed the last wild boar in England, near Rothwell in Yorkshire.

Tall and well built, he was an ardent lover of women as well as the patron of Geoffrey Chaucer and the religious reformer John Wycliffe. He was also possibly the most hated man in England, and was a major target of the Peasants' Revolt of 1381, when his luxurious palace of the Savoy in London was burned.

He died at Leicester Castle and his body was left for forty days, as requested in his will, before being taken to London and buried in St Paul's Cathedral on 16 March, which was Passion Sunday. His remains were interred before the high altar, close to those of Blanche, his first wife.

http://www.historytoday.com/richard-cavendish/
death-john-gaunt#sthash.R510C3PE.dpuf
http://www.britannia.com/bios/royals/jgdklanc.html

4th – Tenants' Permissions

Ragenilda of Bec gives 2*s* for having married without a licence. Pledge, William of Pinner. The same Ragenilda demands of Roger Loft and Juliana his wife a certain messuage [plot of land for a house] which belonged to Robert le Beck and a jury of twelve lawful men is granted her in consideration of the said fine and if she recovers seisin [possession of land] she will give in all 5s ... And they [the jurors] say that Ragenilda has the greater right. Therefore let her have seisin.

William But in mercy for his pigs caught doing damage to the lord. Pledges Robert Maureward and Walter Reaper's son. Fine 6d.

Manor court rolls of the Abbey of Bec,
court held at Ruislip, Middlesex, 1248

Tenants of a lord's manor had to pay a fee to him for permission to marry. To judge from the surnames, despite different spellings, Ragenilda may have been Robert le Beck's widow, daughter or even sister. It is perhaps more likely that she was his daughter because, as his widow, upon her remarriage her rights to the messuage may have been relinquished, but the matter wasn't always certain. Manor courts dealt with all sorts of cases, including stray animals. It was probably William But's pigs who damaged the lord's crops, rather than the man himself.

5th – Fig and Raisin Cream

Here is a medieval recipe for 'Fig and Raisin Cream', or 'rapey' as they called it:

Take half fyges and half raisouns; pike hem and waishe hem in water. Skalde hem in wine, bray hem in a morter and drawe hem thurgh a straynour. Cast hem in a pot and therwith powdur of peper and oother good powdours; alay it up with flour of rys and colour it with saundres. Salt it, seeth it & messe it forth.

M. Black, *The Medieval Cookbook*

The modern recipe suggests using equal quantities of well-soaked dried figs and stoned raisins, about 4 ozs or 125 g of each. Set the soaking liquid aside. Put the fruits in a pan with 10 fl. ozs or 1¼ cups of sweetish red wine. Add a good pinch of black pepper, a dash each of powdered cinnamon and cloves with soft dark brown sugar to taste and bring to the boil. Remove from the heat, cool slightly then put it in a blender. Add a little of the soaking liquid to thin it down, if required.

Cream three teaspoons of rice flour or cornflour with a little of the soaking liquid and add a drop of food colouring – the medieval recipe uses 'saundres' [sandalwood], a red colouring. Blend this 'cream' into the fruit purée, return to the pan and simmer until the mixture thickens slightly. Season with salt and a little more sugar, if liked. Serve hot or cold. It is good with cereals.

6th – English Pogrom

Riots in Lynn in Norfolk spread to Norwich. The riots had begun, so the story goes, when a Jew converted to Christianity and others of the Jewish community in the town attacked him. He fled into sanctuary in the nearest church but the other townsfolk, particularly fishermen and seamen from the port of Lynn, killed many Jews and set fire to Jewish houses in retalliation.

*

Also on this day in 1497, probate was granted for the will of Nicholas Conyers, gentleman of Stokesley, by the Prerogative Court of York. The will is written in Middle English with a very definite northern flavour, using 'qw' where southern English uses 'wh'. Nicholas bequeathed quite a few animals. This is a selection:

I bequeth to Harry my broder a horse or xx [20] shillings. Also to my suster Margaret Pudsay a mair [mare] or x s. Also to my suster Alic[e] Qwarton [Wharton] a mair worth x s. Also I giff John Robinson of Newby a cowe and a calf ... Thomas Robinson my servaunt a cow ... John Wryght a qwhy [heffer] ... to every servaunt [th]at holds the plowgh [plough] xij [12] pence ... every woman servaund viij pence ... to my hyrd [cowherd] [th]at kepis my ky[ne] xij pence ... to my swynard [swineherd] viij pence.

H. Falvey, et al. (eds) *English Wills proved in the Prerogative Court of York, 1477–99*

7th – A New Prince of Wales

The future King of England, Edward II, had been born in Caernarfon Castle, in North Wales on 25 April 1284, the fourteenth (at least) and the youngest child of King Edward I with his first wife, Queen Eleanor of Castile. At the time of the baby's birth, Edward I was almost forty-five and had been King of England for over eleven years. Queen Eleanor was probably forty-two; she died in 1290 when her son was only six. Edward of Caernarfon's three older brothers John, Henry, and Alfonso – named after Queen Eleanor's brother Alfonso X of Castile – died in childhood, making Edward the heir to his father's throne when he was four months old, in August 1284. Five older sisters, Eleanor, Joan, Margaret, Mary and Elizabeth, also survived into adulthood, and there were at least another five daughters who didn't.

On 7 February 1301 at Lincoln, Edward I created his sixteen-year-old heir the Prince of Wales. Previously, Llewelyn the Last had declared himself Prince of Wales in 1258 as he tried to regain territories surrendered to the English after the death of Llewelyn the Great (1194–1240). The title was now recreated in 1301 for Edward of Caernarfon, who had at least been born in Wales. This was the first time the eldest son of the English sovereign was invested as Prince of Wales.

After he came to the throne as Edward II on 8 June 1307, Edward did not pass his Welsh title to his son, Edward III. But his grandson, another Edward, the Black Prince, was created Prince of Wales at the age of twelve in 1343 at Westminster. Since then the title has been held by the eldest surviving son of most English monarchs.

*

Also on this day in 1403, King Henry IV wed Joan of Navarre. Joan had been married in 1386 to John V, Duke of Brittany. The couple had nine children. Her first husband died on 1 November 1399 and for four years Joan acted as regent for her young son John VI.

According to the *Encyclopædia Britannica*, Henry Bolingbroke, heir to the duchy of Lancaster, was at the Breton court, having been banished from England by Richard II. During his visit, he and Joan became close and affectionate. In 1399, Bolingbroke became King of England as Henry IV and Joan married him as his second wife soon thereafter in 1403, after her son had come of age to rule Brittany alone. Joan and Henry had no children, but she is said to have had a good relationship with Henry's children from his first marriage, often taking the side of the future Henry V, 'Prince Hal', in his quarrels with his father.

Nevertheless, during the reign of Henry V, Joan was accused of using witchcraft in an attempt to try to poison her royal stepson. She was convicted in 1419 and imprisoned for about four years in Pevensey Castle in Sussex. After that she lived quietly at Nottingham Castle for the rest of Henry V's reign and into that of his son, Henry VI. She is buried in Canterbury Cathedral beside her second husband, Henry IV.

8th – A Royal Remedy

At some time between the 6 and 21 February, a rather odd entry was made into the account books of Richard III, which otherwise consist mainly of grants of lands and offices. It is a remedy for preventing bladder or kidney stones:

Take a lb [pound weight] of Ripe Cherries and stamp them, stones and all, and put the same into the milk of a Cow being of one colour as you do [with] ale to make a posset and drink it during the Cherry season twice or thrice and that year you shall suffer no pain.

R. Horrox and P. W. Hammond (eds), *B L Harley MS433*

9th – Cinque Ports Storm

On this date in 1287 there were terrible storms in south-east England, especially affecting the important Cinque Ports around the coast of Kent and Sussex. Shipping was lost and there was flooding and wind damage inland.

10th – The St Scholastica Riot

In medieval times, Oxford wasn't always a quiet, peaceful place. For centuries bloodshed, looting and burning were frequent and violence often simmered between the folk of Oxford (Town) and the university students (Gown). For instance, in 1209, soon after the foundation of the university, two students were hanged after one had killed a woman, either intentionally or accidentally. Legend has it that several of their colleagues fled to Cambridge, where they founded a rival university in order to escape further confrontation between Town and Gown.

But on 10 February 1355, the feast of St Scholastica, drink sparked off a riot that continued for three days. Students complained about the quality of the wine served at the Swyndlestock Tavern, on the corner of Queen Street and St Aldates, and 'snappish words' were exchanged between them and the innkeeper; the students threw the wine at the innkeeper's head. In the scuffle that followed, the townsmen rang the bell of their parish church of St Martin's to summon help, while the students rang the bell of the university church of St Mary to gather support on their side. In the riot that raged, about thirty townsmen were killed and sixty-three gownsmen.

In despair, the Mayor of Oxford rode to nearby Woodstock, where Edward III was staying, to seek his support. This didn't work out as the Town had hoped. In fact, the university's privileges were extended, giving them powers to regulate the drinks trade. Most humiliating of all, the mayor and corporation were required to attend a mass at the university church every St Scholastica's Day thereafter and to swear an oath to recognise the privileges of the university forever. They also had to pay the university 5s 3d each year, one penny for every scholar slain, a payment that continued until 1826 when the mayor simply refused to comply.

http://www.oxfordtimes.co.uk/lifestyle/history/9200746.
Rioting_over_wine_led_to_90_deaths/

11th – Against the Peace

On this day in 1358 the peace sessions in Bedford recorded the following:

They say on their oath that Maud Dolle on Sunday night before the feast of St Valentine ... at Eaton Ford assaulted Agnes Pitosfrei and broke her head against the peace. Richard le Sawere of Incomb came to the help of the said Maud and struck one William Sacomb junior against the peace. Maud and Richard were attached [summoned] to answer the lord king. The said Maud made fine and gives to the lord king 2*s* by the pledge of Robert Dolle and Henry Abbot.

P. J. P. Goldberg, *Women in England, c. 1275–1525*

Was Richard le Sawere also fined? The phrase 'against the peace' means unlawfully. In today's terms, we would say 'disturbing the peace'. The language used also makes it sound as though the king (Edward III) was present in person when Maud and Richard have to answer the lord king and Maud pays her fine to him. In fact, the phrase refers to a Justice of the Peace as the king's representative.

12th – Battle of the Herrings

On 12 February 1429 the English fought the Battle of the Herrings, just one incident of the Hundred Years War fought sporadically between England and France. Sir John Fastolf was in command of a convoy of 300 wagons carrying supplies for the English besiegers of Orléans in France, when it was attacked near the town of Rouvray by the French and their Scottish allies. Deploying his wagons as an improvised defence, Fastolf fought off the enemy and eventually drove them from the field. Despite sounding like a sea battle, the engagement owes its unusual name to the fact that the supplies being carried by the convoy included not just cannonballs, arrows and crossbow bolts but also a large quantity of barrels of herrings – particularly important as Lent was approaching, a time when good Christians were forbidden to eat meat.

http://www.historyextra.com/article/what-was-battle-herrings

13th – A Good Ointment for the Gout

A good ointment for the gout. Take an owl and pluck it clean and open it and salt it. Put it in a new pot and cover it with a stone and put it in an oven and let it stand till it be burnt. And then stamp [pound] it with boar's grease and anoint the gout therewith.

W. R. Dawson, *A Leechbook of the Fifteenth Century*

Poor owl! I can't think that this would have helped the patient very much either.

14th – Death of Richard II

It is believed that on or around this date in 1400, the deposed king, Richard II, died in Pontefract Castle in Yorkshire. He had become too much of a liability to the usurper king, his cousin, Henry IV. Still living, Richard could become the focus for rebellion, as had been the case with the Epiphany Rising a month before (see 2 January), endangering Henry's new regime. Quite how Richard met his death isn't certain. Some believe he was left to starve because Henry couldn't bring himself to order that his cousin be killed; others think Henry was less reluctant and royal blood was spilt. We may never know the truth.

15th – The Coroner's Rolls

For 15 February 1339, the Coroners Rolls of the City of London recorded:

Monday the morrow of St Valentine, information [was] given to the coroner and sheriffs that Alice Warde of York lay dead of a death other than her own rightful death in the rent [rented accommodation] of John de Blackwell in Fetter Lane in the parish of St Andrew, Holborn in the ward of Farringdon Without. Thereupon they proceeded there and having summoned the good men of the ward and of the ward of Farringdon Within, they diligently enquired how it happened. The jurors say that on the preceding Sunday at dusk, Geoffrey le Perler, a groom of the craft of lorimers [makers of decorative horse-harness] came to the rent where the aforesaid Alice was living, intending to find Emma de Brakkele, a prostitute, and to lie with her. Failing to find her, a quarrel arose between the said Geoffrey and Alice and thereupon the said Geoffrey secretly drew his knife ... and therewith struck the said Alice on the side under the right arm, inflicting a mortal wound.

P. J. P Goldberg, *Women in England, c. 1275–1525*

16th – Last Will and Testament

Juliane Clerkson of York made her short will on 16 February 1492. She left her soul to God, to Our Lady St Mary and to all the saints of heaven. She wanted to be buried in the churchyard of Holy Cross in York. To the parson, she left her best gown as her 'corsepresande'. This corpse-present was a customary gift from the deceased to the priest who conducted their burial service. Juliane also gave two pounds weight of best wax candles to pay for and to be lit during her burial service and another two pounds of wax to the holy vicar of Brantingham.

She bequeathed a basin and a laver [hand-washing equipment] to Esot Watson and another laver to Esot's daughter, Agnes. Juliane further left to Johnet Clerkson a great brass pot and to her sister, whom she had lived with, a green bed with a man and a woman on it. (Presumably, the man and woman were either carved into the wooden bed frame or embroidered on the green coverlet or hangings.) To Alice Mawman, she bequeathed her best candlestick and her green gown was to go to Margaret Symson.

Juliane appointed John Sponer and William Symson as her executors, and William Clyveland as the overseer of her will. It was witnessed by Thomas Garland and William Rawden.

H. Falvey, et al. (eds) *English Wills proved in the Prerogative Court of York, 1477–99*

Since her will was proven by the Prerogative Court of York on 28 February, less than two weeks later, Juliane must have been on her deathbed when she made this brief testament, of which I have given the full details here. But surely Juliane must have possessed more than these few items – her second best candlestick for one?

17th – The Second Battle of St Albans

Following the Battle of Northampton in 1460, King Henry VI had been captured by the Yorkists leaving his queen, Margaret of Anjou, in charge of the Lancastrian cause. Having recently tasted victory at the Battle of Wakefield, the Lancastrian army advanced on London.

The Yorkists under the command of Richard Neville, Earl of Warwick, moved to block Queen Margaret's march southward, establishing his defences just north of St Albans, on the Watling Street. Learning of Warwick's substantial defences, on the evening of 16 February 1461 Margaret veered her Lancastrian army west, capturing the town of Dunstable. Then, using the cover of darkness to move south-east, the Lancastrians arrived in St Albans early on 17 February, having outflanked Warwick's defences. As they advanced through the narrow streets, the Lancastrians initially suffered heavy casualties from Yorkist archers billeted in the town. The fierce hand-to-hand fighting continued for several hours, but without reinforcements the Yorkist archers were eventually overcome.

Now in control of the town, the Lancastrians turned and attacked the main Yorkist army to the north. Realising he was outmanoeuvred, Warwick ordered a tactical withdrawal, marching with his remaining force to Chipping Norton, Oxfordshire. In retreat, the Yorkists abandoned their vital hostage, the mentally unstable King Henry who apparently had spent the time of the battle sitting under a tree, singing.

http://www.historic-uk.com/HistoryMagazine/DestinationsUK/
The-Second-Battle-of-St-Albans/

18th – Drowning by Wine

On this day in 1478, news was leaked that the brother of King Edward IV, George, Duke of Clarence, had somehow managed to drown in a butt of malmsey wine. Did he fall or was he pushed? A contemporary chronicler, who otherwise seems very well informed, can only write: 'a few days after the execution, whatever its nature may have been, took place … in the Tower of London.'

Croyland Chronicle, c. 1486

George had never been very reliable nor faithful to his brother the king, but when his wife, Isabella, died soon after giving birth, probably of childbed fever, George was convinced that a lady-in-waiting, Ankarette Twynyho, had poisoned her. He tried Ankarette in a rigged court and arranged her execution. King Edward decided George had gone too far by taking the law into his own hands. Then George became involved in a further plot to dethrone Edward. Matters deteriorated when he accused the queen of witchcraft, saying she was behind the death of his wife. Finally, the king lost patience and George was imprisoned in the Tower of London in the summer of 1477.

Brought to trial before Parliament, only the king gave evidence against George, listing all his former mercies to him, how he had pardoned him for previous acts of treachery and showered titles and riches on him, only to receive ingratitude and further treachery in return. Meanwhile, George had spread rumours that the king was a bastard with no right to wear the crown, practising necromancy and poisoning those who displeased him.

Parliament sat in embarrassed silence as the king and his brother accused each other, shouting and arguing in a most unseemly and vulgar display. But the eventual outcome was never going to be in doubt: Parliament found in the king's favour, George was guilty of high treason and sentenced to death. He was returned to the Tower while the king wrestled with his conscience over signing his brother's death warrant, until the Speaker of the House intervened, demanding that sentence be carried out. George, Duke of Clarence, was executed privately in the Tower of London – spared the ignominy of a public beheading.

Rumours spread that Clarence had been drowned in a butt of malmsey wine. A butt is a large barrel and an imperial measure of 100 gallons – more than enough to drown in – but the story is almost certainly a later invention. Perhaps George was partial to the sweet white wine, so the tale was an ironic joke. It has been suggested, perhaps not seriously, that George was allowed to choose his manner of death, or even that a 'well-wisher', wanting to spare the king the grief of committing fratricide, sent Clarence a gift of wine, laced with poison. We will probably never know the truth.

19th – England's First Heresy

On 19 February 1401, William Sawtrey [or Sawtree] was on trial for his life at St Paul's Cathedral in London. William had been a priest at St Margaret's church in Lynn in Norfolk and had become a follower of the ideas of John Wycliffe. Wycliffe believed that the Church had corrupted the teachings of the Bible, so he translated it from Latin into English so that ordinary people could read and understand for themselves words they had previously only been able to hear, second-hand, from priests. William Sawtrey supported this initiative [known as Lollardy] and was first charged with heresy in 1399. Imprisoned, he swore to reject Wycliffe's teachings and was released, but quickly admitted this was a betrayal of Christ. He came to London and began preaching Lollardy once again. This time, he would not falter.

Another Lollard teaching stated that at the consecration of the bread during Mass, although it became the blessed Bread of Life, it remained bread (whereas the Church insisted that it transubstantiated into the Body of Christ, despite still looking and tasting like bread). It was William's denial of this miracle that landed him in court, on trial before Thomas Arundel, the Archbishop of Canterbury. Questioned for hours, William refused to conform. He was found guilty as a relapsed heretic, defrocked (literally stripped of his vestments and metaphorically of his priesthood) and handed over to the secular authorities for sentencing. A new law had recently been passed by Henry IV, urged on by the obsessive Archbishop Arundel, for the crime of heresy to carry a death sentence – a death of the worst kind. William Sawtrey was burned at the stake at Smithfield just outside London, the first English martyr to die for his religious beliefs in this horrible way.

http://www.christianity.com/church/church-history/
timeline/1201-1500/william-sawtrey-1st-lollard-
martyr-11629873.html

20th – Orkney and Shetland

Following the battle of Largs in 1263, the Treaty of Perth in 1266 forced the King of Norway to cede the Western Isles, off the Scottish coast, to the King of Scots. As a result, only Orkney and Shetland remained in Norwegian hands. Although the islands were still officially under Norway's rule, the Scottish earls had more and more control over Orkney, culminating in the appointment of Henry Sinclair, Earl of Roslin, as Earl of Orkney in 1379.

The earldom of Orkney was held from the Norwegian (and later Danish) crown until 1468, when the impoverished Christian I, King of Denmark, Norway and Sweden, gave Orkney to the Scottish crown as part of a marriage agreement with King James III. James was to marry Christian's daughter, Margaret, being given Orkney in lieu of her dowry until King Christian could raise 50,000 Rhenish Florins. At the end of the year, no payment had yet been made so Shetland was pledged (pawned) to the Scots for another 8,000 Florins.

A further two years on, King Christian had still been unable to raise the money and the earldom of Orkney and lordship of Shetland were formally annexed to Scotland on 20 February 1472.

http://www.orkneyjar.com/history/history6.htm

21st – Road Tax

On this date in 1482, the Bishop of Norwich was indicted for failing to maintain the king's highway where its route ran across his land, west of the city of London towards Westminster – a very busy thoroughfare:

For not repairing the highway in the parish of St Martin in the Fields lying between his inn [town house] and the inn of the Bishop of Durham, which way is so overflowed with water that the lords both spiritual and temporal, the King's Justices ... and all persons journeying by that way to Westminster to administer and observe the laws ... are often hindered.

H. S. Bennett, *The Pastons and their England*

This was how roads and bridges were kept in good repair – hopefully. Every householder and landowner was expected to maintain the highway at their front door and on their property at their own expense.

Clearly, as in this case, that didn't always happen. Often people left money in their wills for the upkeep of bridges and road repairs. This was seen as a charitable act, as good for the testator's soul as giving alms to the poor (see 12 August).

*

Also on this date in 1173, Thomas Becket was canonised by Pope Alexander III in record time.

22nd – Pot-Herbs

This was the time of year when the medieval housewife would plant allium bulbs in her garden – whether sweet-perfumed lilies or powerful-smelling onions, leeks and garlic. These 'pot-herbs' were vital to the cook and relatively easy to grow, the stronger tasting, the better – the medieval palate was rarely interested in subtle flavours. Leeks were an especial favourite; in 1333, Thomas of Keynsham, head gardener for Glastonbury Abbey, planted twenty-three beds of leeks in eight gardens, mostly to be consumed by the abbot and his visitors. Here is a fourteenth-century poem extolling the virtues of pot-herbs during Lent, when meat and dairy products were off the menu. Pottage was meant to be thick – a 'stonding' pottage was one in which a spoon would stand upright – and sufficiently filling that you didn't need to have bread as well, making it a cheap meal:

> Now leeks are in season, for pottage full good,
> And spareth the milchcow [milk-cow] and purgeth the blood:
> These having with peason [peas] for pottage in Lent,
> Thou sparest both oatmeal and bread to be spent.

T. McLean, *Medieval English Gardens*

23rd – Blaunche Pore

In the previous entry, I mentioned that pottage was meant to be an economical dish, but the Abbot of Glastonbury and his VIP guests would have expected their pottage to be an elaborate and luxurious dish, even during Lent. Here is a suitable recipe for *blaunche pore,* white pottage which required that the green parts of the leeks were discarded – a waste of good vegetables and something humble folk would never have done. However, the abbot's cook would have wanted to impress:

To make blaunche pore. Take whyte lekys & perboyle hem & hewe hem smale with oynouns. Cast it in a good broth & seethe it up with smale bryddys. Coloure it with safferoun; powdur yt with pouder douce.

M. Black, *The Medieval Cookbook*

Maggie Black suggests chicken stock for the broth, which wouldn't have been permitted in Lent – not officially at least – and she advises that the parboiling of the leeks and onions isn't necessary and to omit the 'smale bryddys'. After all, sparrows are today becoming rarer and would also be barred as meat in Lent. 'Pouder douce' we have seen before in various spellings and recipes and can be made using a pinch each of ground pepper, cinnamon and cloves with a little light brown sugar.

24th – Maud Heath's Causeway

In the damp month of February, the River Avon in Wiltshire was prone to flood the low-lying water meadows around Chippenham. Chippenham was an important local market in medieval times and people came from miles around to shop and buy produce.

In the fifteenth century, an enterprising widow named Maud Heath made her pin-money (a housewife's income) by taking her surplus eggs and homemade butter to Chippenham to sell at the market every week. She had a long walk of four or five miles from her home near Wick Hill and frequently got her feet wet as she crossed the water meadows.

In 1474, when Maud died, in her will she proposed that a causeway should be built through the meadows and bequeathed enough money to pay for its construction and upkeep. Her wishes were carried out and parts of Maud's causeway are still there, allowing travellers to keep their feet dry on the walk to Chippenham market and back.

B. Henisch, *The Medieval Cook*

25th – Anselm's Dispute

The tragic quarrel between King Henry II and Archbishop Thomas Becket is well known (see 29 December) but it wasn't the first of its kind. In the 1090s, King William II of England (known as Rufus) took issue with Anselm, designated to become Archbishop of Canterbury. The subject of the argument was much the same as between Henry and Becket: the king wanted to control both Church and state; the new archbishop insisted that Church authority lay with the Pope.

Anselm's first clash with Rufus occurred within days of his agreeing to take up the office, even before he was officially installed. Rufus was fighting his elder brother, Robert, for possession of Normandy and needed money to pay for the war. Anselm, like other noblemen and churchmen who weren't going to fight at the king's side, was expected to contribute to the cause, in cash. The new archbishop offered Rufus £500, but Rufus insisted on £1,000 – after all, he was permitting Anselm to achieve the highest office. Anselm not only refused, he demanded that the king allow full authority to Church law, that he fill the vacant bishoprics in England and permit bishops to meet freely in councils, and to allow him to clamp down on incestuous marriages – apparently a big issue at the time but probably referring to marriages of cousins, rather than within close family. Rufus commanded Anselm to be silent. When a group of churchmen suggested the king should accept the original offer of £500, Anselm said it was too late, he'd given the money to the poor instead and he wouldn't buy Rufus' favour as he might purchase a horse or an ass. The king's response was: 'I hated him before, I hate him now and shall hate him still more hereafter.' Anselm retired to Canterbury and Rufus went off to fight his brother in Normandy – without the archbishop's money or his blessing, which he blatantly withheld.

When Rufus returned, Anselm informed him that before he was formally installed, he intended to visit the Pope, to receive papal permission and make his position as archbishop official. Rufus refused, insulted by the gesture. After all, as king he had instated Anselm to the post; to be told it required the Pope to second the decision was to question Rufus' authority in England.

On 25 February 1095, the Lords Spiritual and Temporal, i.e. churchmen and nobles, met in council at Rockingham Castle in Northamptonshire, on the border with Rutland and Leicestershire. Rufus now intended to deny Anselm the office of Archbishop of Canterbury; the churchmen, led by the Bishop of Durham, fully supported the king. Surprisingly, the nobles supported Anselm, saying there was no proof he had committed any crime. The conference ended in deadlock.

Rufus then had the idea of selling the office of archbishop to anyone who wanted it. Nobody came forward. So the king offered it to Anselm once more – for a fee. Anselm refused. Finally, Rufus had the archbishop's pallium (outer garment) laid on the altar in Canterbury Cathedral; whoever wanted the job could take it. Anselm took it on 10 June 1095.

Like his later successor, Thomas Becket, Anselm spent time in exile; unlike Becket, he outlived the king with whom he had quarrelled. He died on Holy Wednesday, 21 April 1109 and was buried in Canterbury Cathedral. After his death, again like Becket, Anselm was canonised as a saint; his feast day is 21 April.

26th – The King's Ordnance

Richard III instructed the Constable of the Tower of London to hand over various ordnance supplies:

A warrant to the Constable of the Tower to deliver to Roger Bikley seven serpentines upon carts, twenty-eight hacbusshes with their frames, one barrel of touch powder, two barrels of serpentine powder, 200 bows, 400 sheaves of arrows, ten gross [1,440] bowstrings and 200 bills.

R. Horrox and P. W. Hammond (eds), *British Library Harleian Manuscript 433*

This was some of the latest in weapons technology from the royal armoury at the Tower. Serpentines were small cannon, light enough to trundle around on their purpose-built carts. Hacbusshes (I left the original spelling for this) were harquebuses, the first ever hand-held guns, which came with a frame or tripod to help keep them steady when aiming and firing. The barrels were of gunpowder – obviously there were different types depending on the firearm. Bows, arrows and bills (pole or staff weapons) were still in use as well, although the guns would supersede the longbow in the sixteenth century. Unfortunately, there is no further indication as to who Roger Bikley was, apart from a man it was best to keep as a friend.

27th – A Knight's Last Wishes

On this day in 1378 Sir John Northwode, a knight who lived on the Isle of Sheppey in Kent, wrote his will. These are his last wishes:

To be buried in the Church of the Nuns of Saint Sexburg of Mentre in Scapeya [Minster in Sheppey] in Canterbury Diocese. I will that my wife pay my debts of my goods. I will that Johanna my daughter have of my goods if there are any over after my debts are paid according to the discretion of the said Johanna my wife, William Frogenhale, William Suttone and John de Mere.

   I will that Stephen my son be found *ad scolas* [his education paid for] of my said goods after my debts are paid if there be sufficient to the effect he be moved to be a Religious or take Sacred Orders. I will that two men go on pilgrimage to visit the shrine of the Apostles Peter and Paul and Saint James in Galicia and that they be found [paid for] of my said goods. Residue to Johanne my wife and executrix.

Medieval & Tudor Kent Wills at Lambeth – Book 24

On 13 March 1378, his wife, Dame Johanne, was granted probate on Sir John's will as his executrix.

   Paying for others to go on a pilgrimage in your name, as Sir John does here, was a good way of earning merit for your soul in heaven, even though you couldn't make the journey in person any more.

28th – Medieval Apprenticeships

In York, the Founders' Guild – the guild for metalworkers – ordained:

That no one of the said craft shall have an apprentice for less than a term of seven years and not several at a time, but only one apprentice, except that the said Giles de Bonoyne can have two apprentices at a time because he has no wife.

P. J. P. Goldberg, *Women in England, c. 1275–1525*

Evidently, a wife must have been expected to assist her husband at the forge and we know many did so. However, there was also a requirement that a master had to be married in order to take on an apprentice, the intention being that his wife would feed and care for the youngster in lieu of his or her mother. Giles seems to have been allowed to break this rule for some reason.

29th – Balourgy Broth

Here is a spicy fish recipe called balourgy broth, suitable for Lent (I have modernised the spelling):

Take pikes and spread them on a board and eels if thou hast [them]. Skin and cut them into gobbets and boil them in a liquid: half wine and half water. Take out the pikes and eels and keep them hot, and strain the cooking broth through a cloth. Add powdered ginger, pepper and galingale and cinnamon to the broth and boil it; pour the broth over the pikes and eels and serve it forth.

S. Pegge, *The Forme of Cury*

MARCH

1st – St David's Day

In AD 589, 1 March fell upon a Tuesday and is believed to be the day that David, a Welsh bishop, died. He was canonised as St David by Pope Callixtus II in 1120 and became the patron saint of Wales with his feast day celebrated on 1 March. David was a strict vegetarian and, according to Shakespeare, his badge of a leek was worn by Welshmen from the time of Henry V at least:

Fluellen: If your Majesty is remembered of it, the Welshmen did good service in a garden where leeks did grow, wearing leeks in their Monmouth caps, which your Majesty knows, to this hour is an honourable badge of the service and I do believe, your Majesty takes no scorn to wear the leek upon Saint Tavy's day.

King Henry: I wear it for a memorable honour; for I am Welsh, you know, good countryman.

W. Shakespeare, *Henry V*, Act V: Scene 1

2nd – The Rights of Sanctuary

At about this date in 1313, according to the Eyre roll of Kent (records of the travelling justices), a woman, unnamed, who had already been tried, found guilty and condemned to death for larceny (theft of personal items) was discovered to be pregnant. She was to be kept in prison until the child was born – medieval justice regarded the unborn baby as innocent of its mother's crime, so should not suffer any penalty; after its birth, sentence would be carried out on the mother.

However, in this case, the mother-to-be managed to escape from the prison and fled to a church, seeking sanctuary. Her gaoler found her and dragged her from the church, thus breaking the rights of sanctuary, and took her before the justices, only to find himself in trouble. The justices ordered that the woman be taken back to the church, as sanctuary required, for the full forty days and then allowed to 'abjure the realm' – be banished abroad. Her gaoler was then tried for having broken her rights and the Church's laws of sanctuary.

P. J. P. Goldberg, *Women in England, c. 1275–1525*

3rd – The Statute of Wales

In the reign of King Edward I, the Statute of Rhuddlan was issued on this day in 1284, incorporating the Principality of Wales into England. Sometimes known as the Statute of Wales, this was a royal ordinance, issued personally by King Edward I without any act of Parliament. It was intended to settle the government of Wales after the execution of Dafydd ap Gruffydd in 1283. English criminal law came into effect but Welsh custom and law were to operate in civil proceedings – with certain exceptions. Six English-style counties, each with a sheriff to enforce the new laws in the king's name, were established in Anglesey, Caernarfon, Cardiganshire, Carmarthen, Flint and Merioneth.

http://www.oxfordreference.com/view/10.1093/oi/
authority.20110803100419253

By this statute, Wales was annexed to the crown of England and much of Welsh law abolished. Issues concerning debt, the use of lawyers and attorneys, inquests, pleas, trials and juries were all now to be conducted in accordance with English common law. Edward also established laws dealing with dowers for women (for which there was no arrangement under Welsh law). Under English law, a dower was the portion of her husband's estates allotted to a widow, as a sort of widow's pension to sustain her, either until she married again or for the rest of her life if she remained unwed. Only then could her deceased husband's heirs inherit her portion. And there were new laws to regulate who were those lawful heirs.

Under Welsh law, a man's sons, whether born in or out of wedlock, had the same rights of inheritance, but King Edward specifically forbade bastards to inherit, as was the case under English law. His crackdown on illegitimate offspring may well have been because some of the most troublesome Welsh princes had inherited their fathers' titles despite being bastard-born. This is what the statute says on the matter of dowers and illegitimate sons:

Inheritance shall be made as it was wont [used] to be made with this exception, that bastards from henceforth shall not inherit and also shall not have portions with the lawful heirs ... We will of our especial grace that ... women shall have their portions thereof to be assigned them in our Court, although this be contrary to the custom of Wales before used.

http://www.sarahwoodbury.com/the-statute-of-wales/

4th – King John's Crusade

On this day in 1215, King John of England took an oath to go on Crusade to the Holy Land. John had no intention of leaving England to make such a journey for the country was in uproar, but the promise was meant to gain the support of Pope Innocent III in his quarrel with his unruly barons – a situation that would lead to the drawing up of Magna Carta (see 15 June).

*

Also, on this day in 1461, Edward Plantagenet, Duke of York and Earl of March, claimed the throne of England as King Edward IV (see 13 March). Edward's father Richard, Duke of York had been slain at the battle of

Wakefield the previous December (see 30 December). Richard had a valid claim to the throne which passed to his son, Edward. Edward had already won the battle of Mortimer's Cross against the rival House of Lancaster and would later have the decisive victory at Towton (see 29 March). In the meantime, on his way from Mortimer's Cross in the Welsh borders to continue the fight in the north of England, Edward came to London to stake his claim to the kingdom. His father had once done the same in the previous autumn, only to be greeted by a stony silence, even from his supporters, but by now, England wanted a new, active and capable king to bring peace to the country, Henry VI having proved so disastrous and inept as a monarch. Edward fitted the profile perfectly. Henry was in the Yorkists' custody and in such a situation it was more usual for the opposition to rule in the old king's name. Not this time: Edward claimed the crown in his own right. Londoners cheered him, the Archbishop of Canterbury gave his blessing and the coronation was planned.

5th – Henry II's Birth

In 1133 the future King of England, Henry II, was born at Le Mans in France. He was the son of Geoffrey, Count of Anjou and Matilda, the daughter of King Henry I of England. Matilda had previously been wed to the Emperor of Germany and still liked to call herself 'empress', despite having been widowed and remarried to a lowly count. Her son Henry also liked the idea of his mother being a one-time empress and used the surname 'FitzEmpress'. The young man was also known as Henry Curtmantle (in French: *court-manteau*), because the fashionable long cloaks of the day got in the way when he was rushing about, with Henry preferring a shorter style. Today, he is probably better known as Henry Plantagenet, a surname used by his father Geoffrey, who is thought to have worn a sprig of the broom plant, or *Planta genista,* in his hat as a means of identification in battle – or so the story goes.

Henry eventually ruled as King of England, Lord of Ireland, Duke of Normandy and Aquitaine, Count of Anjou, Maine and Nantes, as well as controlling Wales, Scotland and Brittany. By the age of only fourteen, Henry was actively involved in his mother's efforts to claim the throne of England from her cousin and rival, King Stephen. Henry was made Duke of Normandy at the age of seventeen, inherited Anjou in 1151 and shortly afterwards married Eleanor of Aquitaine, whose marriage to King Louis VII of France had been recently annulled by the Pope. King Stephen agreed to a peace treaty after Henry's attempted military expedition to England in 1153 and the death of Stephen's son and heir, the Lord Eustace. Henry inherited the kingdom on Stephen's death a year later (see 19 Dec).

6th – Spring Bestiary

At about this time of year, as the weather begins to warm the earth, hedgehogs come out of hibernation. In the thirteenth century, bestiary books were especially popular in England. They were the medieval equivalent of nature books, describing all types of animals, both real and mythical. It was believed that God had created every animal with a purpose for mankind. Sheep, cows and horses were of obvious use, but if a creature didn't seem to have a specific benefit for man, it must serve as an object lesson for good Christians. This is what an English bestiary book, taken from MS Bodley 764, has to say about the endearing hedgehog, which wasn't quite what it seemed:

The hedgehog is covered in spines which protect it from its enemies. If it senses danger, it curls up inside its armour. It always builds its den with two holes for ventilation. If the cold north wind blows, it blocks the northern hole; if the south wind blows from hot, dangerous lands, it blocks the southern hole. The hedgehog is quite clever: if it plucks fruit from a grape vine, it rolls onto it, spearing the grapes with its spines and carrying them home to feed its young. In this way the hedgehog is a sinner, skilled in robbery; it steals the fruits of other peoples' labours, taking their food for itself. In the book of Psalms [in the Bible] it says that 'the rocks are the refuge of the hedgehog'. It is like the man bristling with sins who fears the judgement to come and takes safe refuge in the rock of Christ.

R. Barber, *Bestiary*

7th – The Town Drunk Dry

On 7 March 1487, William Paston wrote to John Paston from Sheen (now Richmond, Surrey):

As for the King's [Henry VII] coming ... to Norwich ... Wherefore you need to warn William Gogyne and his fellows to provide themselves with enough wine, for everyone assures me that the town will be drunk dry, as was York when the King was there.

I beseech you to remember the horse that you promised me.

R. Virgoe (ed.), *The Illustrated Letters of the Paston Family*

8th – Herb Fritters

Whatever the date of Easter each year, this day would fall within Lent, the forty day period when the Catholic Church required everyone to fast – that is, to refrain from eating meat and dairy products – yet not every day of Lent was a fast day. Sundays were feast days in the Catholic Church, so the forty-day fast was broken with a respite each Sunday. In the early Church, Saturday was also excluded but, for the remaining days of fasting, here is a Lenten recipe for herb fritters:

Frytour of Erbes
    Take gode erbys; grynde hem and medle hem with flour and water & a lytel yest and salt and frye hem in oyle. And ete hem with clere hony.

S. Pegge, *The Forme of Cury*

A version for modern cooks recommends using these chopped fresh herbs:

1½ teaspoons of thyme, 2½ teaspoons of sage, 1 tablespoon of oregano and 6 tablespoons of parsley
3 cups of flour
2¼ cups of water

¼ teaspoon of yeast
A pinch of salt
Oil for frying
Clear honey

Dissolve the yeast in half a cup of water, add salt to flour; when the yeast is foamy, add it and rest of flour to water. Let sit while herbs are chopped and ground (note that quantities of herbs are after chopping). Add the herbs to the batter. Deep fry in the oil until crispy, using half a tablespoon of batter for each fritter. This makes about thirty-six 2½ inch (6 cm) fritters. Serve drizzled with honey.

9th – Katherine Sage's Bequest

On this day, the will of Katherine Sage of Scarborough in Yorkshire was proved. Katherine had outlived two husbands: Robert Alcock, a merchant and ship-owner, and Thomas Sage.

In 1493, Thomas Sage, a merchant, had been a member of a group commissioned by the king to enquire into the escape of prisoners from the gaol in Scarborough. The prisoners had been involved in the 'spoliation' of a ship belonging to a Londoner – possibly thieving from the cargo – and had made their escape from custody while being detained by Bailiff Shilbotell, who clearly hadn't been up to the task, or else outright aided the miscreants in their getaway. When Thomas died, he had asked to be buried beside his first wife, Alice.

Now Katherine was a wealthy widow and seems to have had quite a collection of jewellery and fine quality clothing. Her son, Robert Alcock, is to receive 100 shillings worth of jewellery, a piece of silver-gilt, three sets of beads, i.e. rosary beads: one of silver, one of gold and one of coral, and a gold ring. Katherine's daughters, Margaret and Elizabeth Sage, are to have £10 worth of jewellery each. Margaret is also bequeathed her mother's two best girdles [belts], a coral rosary, two gold rings, a crimson gown, a gown trimmed with black velvet, a scarlet kirtle [under gown] and a little gold brooch. Elizabeth is bequeathed two girdles, a 'damysyn' girdle (either made of damask or maybe damson-coloured), a 'toking' girdle (I have no idea what 'toking' means), a coral rosary, two gold rings, a silver bell, a lined scarlet gown, a violet gown furred with squirrel and a scarlet kirtle.

And that is just a small sample of Katherine's bequests!

H. Falvey, et al. (eds) *English Wills proved in the*
PC of York, 1477–1499

10th – The Treason Act

The Treason Act 1351 was passed by Parliament at Westminster during the Hilary term of 1351, in the twenty-fifth year of the reign of Edward III, to clarify precisely what was treason. Although the act has been changed significantly over the centuries, it is one of the earliest English statutes still in force today in the United Kingdom. It also still applies in some former British colonies, including New South Wales in Australia.

The act defines two forms of treason: high treason and petty (*petit,* little) treason. High treason covers disloyalty to the sovereign, and the second disloyalty to one of the king's subjects. For high treason, the punishment was death by hanging, drawing and quartering for a man or drawing and burning for a woman; the traitor's property would then belong to the Crown. In the case of petty treason, the penalty was almost as terrible: drawing and hanging without the quartering, or burning without drawing; and the traitor's property went to his overlord, not the Crown. Whatever the case, the traitor was executed. Here is an excerpt from the Treason Act of 1351:

Whereas divers Opinions have been before this Time in what Case Treason shall be said, and in what not; the King, at the Request of the Lords and of the Commons, hath made a Declaration in the Manner as hereafter followeth, that is to say; When a Man doth compass or imagine the Death of our Lord the King, or of our Lady his Queen or of their eldest Son and Heir; or if a Man do violate the King's Companion, or the King's eldest Daughter unmarried, or the Wife of the King's eldest Son and Heir; or if a Man do levy War against our Lord the King in his Realm, or be adherent to the King's Enemies in his Realm, giving to them Aid and Comfort in the Realm, or elsewhere, and thereof be attainted of open Deed by the People of their Condition ... and if a Man slay the Chancellor, Treasurer, or the King's Justices of the one Bench or the other, Justices in Eyre, or Justices of Assize, and all other Justices assigned to hear and determine, being in their Places, doing their Offices: And it is to be understood, that in the Cases above rehearsed, that ought to be judged Treason which extends to our Lord the King ...

Section II, *Treason Act 1351*

Other deeds of high treason included counterfeiting the Great Seal or the Privy Seal, counterfeiting English coinage or importing counterfeit English coins. Under the act, petty treason was defined as the murder of a lawful superior, i.e. if a servant killed his master or his master's wife, or a wife killed her husband – but not if a husband killed his wife – or if a clergyman killed his bishop. The act was originally worded so that if any additional forms of treason arose in the future, they too could be covered by the act, so it legislated for this possibility:

And because that many other like Cases of Treason may happen in Time to come, which a Man cannot think nor declare at this present Time; it is accorded, That if any other Case, supposed Treason, which is not above specified, doth happen before any Justices, the Justices shall tarry without any going to Judgement of the Treason till the Cause be shewed and declared before the King and his Parliament, whether it ought to be judged Treason or other Felony.

Section II, *Treason Act 1351*

11th – Trial of the Pyx

On this day in 1248, the first ever Trial of the Pyx was carried out at Westminster, conducted by Richard, Earl of Cornwall, the brother of King Henry III, to ensure that the new coinage then being minted – all silver pennies – was of a consistent and high standard. Richard was in charge of the Mint at the Tower of London and had taken on the responsibility for sorting out the coins of the realm, many of which had been clipped (had the edges trimmed off) and so were underweight and no longer worth one penny. Unscrupulous people melted down the silver trimmings, adulterated them with cheaper metals and produced forged coins.

To be certain only pure silver was being used, Richard ordered the Master of the Mint to select at random and save for trial one coin for every ten pounds worth of silver minted. A trial was normally conducted every three months. The term 'Pyx' refers to the wooden chest (in Greek *pyxis*) in which the coins were locked for safekeeping until they were presented to the jury. Such trials are still held today, once each year, the ceremony being little changed since 1282, when Edward I set down the procedure to be followed. The trial is conducted as in a court of law, presided over by a judge with an expert jury of assayers – usually goldsmiths – who test the coins for the purity of the metal. Trials are now held at the Hall of the Worshipful Company of Goldsmiths, but in medieval times they took place at the Palace of Westminster. The presiding judge is the King's (or Queen's) Remembrancer, the senior Master of the King's Bench. It is his (or her) responsibility to ensure that the trial is held in accordance with the law and to deliver the jury's final verdict to the monarch. The jury is composed of at least six assayers from the Company of Goldsmiths. They have two months to test the provided coins, and decide whether they have been properly minted.

12th – A Merchant's Last Statement

It was on 12 March 1485 that John de Saire, a merchant of Southampton, drew up a very long will in Latin while lying abed at the house of Ralph Pykart in that town. John's dealings as a merchant were wide ranging, from cloth to wine and tin. John Kenaules seems to have been an important business associate:

John Kenaules holds and should hold 18 large pieces of tin and one small piece of tin belonging to me which weigh 49 hundredweight with a half, a quarter and 13lbs. Also the said John Kenaules has from me 18 pieces of wide white cloth, each piece containing 24 yards or thereabouts, which goods the said John Kenaules holds and should hold until I am able to deliver to him 45 casks of wine now being in two or three cellars in this town [Southampton]. ... Also I acknowledge that I owe the said John Kenaules £14 8s 4d. Also I owe Thomas the servant of John Kenaules 2s 4d. ... For the paying and satisfying of my debts I bequeath into the hands of my executors ... from the said John Kenaules £35 sterling and 10s for wine. Also, moreover, I acknowledge that I owe John Kenaules 13 hundredweight of tin worth 24s a hundredweight. ...

Also the fact is that John Paschall, master of the *hulque,* owes me 54 crowns [£13 10s] of English money because I take upon myself all the chances and outcome of the sea in going and travelling by sea to La Rochelle and also returning to this country ...

L. Boatwright, et al. (eds), *Logge Register*

This last statement shows that John de Saire was acting as a marine insurance broker, covering the risks of importing and exporting goods across the English Channel, chancing piracy, shipwreck, storms and other calamities.

13th – A King's Call for Help

In 1461, King Henry VI wrote a pleading letter to Sir William Plumpton for assistance against Edward Plantagenet, Earl of March, who had claimed the throne of England as King Edward IV earlier in the month, on 4 March. Here is Henry's letter:

Trusty and well-beloved, we greet you well, and for as much as we have knowledge that our great traitor, the late Earl of March, hath made great assemblies of riotous and mischievously disposed people, and to stir and provoke them to draw unto him, he hath cried in his proclamation havoc upon all our true liege people and subjects, their wives, children and goods and is now coming towards us. We therefore pray you and also straightely charge you that anon [immediately] upon the sight hereof [this letter], ye with all such people as ye may make defensively arrayed [armed for war], come unto us in all haste possible, wheresoever we shall be within this our Realm, for to resist the malicious intent and purpose of our said traitor, and fail not hereof as ye love the security of our person, the weal [wellbeing] of yourself and of all our true and faithful subjects.

Given under our signet at our City of York.

T. Stapleton (ed), *The Plumpton Correspondence*

The phrase 'late Earl of March' refers to the fact that Henry had attainted the earl, stripping him of his title. Sir William Plumpton obeyed Henry's call to arms and would fight for the Lancastrian king at the forthcoming Battle of Towton (see 29 March). The Lancastrians were defeated and Sir William's eldest son was among the dead.

14th – Morte d'Malory

On 14 March 1471, Sir Thomas Malory died in London. He had been released from the infamous Newgate Prison, just outside the city walls, a few months previously. He was the author of *Morte d'Arthur* and had written his collection of stories of King Arthur and the Knights of the Round Table while serving time in the gaol.

Thomas Malory was probably born around 1415 at Newbold Revel in Warwickshire. We know nothing of his childhood except that he was a teenager when his father died in 1433 and by October 1441 he had been knighted. His adventures read like a thriller novel.

In 1442, Thomas served in the war in Gascony, but the following year he was accused of robbery with violence, a charge that fell through and didn't stop his election as MP for Warwickshire in 1445. Then, during the recess of Parliament on 4 January 1450, he and twenty-six other armed men allegedly lay in ambush to murder the Duke of Buckingham in the woods near Newbold Revel. This was followed by an eighteen-month crime spree that included extortion, theft, rape, cattle rustling, robbery of the local abbey, deer poaching and damage to property at Caludon Park, the Duke of Norfolk's hunting lodge which Buckingham was using. Malory's attack was a deliberate provocation of Buckingham who hunted him with a large posse and put him at odds with the Duke of Norfolk too. In desperation, Malory turned to the Duke of York, who was trying to bring political pressure to bear on the government and for whose borough of Wareham Thomas was returned to Parliament in September 1450.

It was a bad move. In May 1451, York's efforts collapsed and in July, Buckingham caught up with Malory and committed him to the sheriff who detained him at Coleshill in Warwickshire. Malory escaped by swimming the moat at night, but was recaptured. He was charged with a long list of offences including the attempted murder of Buckingham, but when two juries couldn't reach a verdict, the proceedings were transferred to the King's Bench at Westminster, which is how Thomas ended up in Newgate for the first time.

During Malory's first year in prison, he made his peace with the Duke of Norfolk and was released, but a neighbour's complaint that he had stolen her oxen meant Buckingham was called again to recapture him. Released a second time in 1454, he joined an old crony on a horse-stealing expedition across East Anglia that ended in Colchester Gaol. From there he escaped again, 'using swords, daggers, and halberds', but was recaptured and sent back to London. After that he was shifted frequently from prison to prison and the penalties imposed on his gaolers for his safekeeping reached a record high for medieval England.

In 1455, when King Henry VI suffered a mental collapse, Malory was granted a pardon by the Duke of York as Lord Protector. However, the Lancastrian chief justice dismissed it. When the Yorkists invaded England in 1460, Thomas was moved to a more secure prison, but their victory brought him freedom. He was never tried on any of the charges against him.

The new decade looked more promising. A second pardon cleared the slate and Malory settled down to a peaceful life. Soon after that, for some reason his political sympathies shifted and he became involved in a plot against the Yorkist king, Edward IV, in June 1468. He was arrested and imprisoned in Newgate once again, but spent his time writing his famous book, completing his *Morte d'Arthur* by 3 March 1470. Meanwhile in October 1470 a sudden invasion brought the Lancastrians briefly back to power, who freed all imprisoned members of their own faction, including Thomas. He hadn't much time to enjoy his freedom. Six months later he died in London; he was probably aged fifty-five. He was buried under a marble tombstone in St Francis's Chapel, Greyfriars, Newgate, one of the most fashionable churches in London. When an inquiry was made into his estate, the jurors testified that he had died owning nothing. In a prudent moment, the rash Sir Thomas had made over all his lands to others.

T. Mount, *Everyday Life in Medieval London*

15th – The French Raid

On 15 March 1360 the French attacked Winchelsea on the south coast of England. Present-day Winchelsea, a quiet little place, overlooks the marshes near Rye in East Sussex, but it was once an important town, one of the chain of Cinque Ports that line the coast of south-eastern England. An earlier ancient port of Winchelsea now lies beneath the sea, having been overwhelmed by the waves during storms in the thirteenth century, but King Edward I built a new town on the hilltop to replace it. The new Winchelsea, rebuilt on a steep peninsula, was a popular embarkation point for the royal family. The Cinque Ports were vital to English trade and coastal defence and whenever there was war with our neighbours across the Channel, the French were keen to attack them. Winchelsea was on the front line and a frequent target, being attacked on at least seven occasions.

On this particular Sunday, 2,000 Frenchmen landed and invaded the town. The people were slain at church, the women raped before they were killed. It was a bloodbath repeated in other towns along the coast and repaid by the English on the other side of the Channel in the early years of what we now call the Hundred Years War. Winchelsea's defences hadn't been maintained. In fact, the town was said to have been partially 'waste and uninhabited' due to the ravages of the pestilence, or Black Death, drastically reducing the population. Most fit and able men remaining were either supporting Edward III in France with the Cinque Ports fleet, or patrolling the Thames estuary, in the mistaken belief that the French intended to attack London.

The story runs that the French walked up the hill into town, meeting little resistance, taking the people unawares while they were attending Sunday mass. A more likely version says that, since church bells had been rung all along the south coast of England to warn of the possible

French invasion, the population had taken refuge in the stone-built church of St Giles, where a few defenders might stand a chance of repelling the French. Unfortunately, they were greatly outnumbered and stood no chance; the townsfolk were slaughtered and the church burned.

The French then took their time, looting houses and burning ships in the harbour. In the meantime, the abbot from Battle Abbey was able to bring 300 mounted men to the aid of Winchelsea. Loaded down with their ill-gotten gains, the French were reluctant to contest the issue and attempted to return to their ships. They suffered hundreds of casualties from the arrows of the hastily assembled English archers as they tried to board their ships, but too late for the townsfolk. Three years later, over 400 houses were not yet rebuilt and the loss of the ships burned in the harbour was still affecting trade.

The French returned to attack Winchelsea repeatedly and in 1388, in combination with their Spanish Castillian allies, they virtually obliterated the little town. Although it was rebuilt on a smaller scale, Winchelsea never fully recovered and, as the sea receded, it was left, literally high and dry, a quiet village, a bustling port no longer.

http://www.thehistorypress.co.uk/index.php/updates/
winchelsea-at-war/#sthash.vYfBTkJO.dpuf

16th – Death of Anne Neville

Anne Neville, the wife of King Richard III, died at Westminster Palace on 16 March 1485, aged only twenty-eight. As she lay dying, there was a solar eclipse. The sky grew dark, birds roosted and people felt scared. Some took the eclipse to be an omen of her husband's fall from heavenly grace. Anne was buried in Westminster Abbey to the right of the High Altar, next to the door to the Confessor's Chapel. King Richard is said to have wept at her funeral. Nevertheless, rumours circulated that he had poisoned her in order to marry his niece – rumours he flatly denied. It is more than likely that the queen died of tuberculosis as she had been ailing since the previous Christmas.

17th – The First Duke of Cornwall

King Edward III of England also held the titles Duke of Normandy and Duke of Aquitaine – both being French titles. At the time there were no English dukedoms until Edward of Woodstock, the Black Prince, the eldest son of Edward III, was made the first Duke of Cornwall on 17 March 1337, when he was just seven years old. He had been given the title Earl of Chester in 1333, but as the king's son and heir, Edward wasn't created Prince of Wales until 1343, six years after becoming Duke of Cornwall. The main reason for a monarch to bestow such titles was so that the recipient had an income from the estates which accompanied the title.

The original earldom of Cornwall came with the wealth from the tin mines (stannaries) of the area and was a title that had been given to Henry III's brother, Richard, who had become extremely wealthy on the income. In 1337, the title was vacant, so Edward III took the opportunity to bestow the valuable estates on his eldest son, raising the title to a dukedom.

The dukedom of Cornwall can only be held by the eldest living son of the monarch who is also heir apparent. In the event of a Duke of Cornwall's death, the title merges in the Crown even if he left surviving descendants. The monarch's grandson, even if he is the heir apparent, may become Prince of Wales, but doesn't succeed to the dukedom.

As Duke of Cornwall, the Black Prince was thought of as a decent, caring landlord. Thomas Brinton, Bishop of Rochester, said of the prince:

Where the lords of this world usually oppress and afflict their tenants and landholders, this lord always cares for his tenants, comforting them in many ways.

The 'ways' included letting his Cornish tenants forgo certain payments to him during the time of the Black Death, when the tin miners were particularly hard hit. He had a word with his father, Edward III, concerning pirates who had taken Cornish ships and goods at sea, to get compensation for his people. The duchy owned Dartmoor and the prince ensured that the poorest folk had the right to graze their animals there for free.

Having created one dukedom, Edward III of England created two more: his cousin, Henry of Grosmont, Earl of Lancaster, was promoted to Duke of Lancaster in 1351, and the king's second son, Lionel of Antwerp, was created Duke of Clarence – an Irish title since the young man had acquired other lands and titles there through his marriage to Elizabeth de Burgh, Countess of Ulster – in 1362. At about the same time that Lionel received his dukedom, his younger brother, John of Gaunt, third son of Edward III, became Duke of Lancaster in right of his wife, Blanche of Lancaster, Grosmont's daughter and heiress when Henry died in 1361.

Perhaps another reason for Edward III bestowing dukedoms upon his family was to do with the rules of chivalry. According to the chivalric code, in time of war a man should only be taken captive and held to ransom by his social equal or higher. With the Hundred Years War against France in full swing, French dukes were being taken prisoner by mere knights, squires and men-at-arms. At best, they might be ransomed by an English earl. This was regarded as an insult to chivalry, so a few English dukedoms evened the odds a little. Also, King Edward wanted the French to be well aware that the English nobility was as good as theirs – if not better – and the new rank of duke underlined that (see 26 January).

18th – Ludshot Manor Court

The manor court of Ludshot (Ludshott, Hampshire) was held on the feast of St Edward the Martyr in the fifth year of Henry IV (1404):

John Beell, free tenant, is in default [has not come as ordered], so order is given to distrain him to [appear at the next Court]. William Stede is also guilty of failing to come. Richard Durvet who held one messuage and one ferling and 1½ acres of land in Ludeshot has died, heriot to the Lord 1 cow value 6s 8d. And the said tenement and closes ... to a loss of 3s 4d to the use of the Lord. John Newman allows his tenement to be in disrepair and fails to repair it, so is in mercy; he is ordered etc. William Stede fails to reside on his villein holding so is in mercy; order is given ... The Prior of Selborne has taken over without permission one grove containing about 4 acres in the villein holding called Woodhouse, order given to distrain to next Court. One toft and 2 crofts containing 3 acres, once held by Alice Foghell, remain in the Lord's hands.

Robert Chester and wife Joan take on the tenancy of a cottage & curtilage and one acre of land in Ludshot which William Foghell had; it came into the Lord's hands because no one of the said William Foghell's blood claimed the holding. So Robert takes it on according to the custom of the said manor and gives for a 'fine' ... and does fealty, his surety [for payment] being Peter Longe.

Ludshott Manor Court Rolls, 1400–1833

A heriot was a kind of death duty payment given to the lord of the manor when a tenant died, allowing his heir to take over the tenement. It was the custom that payment was made by giving the tenant's best beast to the lord, in this case a cow – and a very good one – valued at 6s 8d.

19th – Kent's Execution

On this day in 1330, Edmund Plantagenet, Earl of Kent, was beheaded at Winchester. He was the second son of King Edward I and his second queen, Margaret, and was born at Woodstock in Oxfordshire in 1301, when the old king was in his sixties. In 1325, Edmund married Margaret Wake, a cousin of Roger Mortimer, Earl of March. Edmund supported Queen Isabella and her lover, Mortimer, in rebellion against his half-brother, Edward II, but then he fell out with the lovers. Being convinced that his half-brother was still alive, in 1330 Edmund joined a conspiracy to rescue Edward II from imprisonment, despite the fact that the king's funeral had taken place in 1327. The plot was discovered and Isabella and Mortimer had Edmund and his family arrested and imprisoned. Edmund was executed but his widow and three children – Edmund, Margaret and Joan – remained under arrest in Arundel Castle in Sussex, where the widow gave birth to another son, John, shortly after her husband's death. Their daughter Joan would become the famous 'Fair Maid of Kent' (see 29 September).

20th – Shaa's Remorse

In 1450, Edmund Shaa, the son of John Shaa of Dunkinfield, Cheshire, was apprenticed to a London goldsmith, completing his apprenticeship in 1458. He must have been outstanding at his craft because just four years later, in 1462, Edmund was appointed engraver to the Royal Mint at the Tower of London and Calais, holding the office for the next twenty years. He became a Sheriff of London in 1474/75 and Lord Mayor in 1482/83. He was in office when Richard, Duke of Gloucester, was proclaimed king in June 1483 and gave the new monarch his full support, for which he was rewarded with a knighthood.

Edmund outlived the king, making his will on 20 March 1488. He died a month later, on 20 April 1488, and was buried in the Mercers' chapel in the church of St Thomas of Acon in London. Among numerous legacies at his death was a sum to found a grammar school at Stockport, where his parents had been buried; but there was also another matter from long ago which plagued his conscience as his death approached. This is how he described it in his will:

Whereas a kynnysman of mine called Richard Shaa caused me xl [forty] winters passed ... to go wt hym to a mannys ground in the peke [Peak District] in derbyshire to take a distresse ... and we toke ii [two] oxen ... the which I am suer cam never again to his possession that ought [to have] them ... and be cause that dede was doon in my wanton dayes whanne I lakkyd discresyon therefor I have remorce therof now in these days being better advysed.

S. L. Thrupp, *The Merchant Class of Medieval London*

He set aside twenty shillings to be given to the man in compensation, if his executors could find him. If not, they were to take advice on how best to use the money to the benefit of Edmund's soul and to clear his conscience. Forty years seems a long time to delay the search for the Derbyshire man they had robbed of his oxen.

21st – Violets in March

March was the time to pick violets from the hedgerows and woodland edge for medicinal purposes: 'Violet shall be gathered in the month of March and in this month shall sugar of violet be made and syrup.'

W. R. Dawson, *A Leechbook of the Fifteenth Century*

In the thirteenth century, Bogo de Clare (1248–94) was a scandalous young nobleman who became a cleric at the Church Court of Arches at St Mary le Bow in the city of London, despite not having been ordained a priest. He spent his income on luxurious living and had no interest in religious matters whatsoever. Bogo purchased exotic confections, such as violet and rose sugar from the pepperer (grocer) and apothecary, Thomas Romeyn, in Cordwainer Ward. His wardrobe accounts covering his personal expenditure show that Bogo spent almost 20 per cent of his total outgoings of £375 in 1285–86 on spices and finest beeswax for his candles. 55 per cent went on imported textiles, including samite and cloth-of-gold from Italian merchants in Lombard Street and Bucklersbury and furs from a skinner in Walbrook.

M. Prestwich, et al. (eds), *Thirteenth-Century England VII*

The violet sugar, as well as being an after-dinner confection, was also a medicine, sugar of all kinds being good for chest complaints. Syrup of violets was a cure for 'heart straitness', kidney stones and inflamed liver. Violet oil was used on bruises, perhaps because its purple colour was likened to such an injury and taken to be God's indication of its purpose.

http://wildfoodsandmedicines.com/violet/

22nd – A Letter from Joan of Arc

On this day in 1429, King Henry VI, who was only seven years old, and his uncle John, Duke of Bedford and others received a letter from Joan of Arc. Calling herself 'the Maiden', she sent her dictated letter to the English commanders in France. The Hundred Years War was entering its final stages. Under Henry V the English had taken many French towns, but the warrior-king had died in 1422, leaving his little son as King of France – in name at least – as well as England.

At the time that Joan's letter was received by the Duke of Bedford, acting as Regent of France, the English were besieging the town of Orléans. The situation was at a stalemate but would eventually be resolved in French favour and prove to be the turning point in the Hundred Years War. Here are some excerpts from Joan of Arc's letter, amounting to a declaration of war:

King of England and you, Duke of Bedford, who call yourself Regent of the Kingdom of France; you, William de la Pole, Earl of Suffolk, John, Lord of Talbot [he was Earl of Shrewsbury]; and you, Thomas, Lord Scales, who call yourselves Bedford's lieutenants, do right by the King of Heaven. Hand over to the Maiden, who is sent by God the King of Heaven, the keys to all the towns which you have taken and violated in France. She has come here in the name of God to support the Royal family [of France]. She is quite prepared to make peace, if you are willing to do right, so long as you give up France and make amends for occupying it.

And you, archers, soldiers both noble and otherwise, who are around the town of Orleans, in God's name go back to your own lands. And if you will not do so, await word of the Maiden, who will go to see you soon to your very great misfortune. King of England, if you do not do so, I am a commander, and wherever I come across your troops in France, I shall make them go, whether willingly or unwillingly, and if they will not obey, I will have them wiped out ...

Duke of Bedford, the Maiden asks and requests that you will not cause your own downfall. If you will do right, you could yet come in her company to where the French will do the noblest deed which has ever been done for Christianity. And reply if you wish to make peace in the city of Orleans; and if you do not do so, you will shortly contemplate your great misfortunes.

'Letter to the English', Joan of Arc
http://archive.joan-of-arc.org/joanofarc_letter_Mar1429.html

As you can imagine, the English commanders must have had a good laugh over this letter from a country girl who thought she was sent by God to rescue France. Only with hindsight do we know that Joan provided the inspiration and impetus which enabled the French to fight back and finally defeat the English, leaving only Calais in their possession. As for Joan, the outcome wasn't good. The French churchmen distrusted her, being highly suspicious of her claim to being sent by God, and sold her to the English. The English put her on trial in Rouen in Normandy – then the English capital of France – and found her guilty of heresy, which included wearing men's clothing. She was burned at the stake in Rouen on 30 May 1431.

23rd – Plague Possessions

On this day in 1349, as the plague was at its height in the City of London, the wills of Thomas Francis, a wax-chandler from Candlewick ward, and his wife, Agnes, were enrolled at the Court of Hustings. Thomas had made his will in February, leaving his estate to Agnes and asking to be buried in the church of St Clements. Agnes, in her will, states that she is Thomas's widow, so we can infer he died first. Agnes wanted to be buried in the same church and bequeathed her personal effects to her daughter Marion, including a silver cup and six silver spoons, a gown with gold-work and a coverlet powdered with roses and lilies.

Return of the Black Death: Secret History,
Channel 4 TV (23 August 2015)

24th – A Very Fair Maiden

Here is what the *Secretum Secretorum* – a Latin translation of a tenth-century Arabic encyclopaedia – has to say about spring:

The air waxes clear, the wind blows softly, snow dissolves, rivers run. Springs surge up among the mountains, moisture is drawn to the tree-top, branches bud, seeds sprout, grains spring, meadows grow green. Flowers are fair and fresh, trees are clad with new leaves and the soil is arrayed with herbs and grasses. Beasts beget offspring, pastures are covered with growth and resume a new vigour, birds sing, and the nightingale's song sounds and re-echoes. The earth puts on its full and entire raiment and beauty and looks like a lovely bride, a very fair maiden adorned with jewels and clad in many colours ... on her wedding day.

M. Collins and V. Davis, *A Medieval Book of Seasons*

25th – English Drought

This was the first day of what became a terrible drought in southern England of 1241. It lasted all through the hot, dry late spring, summer and early autumn. It didn't break until the 28 October.

http://booty.org.uk/booty.weather/climate/1200_1299.htm

*

25 March was also the feast of the Annunciation, or Lady Day. In medieval times, this was the day on which the calendar year began, when financial accounts were drawn up and the first quarterly rents were paid. The other quarter days were the feast of St John the Baptist (or Midsummer Day) on 24 June, the feast of St Michael and All Angels (or Michaelmas) on 29 September and Christmas Day on 25 December. So in England, the day after 31 December 1420 was 1 January 1420 and the day after 24 March 1420 was 25 March 1421. No wonder historians get confused.

Have you ever wondered why our modern financial year in Britain begins on 6 April? In 1752, the British were still using Julius Caesar's old calendar and were eleven days adrift of the more accurate Gregorian calendar then used in Europe. To put matters straight, eleven days were 'omitted' from the calendar – i.e. the day after 2 September 1752 became 14 September 1752. People were horrified, thinking their lives had been shortened by almost a fortnight, but they soon adapted. However, the Exchequer – in charge of the country's finances – refused to be denied any money and taxes due for those missing days, so they added on eleven days to the end of that financial year, taking it to 5 April, as it remains today.

The year previously, the Act for the Supputation of the Year also changed the first day of the year, so that the day after 31 December 1751 was 1 January 1752. As a consequence, 1751 was a short year – it ran only from 25 March to 31 December.

26th – The Tichborne Dole

On this day in 1150, the Tichborne family began a tradition at Arlesford in Hampshire. The custom became known as the Tichborne Dole and continues today. The dole comprises the handout of a gallon of flour for each adult from the parishes of Tichborne and Cheriton and half a gallon for each child. However, the flour is supposed to come from the wheat grown on a particular piece of land. In the twelfth century, the amount of corn was quite adequate for the occasion, but today the field cannot produce nearly enough flour for the hundreds who turn up to collect their dole. Every March, the family in Tichborne House have to buy in several sackfuls of flour to make up the deficit. Despite the expense, a good reason to continue the tradition is the curse of Lady Mabella Tichborne: she swore on her deathbed in 1150 that, if the family didn't do it, the consequences for them and their house would be catastrophic!

http://www.collectionspicturelibrary.co.uk/
customs/d.php

27th – The Combat of the Thirty

On 27 March 1351, the Battle of the Thirty (in French: *combat des Trentes*), took place near Ploërmel in Brittany and settled the struggle for the succession to the duchy of Brittany. The dukedom was contested by Charles of Blois, supported by the King of France, and John of Montfort, supported by King Edward III of England. Instead of an all out battle, it was a contest between two small groups. It became celebrated in song by an anonymous trouvère or balladier and was later retold by the chronicler Jean Froissart.

In spite of a truce, John Bramborough, the English captain of Ploërmel, carried on ravaging the local district of Josselin, so Jean de Beaumanoir, captain of Josselin and marshal of Brittany, sent Bramborough a challenge. A contest was arranged for 27 March near Ploërmel, with thirty picked knights and squires on either side. Beaumanoir chose thirty Bretons; Bramborough had twenty Englishmen, six German mercenaries and four Brabançons (from Brabant in the Low Countries). The battle was fought with lances, swords, daggers and maces, the outcome decided by Guillaume de Montauban who alone unhorsed seven English knights. The remaining English combatants had no choice but to surrender. Almost all the participants were either dead or seriously wounded, Bramborough being among those killed. Of those who survived their injuries, the English prisoners were well treated and released on payment of a ransom.

http://www.britannica.com/event/Battle-of-the-Thirty

28th – Tart for Lent

Lent is often regarded as the time for giving up luxuries. This recipe, although it contains no meat, is anything but plain. The exotic spices, sugar, figs, raisins, dates and wine were all expensive imports. This unusual dish – A Tart for Lent – was clearly one for the king's table:

Take figs and raisins and wash them in wine and grind them small with apples and pears picked clean. Take them up and cast them into a pot with wine and sugar. Add spices – cubebs, cloves, cinnamon and nutmeg – and salt and boil it. Take boiled salmon, codling [cod] or haddock and beat them small and add to the fruit. When it is boiled enough, take it up [off the heat] and put it into a vessel and let it cool. Make a pie pastry coffin an inch deep and put the mixture into it. Take prunes and damsons, stone them, and dates quartered and cover the pie. Bake it well and serve it forth.

L. J. Sass, *To the King's Taste*

29th – The Battle of Towton

The Battle of Towton was fought in 1461 during the English Wars of the Roses near the village of Towton in Yorkshire. It changed the ruling house of monarchs in England with the victor, the Yorkist Edward, 4th Duke of York and Earl of March, becoming King Edward IV (1461–1483), replacing the Lancastrian Henry VI (1422–1461) as king, driving him and many of his most prominent supporters out of the country. According to the contemporary chroniclers, more than 50,000 soldiers fought for hours in a snowstorm on that Palm Sunday. The blizzard gave the advantage to the Yorkists as it blew into the faces of the advancing Lancastrians, blinding them. A newsletter circulated a week after the battle reported that 28,000 died on the battlefield. It is said that Towton was the largest and longest battle fought on British soil, though it seems likely that the medieval chronicles exaggerated both the numbers engaged and the casualties.

Without doubt, Towton was significant in both military and political terms for it secured the throne for the Yorkists, although the Lancastrian cause was far from dead because King Henry, his extremely ambitious French queen Margaret of Anjou and his son and heir had all escaped.

30th – Edward I Takes Berwick-upon-Tweed

Edward I was at war, fighting the Scots. With his army of 5,000 horsemen and 30,000 foot soldiers, on Wednesday 28 March 1296 he was at Coldstream, camping at the priory. At the time, the strategic trading port of Berwick-upon-Tweed was on the Scottish side of the border (the town changed hands many times, finally becoming English in 1482). Berwick had been the most important town in Scotland, with more money coming into the Scottish exchequer from its exports than from all the other Scottish towns combined. King Edward summoned the burgesses of Berwick to attend him and discuss the town's surrender, but nobody turned up.

On Friday 30 March, the king was encamped near the nunnery at the foot of Halidon Hill with twenty-four ships anchored in the estuary. Somehow, the ships thought they had seen the signal to attack and entered the harbour. In the fight that followed, four ships were burnt and the rest managed to escape on the turning tide. Seeing his ships in flight, Edward attacked from the north. He easily entered the town, having no trouble crossing what was supposed to be a defensive ditch.

The numbers given for people slaughtered by Edward's army vary from 7,000 to 25,000, but must be highly exaggerated since the town's population was perhaps 5,000, at most. Edward stayed in Berwick for a month and ordered a stone wall to be built encircling the town with a ditch eighty feet wide and forty feet deep on the north and east sides of the town. The king intended that any attempt made by the Scots to regain their prize asset wouldn't be so easy for them as it had been for him.

http://berwicktimelines.tumblr.com/post/46665978563/
the-anniversary-of-the-sacking-of-berwick

31st – A Cure for Balding

To restore hair where it faileth:

Take cow-dung and old soles of shoes and burn them to powder in a new earthen pot fast stopped; and then mingle it with raw honey and make an ointment thereof. Therewith anoint thy head and close thereabove [wear] a cap of leather and use this nine days.

W. R. Dawson, *A Leechbook of the Fifteenth Century*

Better to go bald, perhaps?

APRIL

1st – Easter Sunday

The forty days fasting of Lent came to an end on Easter Sunday with a well-deserved feast. The Countess of Leicester, wife of Simon de Montfort, was entertaining two bishops on that Easter Day in 1263 at Odiham Castle in Hampshire and she wanted to impress them with a lavish dinner. The height of luxury where food was concerned was to use spices, sugar and other imported goods. Here is the countess's shopping list of items required from the grocers of London:

6 lbs ginger	15s
8 lbs pepper	18s 8d
6 lbs cinnamon	6s
1 lb saffron	14s – by far the most expensive
12 lbs sugar	12s
6 lbs sugar + mace	6s
1 box gingerbread	2s 4d
10 lbs rice	15s 3d
20 lbs almonds	4s 2d

2nd – Twelve Without Trial

On this day in 1305, twelve monks from Westminster Abbey were finally released after being imprisoned in the Tower for two years.

In those days, the royal treasury was kept in the precincts of Westminster Abbey, by the cloisters. In 1303, a large amount of valuable jewellery was stolen. Edward I was fighting in Scotland and, in June when he heard of the robbery, the king sent Ralph de Sandwich south to Westminster to investigate. Together with the keeper of the king's wardrobe, Ralph entered the treasury and found the coffers broken open and much of the treasure gone.

On 10 October, the king gave orders that Sir Roger Brabazon and Sir William de Bereford should make further enquiries which resulted in the arrest of William Wenlock, the abbot, and eighty of his monks. They were all sent to the Tower, charged with stealing the king's property to the incredible value of £100,000. Later, the abbot and most of the monks were released when much of the jewellery was recovered, but twelve brethren remained imprisoned without trial.

On Lady Day, 25 March 1305, King Edward came to Westminster Abbey to give thanks for his victory over the Scots. To mark the occasion, he graciously ordered that the twelve monks should be discharged from the Tower. However, there was some delay, 'out of malice', and it took over a week before they were freed and returned to Westminster.

G. J. Aungier (ed.), *Chroniques de London*

3rd – Hocktide

The medieval English festival of Hocktide was celebrated on the second Tuesday after Easter. The men of the village would tie up the women and demand a kiss for their release. The following day, things became even more fun: the women would tie up the men and demand money for their release which would go to the parish funds. It is thought that Hocktide recalls the massacre of the Danes in the eleventh century by King Ethelred the Unready.

The practice was banned under King Henry VIII but reintroduced by Elizabeth I in 1575. Hungerford in Berkshire is the only place that still practises the tradition of Hocktide, though in a modified form.

4th – A Simple Exchange of Vows

On this day in 1381, the Dean and Chapter of York recorded that Thomas Tavel, parchment maker, and Ellen de Eskryk were ordered to do penance on the following six Sundays, both to be whipped around their parish church and to lead the procession, wearing only their underclothes and each carrying a candle. Thomas had already been in trouble with another woman the month before:

Thomas Tavel fornicated recidivously [repeatedly] with Ibbot Leche. Both appeared before the penultimate [day] of March ... to purge themselves six-handed. The woman [Ibbot] appeared on that day. She confessed the article and abjured the sin on penalty of standing with a candle in the manner of a penitent at the font of St John del Pyke for twelve Sundays and she has six days for [to make] her confession.

The same Thomas fornicated with Ellen de Eskryk, servant of Thomas Parcheminner. They both appeared on 29 March. He denied the article and had Saturday or Monday to purge himself six-handed. Asked, he claimed a contract of marriage between them. They confessed the article.

P. J. P Goldberg, *Women in England, c. 1275–1525*

It may seem odd that Thomas could claim that he and Ellen – who is described his master's servant, so they may both have been Thomas Parcheminner's apprentices – had a contract of marriage which no one seems to have known about. This was possible in medieval times because a simple exchange of vows between a couple – made in the tavern, the street or even in bed – followed by 'consummation' (sex), was considered a valid marriage in the eyes of the Church. No witnesses were required so it could prove difficult for either party to prove or disprove they were married afterward.

5th – Medieval Cure vs MRSA

A medieval remedy for eye infections, discovered in British Library MS. Royal 12D xvii, has been found to kill the superbug MRSA. Anglo-Saxon expert Dr Christina Lee from the School of English at Nottingham University, transcribed the recipe for the tenth-century potion before handing it over to Dr Freya Harrison and the microbiologists at the Centre for Biomolecular Sciences, also at Nottingham University, to see if it really worked as an antibacterial remedy.

None of the experts expected the potion to work, but when it was tested, they discovered that not only did it clear up styes, it also affected the deadly superbug MRSA – resistant to many modern antibiotics. Researchers believe the antibacterial effect of the recipe is not due to a single ingredient but the combination used and brewing methods. Further research is planned to investigate how and why this works.

In the meantime, here is the remedy from Bald's Leechbook as a medieval physician or apothecary would have prepared it:

For a stye on the eye, take cropleek and garlic, of both equal quantities, pound them well together, take wine and bullocks' gall, of both equal quantities, mix with the leek, put this then into a brazen vessel, let it stand nine days in the brass vessel, wring out through a cloth and clear it well, put it into a horn, and about night time apply it with a feather to the eye.

http://britishlibrary.typepad.co.uk/science/2015/04/a-medieval-medical-marvel.html#sthash.PezBneka.dpuf

6th – Lionheart Breathes His Last

King Richard I, known as the Lionheart, died at Chalûs in France on 6 April 1199. He had been wounded by a crossbow bolt in his shoulder on 25 March and, although his surgeons removed the bolt and did all they could for the king, the wound festered. As the chronicler, Matthew Paris tells us:

A kind of blackness mingled with the swelling, discolouring the region of the wound on every side; this began to give the king intense pain.

The swelling suddenly coming to his heart on April 6th, a day agreed to Mars, the man devoted to martial deeds, breathed his last ...

C. Brewer, *The Death of Kings*

Recent forensic examination, carried out on the remains of King Richard's heart, has shown that he died of septicaemia. Clearly, he needed the cropleek remedy given above.

7th – How to Behave at Table

In the late fifteenth century, a manners book in verse by the poet John Lydgate was printed by William Caxton (Wynkyn de Worde's master) at Westminster. Here is an extract, telling how to behave at table:

> With soup, do not use bread to sop it up,
> Or suck it loudly – that is to transgress,
> Or put your dirty mouth to a clean cup,
> Or pass drinks while your hands are in a mess,
> Or stain your napkin out of carelessness.
> Also, beware at meals of causing strife,
> And do not make a tooth-pick of your knife.

J. Lydgate, *Table Manners for Children*

8th – Maintaining a Palace

The king's palace at Rotherhithe had extensive gardens, needing a considerable workforce during the spring and summer, supervised by 'Philip'. Philip kept detailed accounts about the wages paid to the labourers and the purchases he made for the kitchen gardens. In 1354 he spent:

> 5s 10d on 14 lbs of parsley seed
> 1s on 12 lbs of onion seed
> 3s on 12 lbs of leek seed
> 2s 6d on 72 lbs of hyssop seed and
> 7s on 24 lbs of miscellaneous vegetable seed

He also bought 3s 4d worth of young trees and bushes from John of Preston and Is 10d worth of plants from John Aleyn. The gardens were bordered by woven hedges and hurdles for which Philip bought:

A thousand gross [144,000] twigs costing 20s
8 bundles of small twigs for binding the larger ones, 16d
14s 8d for labourers to cut and gather branches on the Isle of Thanet, in Kent, to hire and load a cart and bring the branches to Rotherhithe.

The total in wages for 1354 was £34 8s 11¾d

During March and April, Philip employed eighteen labourers in the gardens, paying them a good wage of 4d per day, even though some of them were women (who were normally paid less than men). This may be explained by labour shortages after the plague ravaged the country in 1348 and 1349. Not surprisingly, in 1355 Philip also took on an assistant gardener, Richard Beansmith, to help him with the work.

T. McLean, *Medieval English Gardens*

9th – Edward IV's Death

King Edward IV died on 9 April 1483, at Westminster. He was not quite forty-one years old. He had been ill for a few days but no certain diagnosis is possible from what was written at the time. Modern suggestions for the cause range from pneumonia to poison. This is how the Croyland chronicler recorded the event:

The king, neither worn out with old age nor yet seized with any known kind of malady ... took to his bed. This happened about the feast of Easter; and on the ninth day of April, he rendered up his spirit to his Creator at his palace at Westminster, it being the year of our Lord 1483 and the twenty-third of his reign.

P. W. Hammond and A. F. Sutton, *Richard III: The Road to Bosworth Field*

Meanwhile, unaware of the king's death, the Conisbrough Tourn was held at Conisborough in Yorkshire. A 'tourn' was a twice-yearly court held in the presence of the sheriff of the county in each district or 'hundred'. The original Anglo-Saxon hundred was so called because it covered an area of land able to support one hundred households – on more fertile soils the hundred would be smaller than on poorer soils. The hundred-leet or court was usually bigger than a manor-leet which dealt with just one manor, its tenants and labourers. Here is a selection of cases heard at the tourn:

Sandall amercements [fines total] 8*d*. William Brande, constable, and his fellows present that the wife of Nicholas Diconson [fined] 2*d*, brewed ale and sold against the assize. Henry Rawson forfeited a penalty enjoined on him at the last tourn in that he did not cleanse or scour a water course at Symondcraft by the day appointed for him. So he incurs namely 6*d*.

Harthill amercements 22*d*. William Haresand, constable, and his fellows present that Roger Wederell 4*d* and Randall Belgh 4*d* did not attend the tourn; therefore they have each individually put themselves in mercy as above assessed. Also they present that the wife of Edward Wardall 2*d*, the wife of John Whitehede 2*d* and Margaret Barbur 2*d* baked and sold bread against the assize; therefore they have each individually put themselves in mercy as above assessed. Also they present that the wife of John Whitehede 2*d* and Margaret Barbur 2*d* brewed ale and sold against the assize. Therefore they have each individually put themselves in mercy as above assessed. Also they present that John Dawes 2*d* and Richard Bothomley 2*d* butchered and sold meat against the assize. Therefore they have each individually put themselves in mercy as above assessed.

Conisbrough amercements 12*d*. Richard Edmondson, constable, and his fellows present that the wife of John Turnour 2*d* and the wife of John Blomer Junior 2*d* baked and sold bread against the assize; therefore each has put herself in mercy. They also present that the wife of John Turnour 2*d*, the wife of John Blomer Junior 2*d*, the wife of Robert Dunneslay 2*d* and the wife of Thomas Barcroft brewed ale and sold against the assize;

therefore they have each individually put themselves in mercy as above assessed.

Conisbrough Court Roll, 1483
http://www.hrionline.ac.uk/conisbrough/
browse/roll_1483_3.html

The phrase 'against the assize' means that the bread, ale and butchery were substandard and not according to the standard of the law. It might mean the bread was mouldy, the ale watered down or the meat gone bad, or it could be that short measures were being used.

10th – Customs at Calais

This is an export-import licence granted by King Richard III in 1484:

To Mathewe Andrewe a licence to charge a Ship of the portage [carrying] of xlv [forty-five] tonne or under with all manner [of] goods and merchandise to the Staple of Calais ... as oft as he shall like within a whole year and with the same to depart to any outward parts [foreign ports] there to discharge and to recharge again into England. Dated at Nottingham.

R. Horrox and P. Hammond, BL MS Harley 433, vol. I

In early medieval times, 'the staple' meant England's staple export: wool. But it was inconvenient and inefficient for the king's men to collect the customs duties that were payable on the exported wool from every one of the hundreds of little English ports all around the country. London, Bristol, Ipswich and Sandwich were major ports but little ships could sail from any small harbour or river estuary. Therefore, since wherever the ships had sailed from, they were all taking their cargo of wool to Flanders (modern day Belgium and north-east France), it was easier to collect the customs when they arrived at their destination. In 1313, Edward II ordained that all merchants had to land their 'staple' at a port he would designate. During the Hundred Years War, England acquired Calais from the French and from the mid-fifteenth century until 1558 this port became the convenient Calais Staple, where customs duties were collected on all English wool exports.

This licence, granted to Matthew Andrew, let him off the payment of any customs duties at Calais on his cargoes for one year. This was a way in which the permanently cash-strapped Crown sometimes paid off its debts or rewarded people: allowing them to recoup their money by avoiding such taxes on their exports.

11th – Skelton's *Boke of Phyllyp Sparowe*

Sometime around this date, John Skelton, the English poet, wrote a long poem of 1,400 lines called *The Boke of Phyllyp Sparowe* (1499), the lament of Jane Scrope, a young girl in the convent at Carrow, near Norwich, when her pet bird died. Here is an excerpt:

> For the sowle of Phyllyp Sparowe
> That was late slayn at Carowe ...
> I wept and I wayled,
> The tearys downe hayled;
> But nothinge it avayled
> To call Phyllyp agayne
> Whon Gyb our cat hath slayne.

12th – Our Well-Beloved Citizen

On 12 April 1487, the Mayor of York, William Todde, wrote a testimonial for the Christian behaviour of a retired ostler – a horse groom and stable hand – at the Swan Inn. William Maunsell had sent John Borowe to the mayor with a fardel of 'stuff', unspecified (a fardel was a large basket). The contents were to be given as alms and charity to any neighbour who should fall into poverty due to the loss of his goods. The mayor rightly commends Maunsell's actions, calling him 'our well beloved citizen'.

L. C. Attreed, *York House Books*, vol. 2

13th – Instructions for Carving

Here are the instructions for the period from Easter Sunday to Whit Sunday to a servant carving and serving meat:

First you shall serve a boiled calf which has been blessed; then boiled eggs with green sauce and set them before the noble of highest rank who will share them out to those about him. Then serve pottages such as greens, jowtes or brewes with beef, mutton or veal and capons coloured with saffron and bakemeats.

For the second course: jussell with mamony, roasted and glazed pigeons with bakemeats such as tarts, chewets, flans and others as the cooks have decided.

Wynkyn de Worde, *The Boke of Keruinge*

According to Peter Brears's glossary, 'jowtes' is a selection of finely chopped herbs, boiled in a rich broth or almond milk with sugar and salt. 'Brewes' are small pieces of meat stewed with herbs and spices before pouring the stock over cubes of bread. 'Jussell' is a dish of eggs boiled in a broth, thickened with breadcrumbs and flavoured with saffron, sage and salt, and 'mamony' is a dish of finely chopped poultry cooked in spiced wine and/or almond milk. Both brewes and mamony would make use of the less elegant offcuts of meat and poultry, so nothing was wasted.

The *Boke of Keruinge* (Carving) was printed by Wynkyn de Worde in 1508. Wynkyn had been an apprentice to William Caxton, the first man to set up a printing press in England, at Westminster, in 1476. Wynkyn took much of his information for the book from a manuscript, *The Boke of Nurture*, written by John Russell, c. 1430–40 (now Sloane MS 2027, British Library).

14th – The Battle of Barnet

The alliance between King Edward IV and his powerful cousin, the Earl of Warwick, lay in ruins by 1469. Once Edward's most loyal ally, Warwick was now his enemy (see 22 November). This situation was good news for the Lancastrian cause which rumbled on, despite Henry VI being imprisoned in the Tower of London and most of the principal

Lancastrian nobles being in exile abroad. In October 1470, Warwick drove Edward from England and restored Henry to the throne.

In March 1471, Edward returned to England with the assistance of his brother-in-law, the Duke of Burgundy. Landing in Yorkshire by the Humber estuary, Edward assembled his men and equipment and marched south, gathering more troops as he went. He reached London unopposed on 12 April. Aware of Edward's movements, the Earl of Warwick, who had been in the Midlands raising troops, marched towards London to confront him. With a Lancastrian army of some 15,000 troops, he took up position about a mile north of Barnet on 13 April.

Edward arrived that evening with a force of between 10,000 and 12,000 troops and took up position to the south of the Lancastrians. Rather than wait until morning, Edward deployed his troops under cover of darkness, very close to Warwick's lines, down in a marshy valley, instructing his men to light no fires and keep silent. This was either a master stroke of strategy or very fortuitous because it meant the artillery bombardment that Warwick launched at dawn the next day passed straight over the heads of Edward's troops.

The Battle of Barnet was fought on the morning of Easter Day, 14 April 1471. The armies of Edward and Warwick met for the last time at a place called Gladmore Heath. No one is sure where Gladmore Heath was, as the name has long ceased to be used, but it was probably the open ground around the village of Hadley. Early in the morning there was a thick fog, making it impossible to see what was happening as the armies engaged. The Earl of Oxford, one of Warwick's commanders, succeeded in routing Lord Hastings' contingent on the flank of Edward's army, and pursued them all the way back to Barnet. However, while they were gone from the field, in the course of the combat the armies had swung around. On returning, Oxford's banner of a star with streamers was mistaken for Edward's badge of a sun with rays, and the Lancastrians attacked their own side, which panicked and fled. Warwick lost the battle and was killed in the final moments by some over-enthusiastic Yorkists intent on revenge, despite Edward's instructions that he be taken alive, if possible.

http://www.battlefieldstrust.com/resource centre/warsoftheroses/
battleview.asp?BattleFieldId=5
and https://www.barnet.gov.uk/
citizen-home/libraries/local-studies-and-archives/pocket-histories/
barnet/battle-of-barnet

15th – First Sleep, Second Sleep

Without good lighting, medieval folk tended to go to bed with the sun and rise at dawn. In winter in southern England that would mean having about sixteen hours' sleep a night – and even more for those living farther north. No healthy adult needs that much rest, so that medieval sleep patterns were rather different to our modern one. Science has shown that without clocks, timetables or deadlines, we would naturally revert to three sleep periods in twenty-four hours: an afternoon nap, a 'first sleep' and a 'second sleep'. This was the pattern in medieval times [see 4 October].

T. Mount, *Everyday Life in Medieval London*

16th – Primroses and Cowslips

This is the season for primroses and cowslips – both closely related plants and very popular in medieval gardens. Primrose leaves were used as cosmetic skin rubs to prevent blemishes, or applied to cuts to ease the soreness. The petals and leaves were chewed for pain relief and the flowers put into soothing baths. The pale yellow flowers of both plants were often made into wine or 'sweet waters', i.e. cordials, put into puddings and pottages, used in salads or to decorate desserts.

T. McLean, *Medieval English Gardens*

17th – A Prosperous and Dignified Woman

On this day in 1456, the indenture of apprenticeship for Elizabeth Eland was enrolled with London's city chamberlain, Thomas Thornton. Elizabeth had already been apprenticed for two years – the long delay in enrolling the indenture wasn't unusual, to see that the apprentice was going to measure up and be likely to complete the term, as enrolment was expensive. Elizabeth was to be trained as a silkwoman by one Ellen Langwith and her husband John, a London tailor in Walbrook ward, in the parish of St Mary Abchurch.

M. Davis and A. Prescott (eds), *London and the Kingdom*

When John Langwith died – his will was granted probate by the Archbishop of Canterbury at Lambeth Palace on 25 July 1467, although he had drawn it up on 4 December the year before – he wished to be buried in St Mary Abchurch, before the image of St John the Baptist, patron saint of the Tailors' Company of which John was a prominent member. He left everything to his wife, Ellen, including all his lands at Beckenham, in Kent (which may have been her dowry), also making her his executrix.

Godwyn register, No. 20:
John Lang[e]with, 25 July, vii year of Edward IV, PCC 1467

Ellen was now a very wealthy widow without an heir so she too drew up a will, although she would outlive John by over thirteen years. Her will was artfully worded. She left much of her property to the Tailors' Company with the proviso that, if they failed in its adequate administration, all would be forfeit to the Cutlers. In this way she was well favoured by both companies, invited to their feasts on special occasions and sent gifts of food and wine to keep them in mind. In 1476, the tailors spent 2s on a pike and wine for Mistress Ellen Langwith, while the less wealthy cutlers sent her a rabbit and a hen costing 8d.

In her will, Ellen left 10s to pay for her funeral in St Mary Abchurch, which included money to the parish clerk to ring the bells. There were alms to the poor, and the Tailors' Company was to use money from the rents paid to them from the Langwith properties to buy twenty-six quarters of coal for thirteen poor men and women of the parish on the anniversary of Ellen's death. Before she died – sometime between January and June 1481 – she left an additional, modest will, bequeathing most of her household goods to her current apprentice, John Brown (presumably an apprentice tailor). She left 40s to Richard Wiott, the son of a shearman, when he should come of age, and money and goods to her servants, John England and Emmott Bynchester. Otherwise, all her bequests were made to women: Margaret, wife of John Wareng, one of her two executors, was to have a gold ring set with a diamond and an image of Our Lady from Ellen's chamber; Mary, wife of John Jakes the draper, the second executor, was to have her blue silk girdle with silver-gilt decorations; and Katherine, wife of Hugh Pemberton, the overseer of Ellen's will, was to receive a gold ring set with turquoise. A gown of black medley (a wool mixture?), trimmed with white lamb, was left to her cousin Mistress Bowyer of

Northampton, and her best blue gown, trimmed with marten fur, was bequeathed to another cousin, Mistress Bounesley of Nottingham. Her personal belongings, household goods and furnishings mentioned in her will suggest Ellen was a prosperous and dignified elderly woman who had had a very successful career, whether as the wife of a cutler and a tailor or as a craftswoman in her own right.

T. Mount, *Everyday Life in Medieval London*

18th – Letter Home

Sir John Paston wrote to his mother, Margaret, in April 1471 telling her what had happened at the Battle of Barnet, four days earlier (see 14 April). The two brothers – both named John – had fought on the losing Lancastrian side in support of the Earl of Warwick. This is Sir John's letter:

Mother, I recommend me to you, letting you know that, blessed be God, my brother, John, is alive and fares well and is in no peril of death. Nevertheless, he is hurt with an arrow in his right arm beneath the elbow: I have sent him a surgeon who has dressed it and he tells me that he trusts that he shall be all whole in right short time. It is true that John Mylsent is dead, God have mercy on his soul! And William Mylsent is alive and it is likely that his other servants have all escaped. As for me, I am in good case, blessed be God, and in no jeopardy of my life, I think, for I am at my liberty ...

There were killed upon the field, half a mile from Barnet on Easter Day, the Earl of Warwick, the Marquis Montagu [Warwick's brother, John Neville], Sir William Tyrrell, Sir Lewis John and divers other esquires from our country [i.e. Norfolk], such as Godmerston and Bothe. And on King Edward's party, the Lord Cromwell, Lord Say and Sir Humphrey Bourchier of our country, who is much lamented here with other people of both parties to the number of more than a thousand.

As for other tidings, it is understood that Queen Margaret [wife of the Lancastrian king Henry VI, and Warwick's supposed ally] is verily landed with her son in the West Country, and I believe that tomorrow or else the next day the King Edward will depart from here [London] towards her, to drive her out again [see 4 May] …

God has showed Himself marvellously like Him that made all things and can undo again when He pleases; and I can think that in all likelihood He will show Himself again, and that in short time. …

It is so that my brother is unprovided with money. I have helped him to my power and more. Wherefore, as it pleases you, remember him, for, being in the same case, I cannot even provide for myself …

R. Virgoe (ed.), *Illustrated Letters of the Paston Family*

19th – Drowning in the Thames

The Coroner's Rolls recorded on 19 April 1340:

Mary, daughter of Agnes de Billingsgate, aged nine years, lay dead of a death other than her rightful death under the wharf of Thomas de Porkele in the parish of All Hallows the Less, in the ward of Dowgate. Thereupon they [the coroner and sheriffs] proceeded there and having summoned the good men of that ward and the ward of Langbourn where the said Mary lived with her mother, they diligently enquired how it happened. The jurors say that on the preceding Sunday [17 April] after the hour of vespers, the aforesaid Mary filled an earthen pot with water on the aforesaid wharf, the Thames being in flood, when she fell into the water and was drowned.

P. J. P. Goldberg, *Women in England, c. 1275–1525*

20th – Round Table Tournament

King Edward I and his queen, Eleanor of Castile, were fascinated by the legends of King Arthur and his Knights of the Round Table. The royal couple were at Glastonbury Abbey in 1272 for the translation of the bones that were believed to be those of King Arthur and Queen Guinevere.

When the time came for two of Edward's daughters to be married, the months of celebration began with a Round Table Tournament at Winchester on 20 April 1290. The king's accounts show that extensive building works were carried out to refurbish Winchester Castle for the event, including the laying out and planting of a garden of plesaunce for the queen and the payment of 1 mark (13s 4d) to Robert Dote, for levelling the tournament field in a meadow just outside the city. The king's nephew, John of Brittany, was given 1,000 marks to cover his expenses, suggesting he was organising the splendid occasion. Over the three days of the event, the Duke of Brabant's household consumed three tuns (1,088 gallons) of wine. The duke was one of the two bridegrooms-to-be.

J. S. Hamilton, *The Plantagenets: History of a Dynasty*

Perhaps the most costly item for the ceremonies was the Winchester Round Table itself, still hanging on the wall of the great hall of the castle today. Archaeologists have made a detailed study of the table and determined from carbon and tree-ring dating (dendrochronology) that wood for the individual planks was likely to have been cut between 1272 and 1285, being well seasoned before the table was constructed, possibly by Peter, the master carpenter on the castle rebuilding project in 1289. He used the same methods employed in making water-mill wheels and cranes for construction purposes at the time. The table measured eighteen feet in diameter and weighed three-quarters of a ton; it could seat twenty people very comfortably. It was supported on twelve wooden legs around its circumference with a central pillar of either wood, or maybe stone. It may have had a permanent covering, perhaps of leather, nailed in place – the nail holes are still in evidence – but a grand cloth of the finest textile – cloth-of-gold, maybe – would have been used on the great occasion.

M. Biddle and S. Badham, *King Arthur's Round Table: An Archaeological Investigation*

When not in use, the huge tabletop was hung on the wall and is still there, although Henry VIII had it painted 250 years later. The chronicler John Hardyng saw the table in 1463 and noted: 'The Rounde Table at Wynchestere beganne, and ther it ende, and ther it hangeth yet.'

Joan of Acre, Edward and Eleanor's eldest daughter who had been born while the couple was on crusade in Acre, married Gilbert de Clare, Earl of Gloucester, on Sunday 30 April in Westminster Abbey. The lengthy nuptials continued: their daughter Margaret wed John, Duke of Brabant, on Saturday 8 July, also in Westminster Abbey. The celebrations were intended to extend for even longer because the Anglo-Scottish treaty, initially drawn up at Birgham (Berwickshire) on 18 July and ratified at Northampton on 28 August 1290, included the provision for the marriage of Margaret, known as 'the Maid of Norway', granddaughter and successor of Alexander III, to the king's son, Edward of Caernarfon (later Edward II). Sadly, the treaty became irrelevant when little Margaret died in September 1290.

21st – Ospringe Leper Hospital

Ospringe is a village on the old Roman road of Watling Street in north-eastern Kent. In medieval times there was a leper hospital here on the busy thoroughfare, where travellers could make charitable donations to the hospital in return for the prayers of the lepers, to speed them on their journey and keep them safe. Lepers were considered to be already dead to society. When some unfortunate person was officially declared to have leprosy, their last involvement in the community was to attend their own funeral service, before retiring to the nearest leper hospital for the rest of their days. Despite being shut away from society, lepers were thought in their status to be closer to God – being regarded as not of the world of men – their great suffering in this life giving them a fast-track entry into heaven in the next. For this reason, the prayers of lepers were thought to be especially effective and listened to more readily by God, so in turn giving alms to the leper hospital was good insurance for the traveller's soul.

In 1294, the yearly accounts for the hospital in Ospringe show that it had enough grounds to grow flax and hemp, so the women patients could make linen yarn and, perhaps, weave it into cloth, or else prepare the hemp for rope-making. Here is an excerpt from the Master's accounts:

For one spade, iron-bound, 2*d*
For one hoe, 2½*d*

Wages of women picking flax, 1½*d* and picking hemp, 4½*d*
To a man hired to dig the gardens at 1½*d* per day, 3*d*

T. McLean, *Medieval English Gardens*

It would seem that picking hemp was much harder work than gathering flax, or there was far more of it to pick. Clearly the gardens were not very extensive since one man could dig them over in just two days. Gardens were thought to be therapeutic for patients and good for the soul and, in the case of leprosy and other incurable ailments, treating the soul was thought to be far more important than treating the body.

22nd – A London Widow's Will

Margaret Gardyner, a London widow, drew up her will on 22 April 1484, leaving a fine selection of bequests. She wished to be buried in the church of St Thomas's Hospital in Southwark, where her son William was a priest and master of the hospital. To him she left a collection of good silverware, including two salt cellars and eighteen spoons. She bequeathed to him bedding, towels, tablecloths and napkins, a carpet, cushions, a Latin primer and assorted pewter and brass pots and basins, among other things. William was also to receive two of her best gowns, but not the murrey [mulberry-coloured] one with grey fur which was to be sold to raise money to be spent for the good of Margaret's soul. She also donated two kerchiefs – one of cotton, the other of 'launde' (perhaps linen) – to each of the nuns who worked at the hospital. To her niece, Johane Beele, she left her best rosary beads of coral and her scarlet kirtle. To her servant, Elizabeth, Margaret left a black gown with grey fur, a kirtle and a coverlet with red birds and the letter 'M', as well as smocks, naprons (*sic*), kerchiefs and sheets. Johane Crane was to have her crimson kirtle and a girdle of violet, decorated with silver. The will was detailed and quite long, instructing how her money was to be distributed among her friends, family, godchildren and neighbours.

Unfortunately, Margaret gives us no hint of who her husband was, nor how she had come by her wealth and luxurious possessions. Incidentally, 'scarlet' was an expensive cloth that was often, but not necessarily, dyed a fine, bright red, and 'napron' was the original form of the word 'apron'. Over time, 'a napron' became 'an apron'. The same thing happened to 'a norange' (still the Spanish word for the fruit), which became 'an orange'.

L. Boatwright, et al. (eds), *The Logge Register of PCC Wills, 1479–86,* vol. 1

23rd – St George's Day

The Most Noble Order of the Garter is one of the earliest of many orders of chivalry, founded during the Middle Ages in the courts of Europe, and it still survives today. The patron saint of the Order is St George (patron saint of soldiers and also of England), and its spiritual home is St George's Chapel, Windsor. The insignia of the Order have developed over the centuries, starting with a garter and badge depicting St George and the Dragon. A collar was added in the sixteenth century, and the star and broad ribbon in the seventeenth century.

The Order was established because it fitted in well with the interests and politics of its founder, King Edward III. Because Edward's mother, Isabella, as the daughter of the King of France, had a legitimate claim to the French crown, he laid his claim to the French throne as his mother's heir. Since all Isabella's brothers had died without legitimate male offspring, Edward might have had a valid point, except for French Salic law which didn't recognise a woman's right. However, the English didn't have this law and Edward, who had a formidable reputation as a soldier, was determined to assert his claim. So began the long-running, intermittent hostility between England and France we call the Hundred Years War.

War wasn't Edward's only interest: he was fascinated by the stories of King Arthur, that paragon of kingly and knightly virtue. In 1344, he held a spectacular joust at Windsor, promising to recreate King Arthur's famous fraternity of 300 Knights of the Round Table. Work began on a huge circular building within Windsor Castle to house the Order of the Round Table, but war with France diverted both money and manpower and the project was shelved but not abandoned.

Instead, in 1348 Edward decided on something smaller and more exclusive. He founded a new college of St George at Windsor to include a select group of knights, each one provided with a stall in the chapel. There would be only twenty-five members, with the king at their head, to be known as the Order of the Garter, after the symbol of the garter worn by each knight. The popular legend tells how the Countess of Salisbury lost her garter during a court ball at Calais and King Edward retrieved it, saving her modesty and rebuking those who had laughed at her embarrassment, saying: *Honi soit qui mal y pense* – 'Shame on him who thinks evil of it'. This phrase became the motto of the order, but actually refers to the king's claim to the French throne, a claim the Knights of the Garter were created to pursue.

The Order always included among the Companions, Knights Subject, who were subjects of the English Crown, and Stranger Knights. Women were also associated with the Order in the Middle Ages and issued with its robes, although they were not counted as Companions. One of the last medieval ladies to be honoured was Lady Margaret Beaufort, mother of Henry VII and grandmother of Henry VIII. After her death in 1509 the Order remained exclusively male, except for reigning queens as Sovereign of the Order, until 1901 when Edward VII made Queen Alexandra a lady of the Order.

http://www.royal.gov.uk/monarchUK/honours/Orderofthegarter/
orderofthegarter.aspx

24th – An Apothecary's Last Prescription

On 24 April 1492 Laurence Swattock, an apothecary and one time mayor of Kingston upon Hull [see 5 November], made his will. His daughter, Agnes, was now married and living in London but he bequeathed to her his everyday silver salt cellar, a chased piece of silver and a maser (a two-handled cup) with an image of Jesus imprinted on it. To his sister's son, Thomas Fisher, Laurence left his best Latin primer and 6s 8d that he might pray for his uncle's soul. He also gave his servant (probably his apprentice, despite the word used), Harry Wytrick, his two books of 'fesik called Nicholesse', i.e. the medical text books he used as an apothecary in making medicines, so long as Harry was good to Janet, Laurence's widow, after his death. He bequeathed a gold ring to his sister, Elizabeth Dalton, and the remainder of his goods, after his debts and funeral expenses were paid, were to go to Janet.

H. Falvey, et al. (eds), *English Wills proved in the Prerogative Court of York*

25th – Vending License

William Wynter of York, founder and fishmonger, and Nicholas Postilthwaite of York, fishmonger, appeared before the mayor and chamberlains and paid for a licence to sell fresh salmon from Foss bridge from this day in 1476 till the end of their lives, paying the chamberlains 26s 8d in two equal portions at Michaelmas (29 September) and the feast of St Andrew (30 November) for the first year, and 4s 6d each year thereafter.

L. C. Attreed, *York House Books,* vol. 1

26th – Murder at Brasenose College

It happened that on Sunday before the feast of the Apostles Philip and James [1 May] in the twenty-seventh year of the reign of King Edward [I] that Margery de Hereford died in the parish of St Aldgate, Oxford, and was viewed the same day by the coroner John de Oseneye and she had a wound next the left breast an inch wide and five inches deep and the same day an inquest was held ... And all the jurors say on their oath that on the previous Friday a clerk [either a cleric or a university student], whose name is not known, took the aforesaid Margery about the time of lighting lamps to King's Hall [now Brasenose College] and there lay with her carnally, and because she asked her fee of him, he drew his knife and wounded her next the left breast whence she died as said before, but she had all ecclesiastical rites and the said clerk immediately escaped from her so that he could not be arrested nor his name be discovered.

P. J. P. Goldberg, *Women in England, c. 1275–1525*

This passage is translated from the Latin of *Oxford City Documents* for 1299. The details are confusing because it says 'it happened on Sunday' but then tells how poor Margery was assaulted on 'the previous Friday', so maybe she lived for two days after she was stabbed. Certainly, there was time for her to receive the appropriate religious rites. Apparently, the area of modern Brasenose College in Oxford was the town's 'red-light district' in the thirteenth century.

27th – An Accidental Death

On about this date in 1367, twenty-four-year-old John, son of Randalph Rykkes of Thursford in Norfolk, suffering from both epilepsy and being out of his mind, left his bed and ran to the village where he dived into a well and died.

S. M. Butler, *Forensic Medicine and Death Investigation in Medieval England*

28th – The Corpus Christi Pageant

On 28 April 1484, a document was drawn up, giving details of the inn-holders' (innkeepers) company's contribution to the forthcoming Corpus Christi pageant. Every year, in May or June, York produced a spectacular show. Each city guild and company performed a play telling part of the Bible story, acting it out on a mobile stage, or pageant-wagon, for which they were responsible. Throughout the day, the pageants would trundle through the city, telling their individual stories in sequence, relating the Bible epic, from Genesis to the Last Judgement. The inn-holders, together with the ostlers (who tended the horses of those who stayed at the inns) were required to tell of the coronation of the Virgin Mary as Queen of Heaven. I have modernised the spelling:

John Strynger, Robert Shyrley and Androw Blyth have taken charge of bringing forth the pageant [wagon] of the inn-holders.

Memorandum that the twenty-eighth day of the month of April in the first year of the reign of King Richard the third, John Strynger, William Robynson, inn-holder, Robert Shyrley, glazier and inn-holder, and Androw Blyth, weaver, and Adam Siggeswik, barber, come before Thomas Wrangwysh, then being mayor of this city [York] and by the assent of all the inn-holders of this city took upon them to bring forth yearly, for the term of the next eight years, fulfilling the pageant of the coronation of our lady, pertaining to the said inn-holders, and also to the repair of the pageant [wagon], seeing that the holders of inns and keepers [pay] every[one] of them by the year 4*d*. Also every person that grooms horses of strangers that come to this city pay in likewise every year 4*d* for bringing forth the said pageant and that also the said John Strynger, William Robynson, Robert Shyrley and Androw Blyth have yearly of the chamber of this city [i.e. the corporation] during the said eight years, for bringing forth the said pageant according to the ordinance thereof made, that is to say 2*s*.

L. C. Attreed, *York House Books,* vol. 2

*

Also on this date in 1489, news was brought to the mayor, John Harper, and the aldermen of York that Henry Percy, Earl of Northumberland had been killed:

At the which day assembled, one Thomas Fissher, tailor, coming, as he said, in all goodly haste from Thirsk, and there and then showing that [there was an] affray this same day in a place beside Thirsk [actually at the earl's manor of Topcliffe] and there and then, as he said, my lord of Northumberland [was] taken and hurt by certain commons of the country thereabouts [i.e. local folk]. For the surety [safety] of this city, it is determined that proclamations shall be made for the king in diverse parts within the same [i.e. in York].

L. C. Attreed, *York House Books*, vol. 2

Northumberland was killed by his own tenants and, possibly, members of his household were involved, or at least did little to protect him. The earl was King Henry VII's heavy-handed tax-gatherer and enthusiastic enforcer of the law. Many Yorkshiremen resented him because he had done nothing to support King Richard III – popular in Yorkshire – at the battle of Bosworth (see 22 August). The city of York feared the king might see the mayor and aldermen as having been complicit in the earl's death, hence their hurried proclamations of loyalty to the Crown.

29th – Medieval Bestiary

Here is an entry from a bestiary book – a medieval book about creatures, whether real or mythological – explaining about the unicorn:

The unicorn, which is also called rhinoceros in Greek, has this nature: it is a little beast, not unlike a young goat, and extraordinarily swift. It has a horn in the middle of its brow and no hunter can catch it. But it can be caught in the following fashion: a maiden who is a virgin is led to the place where it dwells and is left there alone in the forest. As soon as the unicorn sees her, it leaps into her lap and embraces her and goes to sleep there; then the hunters capture it and display it in the king's palace.

Our Lord Jesus Christ is the spiritual unicorn of whom it is said: 'My beloved is like the son of the unicorns' [Song of Songs ch. 2, v. 9]; and in the Psalms: 'My horn shalt thou exalt like the horn of an unicorn [ch. 92, v. 10] ...

The unicorn often fights elephants; it wounds them in the stomach and kills them.

R. Barber, *Bestiary*

30th – Medieval Groceries

Using a list of expenses of 'strangers from France' who stayed at the hostel of the Black Friars in London, Martha Carlin, in her essay 'Putting dinner on the table in medieval London', has drawn up a weekly shopping basket for a modest household in the city earning an income of 5*d* per day, six days a week (total 2*s* 6*d*):

14 loaves of brown bread at ¼*d* per loaf	3½*d*
7 gallons 'second' ale	7*d*
2 quarts dried peas	½*d*
1 gallon onions	1½*d*
½ gallon oatmeal	¾*d*
2 lbs rice	½*d*
A calf's head	1½*d*
18 eggs	1*d*
1 gallon milk	1*d*
½ lb butter	1½*d*
4-5 salted herrings	½*d*
½ pint mustard	¼*d*
¼ lb currants	1*d*
Cheese, cabbage, apples, salt, etc.	½*d*
Total	1*s* 9*d*

M. Davies and A. Prescott (eds), *London and the Kingdom*

An income of 5*d* per day might be earned if the breadwinner was a master carpenter, mason or skilled craftsman paid 4*d* per day and his wife earned 1*d*, perhaps weeding a lord's garden or selling herbs she had grown, or from working as a laundress, although this last occupation was often more poorly paid.

Brown bread was the most economical to buy, a standard priced loaf weighing between 1½ lbs – 2¼ lbs, depending on the price of the grain used to make the flour. The 'second' ale would be cheaper and less potent than 'first' ale which was made from malt being used for the first time; good quality malt might even be used for a third brewing but this would be very weak and suitable only for young children. Peas, onions and oatmeal were the basic ingredients of any pottage – a sort of vegetable soup thickened with oatmeal – the daily dish for dinner with a little meat added for flavour. The calf's head is the only meat bought in but the household might have had its own supply of salted or smoked bacon from last year's Martinmas pig. The herrings would have been for the fast days – Wednesday and Friday and other holy days that specified fasting the day before. Rice was now quite a cheap staple compared to a century earlier, when the Countess of Leicester had bought it as a luxury (see 1 April). The only luxury on this list is currants at 1*d* for 4 ozs. Currants are sometimes listed in recipes as 'raisins of Corinth' – Corinth becoming corrupted to currants.

The only medieval recipe which I've found using raysonys of Coraunce that might just be affordable for an ordinary household is 'a potage of Raysonys':

Take Raysonys & do away the kyrnellys; & take a part Applys & do away the corys & the pare [peel] & bray [t]hem in a morter & temper [t]hem with Almande Mylke, & melle [t]hem with flowre [flour] of Rys that it be clene chargeant [perhaps leaving the sides of the bowl clean] & straw [strew] uppe-on pouder of Galyngale & of gyngere & serve it forth.

T. Austin, *Two Fifteenth-Century Cookery-Books*

Apart from the spices to 'straw uppe-on' it, this pottage could be made from the ingredients in the shopping basket above. However, the apples would need to be sweet ones as the currants are the only sweetener otherwise – no honey or sugar was included (an expensive luxury anyway). There doesn't seem to be any cooking involved either and I'm not sure that the uncooked rice flour wouldn't taste rather like ... well, uncooked flour.

MAY

1st – May Day

May Day traditions were celebrated as a strange combination of pagan and Christian ideas. Long ago, the pagans had held a fertility festival on 1 May as the first day of summer, the focus of the event being a young virgin crowned as the May Queen. To put a suitable Christian twist on a festival that was too popular to be abandoned, the Catholic Church made it the day on which to celebrate the Virgin Mary as Queen of Heaven, with a festival of flowers in her honour. However, the May Queen's procession, which came to include musicians, Jack-in-the-Green (who in pagan times would have deflowered the May Queen at some point), St George, Robin Hood and Maid Marian, to name a few, would end up dancing round the pagan symbol of the maypole. London had a number of maypoles, one of which was stored at the church of St Andrew Undershaft, i.e. under the maypole. Merrymaking was the order of the day with sporting events, such as wrestling, bowling, horse racing, archery and cock-fighting, and entertainments, like Morris dancing (a corrupted derivation of Moorish dancing, because the dancers blackened their faces for disguise) and mummers' plays.

2nd – Summer Clothes

It was traditional for everyone to get a new outfit for summer at the beginning of May. Lords gave their servants a new set of livery – a sort of uniform or football strip – in his colours and of a suitable standard appropriate to the servants' status; the steward got a high quality gown but the kitchen staff got something much cheaper. For anyone who could afford it, this was the time to put on your summer clothes. The old saying, 'ne'er cast a clout 'til may be out', refers to not throwing aside your winter clothes until the may-tree (or hawthorn) blossoms are in flower.

3rd – Love Meets Disapproval

Margery, the eldest daughter of Margaret Paston, had done the unthinkable and fallen in love with the family's steward, Richard Calle (see 3 October). The family utterly disapproved, as is evident in this letter written by Margery's brother, John, to their eldest brother, Sir John (RC is Richard Calle), dated 3 May 1469:

Sir, I understand by your letter which you sent me that you have heard of RC's labour that he makes with the assent of our ungracious sister. But, whereas they write that they have my goodwill therein, they falsely lie ... Lovell asked me once a question, whether I understood how it was between RC and my sister. I believe this was by Calle's suggestion, for when I asked him ... he avoided answering by hums and hays ... Wherefore, so that he nor they should take no comfort from me, I answered him that if my father, whom God assoil, were alive, and had consented thereto and my mother and you also, he should never have my goodwill to make my sister sell candles and mustard at Framlingham.

R. Virgoe, *The Illustrated Letters of the Paston Family*

The mention of his sister selling candles and mustard is a dig at Richard Calle's family who were respectable and reasonably well off merchants in Framlingham. John was clearly a snob: the Pastons themselves had great pretensions but were only a couple of generations on from yeoman farmers.

4th – The Battle of Tewkesbury

On the same day as the Lancastrians were defeated at the Battle of Barnet (see 14 April), Queen Margaret, wife of the Lancastrian King Henry VI, arrived back in England from exile in France with their son Prince Edward and supporters in tow. Landing at Weymouth, the queen was joined by a Lancastrian army led by the Duke of Somerset. In order to reinforce his army, Somerset was determined to head for Wales, where he could count upon the support of Jasper Tudor.

Meanwhile, the Yorkist king Edward IV was in London and, learning of the Lancastrian manoeuvres, headed for the West Country intending to intercept the queen and Somerset before they could reach Wales. The Lancastrian advance to Wales was delayed, firstly when they made a detour to Bristol for much needed supplies and secondly when the city of Gloucester refused to open its gates to them and allow them to cross the River Severn there; the Lancastrians were forced to go north to make the crossing of the Severn at Tewkesbury. King Edward, having narrowly missed an opportunity to confront the enemy at Sodbury, followed in pursuit.

The Lancastrians arrived at Tewkesbury first on 3 May. They had marched hard and fast for several days, covering the last twenty-four miles in just sixteen hours. The weather was hot and their troops exhausted. Edward's men weren't far behind and were equally tired but Somerset chose to stand and fight, rather than risk his army being caught in a vulnerable position as they attempted the difficult crossing of the Severn at Lower Lode, a mile to the south of Tewkesbury Abbey. Somerset had the choice of ground and set up camp in the pastures south of the abbey. The next morning, 4 May, Edward arrived to find the Lancastrians already deployed, and so he arrayed his army to the south of and parallel to Somerset's.

The Battle of Tewkesbury was to prove a decisive encounter which ended the second phase of the Wars of the Roses in 1471. Edward IV's victory and the death of Henry VI's son and heir, shortly followed by Henry's own death and Queen Margaret's imprisonment, destroyed hopes of a Lancastrian succession and led to fourteen years of peace.

http://www.battlefieldstrust.com/resource-centre/
warsoftheroses/battleview.asp?BattleFieldId=45

Upon the morrow following, Saturday the 4th day of May, [the king] apparelled himself, and all his host set in good array; ordained three wards [divisions]; displayed his banners; did blow up the trumpets; committed his cause and quarrel to Almighty God, to our most blessed lady his mother, Virgin Mary, the glorious martyr Saint George, and all the saints; and advanced directly upon his enemies; approaching to their field, which was strongly in a marvellously strong ground pight [placed], full difficult to be assailed.

Somerset commanded the right of the Lancastrian line; command of the centre was entrusted to Prince Edward, aged seventeen. King Henry and Queen Margaret's son had been raised with a hatred for the Yorkists and a thirst for their blood. Today he would have his chance, advised by the veteran Lord Wenlock. Between the two armies:

Were so evil lanes, and deep dykes, so many hedges, trees and bushes, that it was right hard to approach them near, and come to hands: but Edmund, called Duke of Somerset, having that day the vaward [vanguard] … advanced himself with his fellowship, somewhat aside-hand the king's vaward, and, by certain paths and ways therefore afore purveyed, and to the king's party unknown, he departed out of the field, passed a lane [the Gloucester road], and came into a fair place or close, even afore the king where he was embattled and, from the hill that was in that one of the closes, he set right fiercely upon th'end of the king's battle. The king, full manly, set forth even upon them, entered and won the dyke, and hedge upon them, into the close, and with great violence, put them up towards the hill and, so also, the king's vaward, being in the rule of the Duke of Gloucester.

The crisis point for the Yorkists came and passed and Lord Wenlock didn't move. Gloucester's men advanced on Somerset's who, unsupported, refused to stand. Their rout was pursued by the Yorkists across the aptly named Bloody Meadow. Somerset survived to confront Wenlock, a former Yorkist, for his inactivity. The duke, suspecting betrayal, dashed out his subordinate's brains. The flimsy morale of the remaining Lancastrians broke as they fled through the streets of Tewkesbury:

In the winning of the field such as abode hand-strokes were slain incontinent; Edward, called Prince was taken, fleeing to the town wards, and slain, in the field.

Lancastrian survivors, including Somerset, fled to the abbey seeking to claim sanctuary. Presently, they were joined by King Edward who came to give thanks to God for his victory. Feeling magnanimous, he pardoned his enemies. However, it was revealed that the abbey didn't have the legal status to grant sanctuary. The Lancastrians learned their pardons were worth nothing and they couldn't hide from Yorkist retribution.

On 6 May, they were tried by the Duke of Gloucester as Constable and the Duke of Norfolk as Marshal, inevitably being convicted of high treason. Edmund Beaufort, Duke of Somerset, along with several others, went to the block.

Three Chronicles of the Reign of Edward IV

5th – In the Month of May

In the month of May, arise early and eat and drink early and sleep not at noon. Use [eat] hot meats but eat not the head nor the feet of any beast for their brain wasteth and their marrow consumeth and all living things become faint and feeble in this month. There be four [*sic*] days of peril: the seventh, fifteenth and the twentieth. And let the blood at the end of May [from] whichever arm thou wilt. And thou shall be safe from all evils that year.

W. R. Dawson, *A Leechbook of the Fifteenth Century*

6th – The Countess's Kitchen

On the Wednesday of 6 May 1263, the household accounts for Eleanor, Countess of Leicester, read: For the kitchen – fish, 6s 11d; a calf, 12d; for 400 eggs, 15d; cheese for tarts, 9d; fifty herring from stores.

Medieval folk had a rhyme about cheese, to make sure the housewife chose well when buying a cheese at the market:

> Not white as snow, like fair Helen,
> Nor moist like tearful Magdalen,
> Nor like Argus, full of eyes,
> But heavy, like a bull of prize,
> Well resisting a thumb pressed in,
> And let it have a scaly skin,
> Eyeless and tearless, in colour not white,
> Scaly, resisting and weighing not light.

M. W. Labarge, *Mistress, Maids and Men*

Here is a recipe for a medieval cheese tart:

Lese fryes. Take cheese and pare it clean [take off the rind] and grind it small in a mortar. Draw yolks and whites of eggs through a strainer and cast thereto and mix them together [with the cheese]. Then add sugar, butter and salt and put all together in a coffin of fair paste [i.e. a pastry case] and let it bake enough and then serve it forth.

T. Austin (ed.), *Two Fifteenth-Century Cookery-Books*

7th – Suffolk Abandons Orléans

The siege of Orléans was begun by Thomas de Montacute, Earl of Salisbury, on 12 October 1428, after the English had conquered Maine, a border region between the lands recognising Henry VI of England as King of France and those recognising the Dauphin, Charles VII. But Salisbury's actions went against the advice of Henry VI's regent in France, John, Duke of Bedford, who wanted the English to march into Anjou instead. Salisbury captured some important places upstream and downstream from Orléans, along with the bridgehead fort on the south bank of the River Loire, opposite the city. But then Salisbury died of a wound on 3 November. His successor in command, William de la Pole, Earl of Suffolk, did nothing to promote the operation until December, when John Talbot (later Earl of Shrewsbury) arrived. Talbot constructed some impressive siege works, including several forts, but weeks went by without much military action. A French attempt to cut the besiegers' line of supply was defeated (see 12 February) and the defenders, under Jean d'Orléans, Count de Dunois, were about to surrender when Joan of Arc persuaded Charles VII to send an army to relieve the city. Diversionary action five miles upstream against one of the English forts enabled Joan to enter Orléans with supplies on 30 April. In the following week, the English forts were stormed, and Suffolk abandoned the siege on 7 May 1429. This proved to be the turning point in the Hundred Years War against the French.

http://www.britannica.com/event/Siege-of-Orleans

8th – Jack Cade's Rebellion

Jack Cade's name is quite well known but he is a man of mystery; even his real name is uncertain. Some of his followers called him John Mortimer and claimed he was related to Richard, Duke of York. He comes to notice in the spring of 1450, and by means of a forceful personality is recognised as the leader of a group of Kentish rebels. Jack Cade's rebellion was an uprising against the chaotic government of Henry VI.

The majority of the rebels were small landowners from Kent who objected to forced labour services, corrupt courts, the seizure of land by nobles, the loss of royal lands in France and heavy taxation. Led by Cade, an ex-soldier, a mob gathered in Kent. Troops were sent to disperse them, meeting up with Cade and his men at Sevenoaks, but the rebels got the better of the king's men. Triumphant, Cade led his men on to London, where they were welcomed by the sympathetic citizens who let them cross London Bridge. The rebels then stormed the Tower of London. Although they didn't manage to seize the Tower, they killed the Archbishop of Canterbury, the king's treasurer, Sir James Fiennes, and the Sheriff of Kent. The archbishop and the treasurer had their heads cut off and placed on placed on poles kissing each other. The royal troops regrouped and opposed the rebels. Under truce, Cade presented the king's officers with a list of his demands. Assured that his demands would be met, Cade also handed them a list of his men, so that each could receive a royal pardon. The men accepted the promise of a pardon and went home. But it was a trick. The king hadn't agreed to any of Cade's demands, nor had he promised a pardon. Instead, Henry VI demanded the arrest of Cade and all those named on the list. The rebel leader fled from London but there was no place of safety left to him (see 12 July).

http://www.britainexpress.com/History/medieval/cade.htm

9th – The Treaty of Windsor

This day in 1096 saw the consecration of the first cathedral at Lincoln.

Also on this day in 1386, the treaty of Windsor was signed in the Chapter House of St George's Chapel in Windsor Castle, sealed by Richard II and the envoys of King John I of Portugal. This was the start of the great alliance and pact of perpetual friendship between Portugal and England – the oldest diplomatic alliance in the world to still be in force.

In 1386, John of Gaunt, Duke of Lancaster, son of King Edward III of England and father of future king Henry IV, landed in Galicia with an expeditionary force to press his claim to the crown of Castile with Portuguese aid. He was attempting to claim his supposed right to Castile because he was wed to the co-heiress to the kingdom, Constance of Castile – the other co-heiress, Constance's sister, Isabella of Castile, was wed to Gaunt's brother, Edmund of Langley, Duke of York, but he wasn't interested in staking any claim to Castile. In order to ensure Portugal's assistance, John of Gaunt agreed that his elder daughter, Philippa, would marry King John I of Portugal. Their marriage was celebrated in 1387.

http://www.angloportuguesesociety.org.uk/
alliance-history

10th – A Village Dispute

On this day, at Woodbridge in Suffolk, a dispute arose between William the Piper, aged twenty-four years and more, and John

Scanlon of the same [place], and they struck each other with their fists ... John Bray, chaplain, and others took John Scanlon by the neck ... He resisted and William struck John Scanlon while he was being held ... forthwith, John Scanlon took a knife out of the sheath of John Bray without [him] knowing it and struck William feloniously with a wound in the chest nine inches deep and one inch in latitude from which wound William died, languishing for nine days following the dispute ... Alice, wife of William was with him in his home when he died.

S. M. Butler, *Forensic Medicine and Death*
Investigation in Medieval England

This is an edited excerpt from a very detailed report written by the coroner Richard of Martlesham in May 1356. He noted that John Scanlon had fled the village of Woodbridge which was left to pay a fine from Scanlon's forty penceworth of goods. The fine demanded was of eighteen pence – the value of the knife used as the murder weapon – with John Shepherd, Reginald the Cook, Henry the Smith and John the Baker, those villagers who were his nearest neighbours, having to answer because they had failed to apprehend the culprit.

*

Also on this date in 1486, probate was granted on the will of John Mapilton, parson of Halstow in Kent. He had written his short will on 5 March, requesting burial in the chancel of his own church 'before St Margaret'. His most trusted friend seemed also to be his servant, Richard Longman, who was to have a painted cloth with the image of a shepherd and sheep and Mapilton's 'best jewel' for his long and true service. He left a primer (book) and an 'Onglish' book to his godsons. His lands in Yorkshire were to go to his cousin, John of Maldon, 'and my sister's son to be excluded thereof for evermore'.

L. Boatwright, et al. (eds), *The Logge Register of*
PCC Wills, 1479–86, vol. 2

You can't help but wonder what the parson's nephew had done to cause his uncle to include that clause.

11th – Medieval Beds

How comfortable was a medieval bed? Although the poorest folk slept on straw or bracken-stuffed sacks, most townsfolk could probably afford a bed, even if it meant sharing with people other than your spouse. If you had guests staying, you didn't vacate your bed for them. That would be an insult, implying they weren't your equals. So you all climbed in together, wives as well, showing that you trusted your guests to behave. Most folk slept naked apart from a head-covering, but if you wished your partner to know that love-making wasn't an option that night, then you kept your shirt or shift on.

The ditty: 'Good night, sleep tight; don't let the bedbugs bite', dates from medieval times. 'Sleep tight' refers to the ropes beneath the mattress that were strung through the bed frame – they had to be tightened to stop the mattress sagging. Mattresses could be stuffed with feathers, horsehair, sheep's wool or rags, with lavender, fleabane or some other bug-repellent herb included between the mattress and the woven mat which prevented the mattress from bulging down between the ropes. Medieval beds often look rather short. This isn't because medieval people were small – they were much like us in stature – but because folk usually slept propped up on pillows. They feared that if you lay on your back your mouth might fall open, and a gaping mouth was – literally – an open invitation to the Devil to enter your body and steal your soul!

T. Mount, *Everyday Life in Medieval London*

12th – Cherrylips

On this day in 1483, the borough court of York recorded the following:

Memorandum ... the whole parish of St Martin's in Micklegate came before my lord the mayor and complained upon Margery Gray, otherwise called Cherrylips, that she was a woman ill disposed of her body to whom ill disposed men resorted [a prostitute, in other words], to the nuisance of her neighbours.

However, that isn't the last we hear of Cherrylips. On 28 July 1483, she is back before the mayor. This time, a great many people from the parish of St Gregory in Micklegate say that Margery Gray, alias Cherrylips, is of bad disposition and governance of her body; she is also reported to be a scold with her neighbours. On this occasion, she was ordered by the mayor to remove herself beyond the boundaries of the city by the evening of the following day and not to live in the city again, under penalty of imprisonment at the will of the mayor.

L. C. Attreed, *York House Books,* vol. 2

13th – Three Depositions

On 13 May 1430 a court in York heard the depositions of three witnesses: Agnes Crispyn, her husband, John Crispyn, and Joan Scharp, the servant of Robert Lascels. The case concerned Margaret Herman who owed money to Robert.

Agnes Crispyn, aged twenty-six, wife of John Crispyn, a cutler, told how, on the Monday before the feast of St Mary Magdalene the previous year (18 July), she was at Robert Lascel's house in Petergate, York, with Robert, his wife, Isabel Lascels, Margaret Herman and her husband, Thomas, since deceased, dining together with other friends. At some point, Margaret bought some candlewick from Robert, a merchant, to the value of 23s 10d, promising he would receive payment on or before next Michaelmas (29 September).

Joan Scharp, aged twenty, a servant to Robert, related how on that Monday, between three and four o'clock, Margaret bought the candlewick in her master's shop. She saw her master and Margaret weighing out the candlewick and Alice Bawmburgh, another of Robert's servants, witnessed them too. Then Margaret's servant carried the wick home for her. Meanwhile, Joan (who was more likely an apprentice, rather than just a servant) with Agnes Crispyn, Margaret and Thomas Herman, Robert and Isabel Lascels and the wife (unnamed) of William Warde, a York tailor, sat together 'in the summer hall', eating, drinking and relaxing; all of them heard Margaret promise to pay Robert for the wick by Michaelmas. However, the bill wasn't paid and sometime before Martinmas (11 November), Robert sent Joan to Margaret Herman to ask for the money. Margaret told her she didn't have that amount ready but would arrange to pay Robert as soon as she was able.

John Crispyn, a forty-year-old cutler and husband to Agnes, told how Robert had come to him, complaining that he had been summoned to the sheriffs' court in York to answer a case brought by Margaret Herman against him, claiming that he owed her 6 marks (£4 2s). Robert wanted John to accompany him to Margaret's house in Little Peter Lane to sort out the matter. Robert tried first to persuade Margaret that he should pay her the 6 marks minus the 23s 10d that she owed him. Margaret refused, saying that she wanted the entire 6 marks and *then* she would pay him what she owed for the wick. Robert agreed.

John went home with Robert and Robert got together the 6 marks. Then along with other witnesses, Henry Rothwell, a merchant, Robert Trewlofe, since deceased, and William Warde, a tailor and the parish clerk, they all assembled in the porch of St Peter the Little to see Robert Lascels pay Margaret Herman her 6 marks. This he did and then asked her to pay his bill. Margaret refused, saying she would not pay him one penny since she had been advised not to. John Crispyn swore this was a true deposition; he had not been bribed, instructed or corrupted.

P. J. P. Goldberg (ed.), *Women in England, c. 1275–1525*

As so often with such cases, we don't know the final outcome of the protracted dispute.

14th – The Battle of Lewes

In 1264, the battle of Lewes was fought on this day in Sussex. Simon de Montfort, Earl of Leicester, and the rebel barons defeated the English king, Henry III.

*

Also on this day in 1420, a child was kidnapped in Wiltshire and held in Oxfordshire:

William Burton, servant to Master Robert Burton, clerk, one of your [the Lord Chancellor's] chaplains, most humbly beseeches and grievously complains of Lewis Gryville of the county of Oxford, that Robert Archer of Winchester, merchant, did, on the Tuesday before the feast of the Ascension of our Lord in the eighth year of the reign of our sovereign lord king [Henry V], ravish [i.e. abduct or kidnap] one Alice Wodeloke, daughter and heir apparent of Parnell, the wife of the said suppliant [William], the same daughter being aged seven years, and being at Collingburn in the county of Wiltshire in the guardianship of John Santon, to whose care she had been committed by William, and [Robert Archer] brought her thence to the house of the said Lewis at Drayton in Oxfordshire.

And the said Lewis still detains Alice wrongfully and against the law, right and good conscience and against the will of the said suppliant [William], and will not deliver Alice to William unless he will make fine [pay a ransom] to Lewis for forty marks and release by his writing to Robert Archer all the debt which Robert owes William.

May it please your most gracious lordship to consider this matter and thereupon to ordain that the suppliant [William] may have restitution of the said Alice as law and conscience demand, with their damages in this behalf, for God and as a work of charity.

W. P. Baildon, *Selected Cases in Chancery AD 1364 to 1471*
(Seldon Society, X, 1896)

15th – A Simple Dessert

Here is a nice simple recipe for a dessert:

Take good almond milk and let it boil. Thicken it with rice flour and colour it with saffron. Decorate it with pomegranate seeds, or raisins, if you have nothing else. Sprinkle with sugar and serve it forth.

S. Pegge, *The Forme of Cury*

16th – Cely's Marriage Reception

Between the 13th and 22nd of this month in 1484, George, youngest son of the Cely family of wool merchants in London, was celebrating his marriage to Margery Rygon with a series of special dinners. According to the family's accounts book, their cook did most of the preparation but extra help was hired. The handwashing which preceded a meal could be an elaborate ceremony on such occasions and extra water was needed, both for these ablutions and for the washing up afterwards. Since it all had to be carried in from a well or conduit outside their house, the Celys paid the considerable sum of 2s 1d 'unto Steven Water-bearer' for doing the job, and four extra men were paid 2d each for washing the dishes at the end of the meal.

Not every dish was made from scratch by the cook: sauces were bought in from outside caterers, ready-made. Table decorations, ribbons and garlands cost 4d and a painter was paid 18d to give the dining hall a coat of 'part-gold' paint to add a touch of sophistication. Rather less sophisticated was the entertainment: a poulterer was paid to bring along three dozen rabbits for the meal and an additional 6d for three live bunnies as well. These lively little animals were to be released during the meal, to add a bit of fun and drama and, perhaps, to hint at the future fertility of the bride.

B. Henisch, *The Medieval Cook*

17th – A Proper Coronation

On 17 May 1220, King Henry III of England was crowned for the second time. This was his official coronation but a hasty ceremony had been held previously on 28 October 1216 in Gloucester Cathedral, using a makeshift jewelled circlet for a crown. One source says it was his mother's circlet; others state that it was borrowed from an image of the Virgin Mary as Queen of Heaven. Henry was just nine years old; his father, King John, had died suddenly a few days before and England was in a state of civil war. A hasty coronation had been vital but now, over three years on, England was at peace and a proper coronation, with all due ceremonial and pageantry, was celebrated.

Exactly twenty-seven years later, in 1257, Henry's younger brother Richard, Earl of Cornwall, was so rich from his ownership of the Cornish tin mines that he could buy the votes required to get himself elected as King of the Romans. He was crowned in Aachen, seat of the Emperor Charlemagne, in a glorious ceremony. But it was an empty title, despite usually being a precursor to election as the Holy Roman Emperor. Richard never rose to that office and, at home in England, had to be content with the title of 'earl'. Henry forbade him from using any kingly title that might rival his own status.

18th – Eleanor and Henry

Eleanor, Duchess of Aquitaine in her own right, having inherited her father's enormous estates as a young girl, had been Queen of France for fifteen years. Her husband, Louis VII of France, couldn't cope with her fiery personality. She had gone on crusade with him and given him two daughters but her disobedience and failure to produce a male heir proved too much. Their marriage was annulled in March 1152 on the grounds of consanguinity, i.e. they were too closely related by blood.

The annulment returned Aquitaine and Poitou to Eleanor, so although she was almost thirty, she was still quite a prize in the marriage market. On this day, just eight weeks later, she wed nineteen-year-old Henry Plantagenet, Duke of Normandy and Count of Anjou, despite being as closely related to him as she had been to Louis. Henry was described as stocky and freckled, a man of energy and charm but impatient and with a terrible temper. Two such wilful people locked in matrimony was bound to lead to strife.

Eleanor left Paris as soon as her marriage to Louis was annulled and hurried south with an escort of her own men. Warned, she avoided an ambush by Henry's younger brother, Geoffrey, who had hoped to marry her himself. Safe in her own capital of Poitiers, Eleanor immediately sent word to Henry to come and marry her. He joined her in Poitiers and they were married in the cathedral on Whit Sunday in a simple ceremony with surprisingly little show.

King Louis was furious. Neither the bride nor groom had asked his consent, which they were obliged to do as his vassals; he would have refused, of course. It must also have been a huge concern that when Henry succeeded to the throne of England in 1154, he now had dominions in France stretching from the English Channel to the Pyrenees and covering ten times as much of the country as the French king possessed.

Over the next twelve years Eleanor gave Henry five sons and three daughters. Two of their sons, Richard and John, would be kings of England. Not surprisingly, her marriage with Henry was a stormy affair. She encouraged her sons to rebel against their father in 1173, and after that Henry kept her a prisoner in England until he died in 1189. Under both Richard and John she remained active in matters of state; she died eventually in a nunnery at Fontrevault in Anjou in her early eighties in 1204, having been for much of her life the most powerful woman in Europe.

R. Cavendish, http://www.historytoday.com/richard-cavendish/
eleanor-aquitaine-marries-henry-anjou

19th – St Dunstan's Day

St Dunstan's day celebrated the feast of a tenth-century Archbishop of Canterbury. Although he was born the son of a Saxon nobleman, Dunstan decided not to become a courtier but joined Glastonbury Abbey as a monk. He was chosen to become the abbot by his fellow monks around AD 943 and under his leadership Glastonbury developed as one of the most important centres of education and religious studies in England.

Dunstan was promoted to be Bishop of Worcester and then Bishop of London and in 959 he became Archbishop of Canterbury. Because many abbeys had been destroyed by Viking raiders in the previous century, Dunstan founded more than forty new ones, including Peterborough,

Ely (on the Isle of Eels in the Fens) and Thorney (on the Isle of Thorn Bushes, better known as Westminster).

Despite his noble birth, legend says that Dunstan was skilled at metalwork. One day while making a gold chalice, the devil appeared to Dunstan and tried to tempt him. Although he came disguised as a beautiful maiden, the saintly Dunstan recognised the devil and pinched his nose with a pair of red-hot tongs – serve him right! Because of his skills, St Dunstan was chosen as the patron saint of goldsmiths. He once said:

God forbid that for the sake of any mortal man or to save my own life, I should set aside the law which Christ my Lord, the Son of God, established in His Church.

Cowie and Gummer, *The Christian Calendar*

20th – Prince Louis Defeated

On this day in 1217, a battle was fought near Lincoln, England, resulting in the defeat of Prince Louis of France by William Marshal, Earl of Pembroke. The civil wars of King John's reign and French interference were ended at last.

*

Also on this day in 1481, Mawde Undirhill, a widow of Waterlambeth in Surrey, wrote her long, detailed will. Among her bequests of clothing, Mawde left to William Hethe's wife (unnamed) a crimson gown with grey fur, enough spare fabric to make new sleeves for it and a girdle 'powdered' with gold, silver and gilt and a double buckle. To Joanne Garwale, she left a kirtle [underdress] of scarlet, a blue gown furred with lettuce [a pale grey fur] and a scarlet hood. Helen Garwale, Joanne's sister, was to have a green gown and a black kirtle, and Anne Martyn was to have a murrey (mulberry-coloured) gown and a red girdle belt decorated with silver. Mawde's brother-in-law was to have her husband's best worsted doublet and a crimson gown with matching tippets (detachable trailing sleeves). Alice Boure, who lived in St Mary Magdalene's churchyard in Southwark, was to have Mawde's musterdevillers (a grey woollen cloth) gown with grey fur and fur-lined cuffs. Agnes Baren was bequeathed a blue gown lined with buckrum and satin and a violet kirtle.

L. Boatwright, et al. (eds), *The Logge Register of PCC Wills*, vol. 1

This is only a tiny sample of Mawde's bequests. She must have been a very wealthy woman with an extensive wardrobe.

21st – The Treaty of Troyes

On this day in 1420 the Treaty of Troyes was signed, following the English victory at Agincourt more than four years earlier [see 25 October]. The treaty determined that Henry V of England and his heirs would inherit the throne of France upon the death of King Charles VI of France and was sealed by Henry's marriage to Katherine de Valois, Charles' youngest daughter.

*

Also on this day in 1466, John Paston senior died in London. His body remained in London for a week before beginning a six day procession back to Norfolk to be buried in Bromholm Priory. No expense was spared: it is noted that 'a woman who accompanied the corpse from London to Norwich was paid 6s 8d and thirty-nine children were paid 4s 4d to attend the church service. A glazier was paid 20d to remove two panes of stained glass from the church windows to allow the smoke from so many candles and torches to escape and not choke the mourners, and then to solder the lead to fix the panes back in place after the funeral.

R. Virgoe, *The Illustrated Paston Letters*

22nd – The First Battle of St Albans

England's thirty years of civil strife – known to us as the Wars of the Roses but called then the Cousins' War – began on this day in 1455 with the First Battle of St Albans, when Richard, Duke of York, finally rebelled against the mentally unstable Lancastrian king, Henry VI. After years of snubs and with the Crown owing him a fortune in money spent from his own purse in attempting to maintain England's French possessions without support from Henry, York was frustrated. Despite his efforts, England's territories across the Channel, bar Calais, were lost by 1453. The English nobility, without a foreign war to fight, began quarrelling among themselves and with the Crown.

Following their exclusion from court, the Duke of York and his ally Richard Neville, Earl of Warwick, gathered their private armies in the north and marched south towards London. They confronted King Henry at St Albans, just north of the capital. The Lancastrian army of 2,000 men, commanded by the Duke of Buckingham, arrived at the town first and set about organising its defences. Following hours of negotiations that achieved nothing, the slightly larger Yorkist force launched a frontal assault on the town.

In the vicious fighting that followed through the narrow streets of St Albans, the Yorkists suffered heavy casualties. A small group under the Earl of Warwick crept through the lanes and back gardens to make a surprise attack on Henry's main army, held in reserve in the market square. The Lancastrian defenders, realising they had been outflanked, abandoned their barricades and fled. Warwick's longbowmen loosed arrows at Henry's bodyguard, killing Buckingham and several other influential Lancastrian nobles and slightly wounding the king. Henry was escorted back to London by the victorious York and Warwick.

With York as Lord Protector of England, he now effectively ruled the country. Henry's wife, Queen Margaret, along with their young son Edward of Westminster, fled into exile.

E. Castelow, http://www.historic-uk.com/HistoryMagazine/
DestinationsUK/The-First-Battle-of-St-Albans/

23rd – A Day in Court

A sitting of the Wakefield Manor Court was held at Halifax in Yorkshire on the Tuesday before Ascension Day in 1275. A jury of twelve men was sworn in to hear a series of cases. The matters brought before the court varied from trespass in the lord's forest, poaching, leaving the manor without the lord's permission, to assault. On this occasion it would seem that certain women had been up to no good:

They [the twelve men of the jury] say on their oath that Cicely, daughter of William Norman, burgled the house of Margery de Pendaunt by night, and took flour, butter, cheese and a smock and carried them all to the house of John, son of Adam the Miller, her husband without his knowledge. She is to be arrested if she can be found.

Also that Nalle, daughter of Richard the Kittewritt of Norlaund, stole a sheet from the hedge of Robert de Saltunstal and a hood and a ring from the chamber of Adam de Miggele and 4½ ells of linen from John de Noteschawe. She is to be arrested if she can be found. They do not know where she was harboured.

Court Rolls of the Manor of Wakefield, 1274–1297

It may seem strange to us that the jury apparently brought the charges against the defendants, but medieval court cases were conducted quite differently from our contemporary system. In a modern court of law, the jury is expected to be utterly impartial, having no prior knowledge of the defendant, the situation or background to the crime. In medieval times, the jury was made up of local men – always men and not women – who knew the defendant, his/her family and, often, the victim of the crime as well. They were required to use their local knowledge in judging the guilt or innocence of the accused.

In the cases mentioned here, Cicely Norman and Nalle Kittewritt had run off with their ill-gotten goods. Among other items, Nalle had stolen a sheet that was spread to dry on a hedge. In medieval England, thorn hedges were used instead of washing lines and pegs. In Yorkshire, even into the twentieth century, a rack for drying washing in front of the fire was still called a 'winter hedge'.

24th – The King from Dublin

On this day, Ascension Day 1487, a young man was crowned as King Edward of England in Christ Church Cathedral, Dublin. The lad was supposed to be Edward, Earl of Warwick, but he was actually an imposter, Lambert Simnel. Nonetheless, Irish lords and Yorkist nobility, even the Mayor of Dublin, attended the ceremony. Richard III's designated heir, his nephew John, Earl of Lincoln, and the dead monarch's chamberlain, Francis, Viscount Lovell, both took an active role in the coronation. Afterwards, the new king sealed documents with the seal belonging to King Edward V, one of the Princes in the Tower. So who was he? We may never know but the Yorkists wouldn't have insulted God by presenting some lowly person as His anointed representative on earth. Whoever he was, the young man disappeared from history, perhaps slain at the battle of Stoke Field (see 16 June).

25th – Crowned with Eggs

Here is a recipe from the 1390s for capons or chicken crowned with eggs, written by the Goodman of Paris:

Take capouns and rost hem right hoot that they not half ynough and hewe hem to gobbettes and cast hem in a pot; do therto clene broth. Seeth hem that they be tendre. Take brede and the broth and draw it up yfere; take strong powdour and safroun and salt and cast therto. Take ayren [eggs] and seeth hem harde; take out the yolkes and hew the whyte, take the pot fro the fyre and cast the whyte therinne. Mess the dysshes therwith and lay the yolkes aboue hool [on top whole] and flour it with clowes [dust with powdered cloves].

Maggie Black suggests the following method:

Roast the bird in a hot oven until just browning. Allow to cool a little before cutting the meat into bite-sized pieces and removing the bones. Put the meat into a pan and cover with chicken stock. Cook gently until cooked through. Take a little stock and steep ¼ teaspoon of saffron strands in it. Strain the rest of the stock from the meat, into a clean pan. Add the saffron stock, 125 g white bread crumbs, salt, ground black pepper, cinnamon and ginger. Stir until thickened. Pour the sauce over the meat and serve garnished with chopped whites of hard boiled eggs, keeping the yolks whole to crown the dish. Sprinkle with ground cloves.

M. Black, *The Medieval Cookbook*

26th – Of Weasels

Here is an intriguing entry from a thirteenth-century bestiary book:

The weasel is a sort of long mouse. It is very cunning; when it gives birth to its young, it carries them from one place to another and puts them somewhere different each time. It attacks serpents and mice ... Some people say the weasel conceives through the ear and gives birth through the mouth; others say it is the opposite. The weasel is said to be skilled in healing, so that if its young have been killed, it can bring them to life again.

R. Barber, *Bestiary*

27th – King John's Coronation

King John brought trouble on himself, choosing a moveable feast for his coronation on Ascension Day, 27 May 1199. Churchmen warned him of the consequences of such an 'inconstant' day. Matters had already began badly when John had dropped the spear given to him as the emblem of his investiture as Duke of Normandy; he quickly lost the duchy to the French. He giggled throughout the coronation ceremony and didn't bother to take the sacrament during the Mass. In a time when ill-omens were taken very seriously, is it any wonder he turned out to be a disastrous monarch?

Because John numbered the years of his reign from his coronation day, the start date for each regnal year changed – a nightmare for historians trying to work out the year AD for various documents in John's time, if they refer to May or June — for instance, the third year of his reign began on 3 May 1201, but the sixth year of his reign began on 3 June; some regnal years were longer than others.

28th – A Common Procuress

On 28 May 1385, Elizabeth, the wife of Henry Moring, was brought before the Lord Mayor of London, Sir Nicholas Brembre, and the aldermen and sheriffs at the Guildhall. Elizabeth was accused of taking on Joan and other female apprentices to be trained as silkwomen when, in fact, she incited them 'to live a dishonourable life and to consort with friars, chaplains and all other such men as desired to have their company both in her own house in the parish of All Hallows near the Wall, in the ward of Broad Street in London, and elsewhere.'

The report continues at length, telling how Elizabeth ordered Joan to steal a book from one of the chaplains and then sold it for profit. The sheriffs were instructed to summon a jury of twelve good men of the district:

Who said upon their oath that the same Elizabeth was guilty of all the above matters of which she was accused and that she was a common prostitute and a common procuress [a woman who procures other women to provide sex for men] ... In order that other women might beware of so acting, it was ruled that the said Elizabeth should be taken from the guildhall to Cornhill and put in the 'thewe', to remain there for one hour ... being proclaimed publicly and afterwards to be taken to some gate of the city and there be made to forswear the city and liberty thereof.

P. J. P. Goldberg, *Women in England c. 1275–1525*

The 'thewe' was a pillory specially made for punishing women. Apart from execution, being thrown out of London and denied citizenship was the worst sentence that could be passed on an accused.

*

Also on this day in 1483, Conisbrough Court was held in Yorkshire, giving the date as the twenty-eighth day of May in the first year of the reign of King Edward V after the conquest. It is interesting that the same court, meeting previously, was dated the last day of April in the [blank] year of the reign of King [blank], following the death of Edward IV earlier that month. Clearly, there had been some doubt as to who should be the next king, but this was now resolved. Here is the only case heard:

Conisbrough fine 4*d*. Agnes Todd in her widowhood, by John Swetyng, tenant and sworn, surrenders into the hands of the lord one toft with buildings on it, the moiety of one garden as it is divided off by hedges and boundary-posts planted and positioned there, with appurtenances in Conisbrough, to the use of William Baldirstone and Joan his wife, daughter of the said Agnes, and the heirs lawfully begotten between the same William and Joan. Which are granted to William and Joan, to hold to them and their heirs for ever for services according to the custom of the manor. And they give to the lord the entry fine 4*d*.

http://www.hrionline.ac.uk/conisbrough/
browse/roll_1483_3.html

To conclude the story of dating years to the reign of the king, the subsequent Conisbrough Court was held on the twentieth day of June in the first year of the reign of King Richard III after the conquest. This suggests that whoever wrote up these records did so from notes taken in court at the time, whereof there was evidently some delay in doing so, because King Richard's reign did not commence until 26 June, so the scribe was writing with hindsight – he should still have dated it more correctly to the first year of the reign of King Edward V.

29th – A Kent Landowner

On this day in 1483, John Pokyll senior of Bearsted in Kent wrote his will – in Latin. He owned a good deal of land in the Maidstone area and also at Rainham in the same county. His wealth was such that he could bequeath sizeable holdings to his son, John, when John should reach the age of twenty-two, and still have enough for his daughters' marriage dowries and to make provision for the unborn child which his wife, Alice, was currently carrying, whether a boy or girl. Son John got the largest share of lands but a daughter, Godelina, was to have the land called Melfield as her dowry. Wife Alice got the lands at Rainham and another daughter, Joanna, was to have £10 towards her marriage.

L. Boatwright, et al. (eds), *The Logge Register of PCC Wills,* vol. I

30th – The Peasants' Revolt

On this day in 1381, the English commons rose up in what is now called the Peasants' Revolt – one of the most dramatic events in English history. What began as a local dispute in Essex, when a group of common folk in Brentwood reacted to an over-zealous poll-tax collector, spread to neighbouring villages, while across Kent, Suffolk, Hertfordshire and Norfolk, armed bands of villagers and townsmen also rose up and attacked manors and religious houses.

The authorities could hardly believe what was happening. How could illiterate, unlettered, ignorant commoners organise themselves so efficiently in a concerted uprising? How could the people of Essex and Kent communicate with each other to coordinate their actions, without London knowing about it? It seems that those in power were utterly out of touch with the common folk, unaware that boats frequently crossed the Thames downriver between Kent and Essex transporting livestock, goods and, most crucially, information. The authorities were also slow to realise the extent to which priests and friars were involved in the organisation with their valuable ability to write letters and note down plans (see 14 June).

*

Also on this day in 1431, England's nemesis in France, Joan of Arc, was burned at the stake in Rouen, Normandy.

31st – *Supersedeas*

The Mayor and the City Council noted:

All the aforesaid gathered and unanimously agreed that Richard
Marston, one of the sheriffs of the city, should be committed to
prison for his disobedience to the mayor concerning a writ of
supersedeas sent to Richard by the mayor, which writ Richard
refused to admit and allow.

L. C. Attreed, *York House Books*

A writ of *supersedeas* could be either a common-law writ commanding
a stay of legal proceedings that was issued to prevent an officer – in this
case a sheriff – from proceeding under another writ, i.e. it superseded
the earlier writ. Or it may have been an order from a higher court
staying the proceedings of a lower court.

JUNE

1st – Summer's Arrival

With summer's arrival, it was the season of cuckoos and roses. A merry song has survived the centuries. This piece is meant to be sung in a round by four singers, each singing the same melody one after the other, each starting when the previous singer reaches the end of the first line. While this is happening, two lower voices repeat the words 'sing cuccu'. It is lively and meant to be danced to – correctly called 'a carol'. Instructions on how to perform the song were given. It comes from a volume of mid-thirteenth-century manuscripts from Reading Abbey (British Library, Harley MS.978, f.12v). Below are the original Middle English words followed by the modern version:

> Sumer is icumen in,
> Lhude sing cuccu!
> Groweþ sed and bloweþ med
> And springþ þe wde nu,
> Sing cuccu!
>
> Awe bleteþ after lomb,
> Lhouþ after calue cu.
> Bulluc sterteþ, bucke uerteþ,
> Murie sing cuccu!
> Cuccu, cuccu, wel singes þu cuccu;
> Ne swik þu nauer nu.

Sing cuccu nu. Sing cuccu.
Sing cuccu. Sing cuccu nu!

Modern version:

Summer has come in,
Loudly sing, Cuckoo!
The seed grows and the meadow blooms
And the wood springs anew,
Sing, Cuckoo!

The ewe bleats after the lamb,
The cow lows after the calf.
The bullock stirs, the stag farts,
Merrily sing, Cuckoo!
Cuckoo, cuckoo, well you sing, cuckoo;
Don't you ever stop now.

Sing cuckoo now. Sing, Cuckoo.
Sing Cuckoo. Sing cuckoo now!

2nd – Edible Roses

Here is a fourteenth-century recipe to make use of all those beautifully scented rose petals:

For to make Rosee. Tak the flowris of Rosys and wasch hem wel in water and after bray hem wel in a morter and then tak Almondys and temper hem and seth hem and after tak flesch of capons or of hennys and hac yt smale and than bray hem wel in a morter and than do yt in the Rosee so that the flesch acord wyth the mylk and so that the mete be charchaunt and after do yt to the fyre to boyle and do therto sugur and safroun that yt be wel ycolowrd and rosy of levys and of the forseyde flowrys and serve yt forth.

S. Pegg, *The Forme of Cury*

As with most medieval recipes, no amounts of ingredients are given but as the rose petals cook down to almost nothing, you can be generous with them – red ones keep their colour best. Wash the flowers and crush them in a mortar. Take almonds, pound them and boil them in a pan of water to make 'almond milk'. You can use this just like cows' milk to make and thicken the sauce. Take chicken meat, chop it, grind it in the mortar and add it to the milk with the roses and mix well. Put the pan back on the heat until the chicken is cooked and the sauce thickens – take 15 to 20 minutes according to how much you are making. Add sugar to taste and saffron to flavour and colour the rosee. As an option, a little rosewater can be added to increase the flowery taste. Garnish with rose leaves and petals and serve.

3rd – Abelard the Heretic

The French scholar and lover of Heloise, Peter Abelard, was tried and found guilty of heresy on this day in 1140. He died two years later on 21 April.

4th – Corpus Christi

The earliest possible date for the feast of Corpus Christi is 21 May and the latest is on 24 June, with the Sunday celebrations three days later; in 2015, the feast falls on 4 June and in 2016 it will be on 26 May. The feast of Corpus Christi (Latin for 'Body of Christ') celebrates the tradition and belief in the body and blood of Jesus Christ and his real presence in the Eucharist.

The feast is celebrated on the Thursday after Trinity Sunday and sixty days after Easter, so it is another moveable feast. The feast day didn't exist officially until Pope Urban IV instituted the Solemnity of Corpus Christi on the Thursday after Pentecost in 1264. In medieval times, across many towns in England and Europe, the festival of Corpus Christi saw the performance of cycles of mystery plays. These plays, often staged by local guilds, told the Bible story from the Creation to the Last Judgement.

5th – Hayfever Remedy

In the month of June, every day a draught of water is good to drink
fasting. Ale and meat in moderate measure eat and drink and eat
lettuce and sage.

W. R. Dawson, *A Leechbook of the Fifteenth Century*

For sufferers of that summer blight, hay fever, these remedies were
supposed to help:

For eyes that be red and running. Take the red cabbage leaf and
anoint it with the white of an egg and lay to thine eyes when thou
goest to bed.

For a running nose. Take the juice of mint and the juice of rue,
tempered together, and put it in thy nostrils oft, and it will much
amend and cast out the filth of the brain whence it cometh.

W. R. Dawson, *A Leechbook of the Fifteenth Century*

6th – A Mercer's Will

On this day in 1487 probate was granted on the will of Guy Malyerd,
a mercer from Beverley in Yorkshire. To judge from his bequests,
Guy was quite well off and an active member of the Mercers' Guild.
He leaves thirty 'squared trees' and fifty wainscots ready to repair
the choir stalls of St Mary's, Beverley, gold rings to a number of
beneficiaries and a silver-decorated sword to Alexander Smythley. An
unusual bequest of three yards of russet – a fine woollen cloth – 'of
my wyves making', is left to Guy's godfather, John Trelles, so it seems
that Guy's wife, Cecill as he refers to her, may have been a webster, a
female weaver.

H. Falvey, et al. (eds), *English Wills proved in the
Prerogative Court of York, 1477–99*

7th – 'Spells Contrary to the Universal Church'

Sometime around 7 June 1481 the Church Court of London, which usually met in St Paul's Cathedral, heard a case from the parish of St Sepulchre in the city:

Joan Beverley, or Lessell, or Cowcross, is a witch and she asked two accomplice witches to work together, so that Robert Stantone and another gentle-born of Gray's Inn should love her and no other. And they committed adultery with her and, as it is said, fought for her, and one almost killed the other. Her husband does not dare stay with her on account of these two men. She is a common whore and a procuress and she wants to poison men.

Joan's punishment is unrecorded but Katherine Martyn of Colnbrook was sentenced by the Church Court of Buckingham in 1495 'concerning spells contrary to the universal Church'. She was beaten three times through the church and dismissed.

P. J. P. Goldberg, *Women in England, c. 1275–1525*

It seems that the authorities in the later fifteenth century in England were far more lenient with supposed witches than the Irish had been on the unfortunate Petronilla de Meath in the early fourteenth (see 3 November).

8th – The Black Prince Dies

Edward of Woodstock, known as the Black Prince, Duke of Aquitaine and Duke of Cornwall, and the eldest son and heir to King Edward III, died on this day in 1376. Renowned as a soldier, first having earned his spurs at the battle of Crecy and adding to this the victory over the French at Poitiers, the prince was England's hope for a superb future king. This was of paramount importance and his succession was eagerly awaited as his father, Edward III, was less active after 1364, becoming increasingly senile after the death of Queen Philippa in 1369.

The Black Prince had been born on 15 June 1330 and seemed to be in good health until 1366. That year, he was on campaign in Spain to restore Don Pedro the Cruel to the throne of Castille when he became ill. During this campaign, the entire army suffered terribly from dysentery and it was said that one in five Englishmen on that expedition never returned home. The Black Prince, aged just thirty-six, contracted an illness in Spain that would afflict him for the rest of his life.

Some modern medical experts and historians believe that he contracted amoebic dysentery but others argue against the possibility of surviving for another ten years with such an illness. Other possible diagnoses include oedema (dropsy, from which his mother had died), nephritis, or a combination of these. Though severely debilitated, in 1370 the prince had to leave his sick bed in Bordeaux and raise an army to defend his duchy of Aquitaine against Charles V of France. The following year, his health deteriorated further and his physicians advised him to leave Bordeaux and return home to England. After months of rest and special diets in England, there was some improvement in his health, sufficient that in 1372 he sailed on an expedition with King Edward III, but they were unable to land in France due to contrary winds. This failed expedition with his father caused the health of both men to decline drastically. It was said that the prince would often faint because of weakness, a sad situation that continued until his death in 1376, just short of his forty-sixth birthday.

Edward the Black Prince died at Westminster Palace on 8 June. As Thomas Walsingham said at the time: 'Thus died hope for the English.' The prince requested to be buried in the crypt of Canterbury Cathedral and a chapel was prepared there as a chantry for him and his wife, Joan of Kent. (This is now the French Protestant Chapel, and contains ceiling bosses of her face and of their coats of arms.) However, his wish was overruled after his death – the crypt was thought too lowly a place for a hero's burial – and he was buried instead on the south side of the shrine of Thomas Becket, behind the choir. His tomb consists of a bronze effigy beneath a tester (canopy) depicting the Holy Trinity, with his heraldic achievements hung over the tester. The achievements have now been replaced by replicas, although the originals can still be seen nearby. An epitaph was inscribed in French around his effigy, as he had instructed. In translation it reads:

Such as thou art, sometime was I.
Such as I am, such shalt thou be.
I thought little on th'our of Death
So long as I enjoyed breath.
On earth I had great riches
Land, houses, great treasure, horses, money and gold.
But now a wretched captive am I,
Deep in the ground, lo here I lie.
My beauty great, is all quite gone,
My flesh is wasted to the bone.

9th – Halley's Comet

The comet we know as Halley's comet appeared in the sky in 1456.

10th – A Writ of Protection

Thomas Plouden, citizen, gentleman, brewer and grocer of London, requested a writ of protection (a sort of passport and safe passage) from King Richard III on the pretext that he was going to Picardy to carry out victualling and defence work on the king's castle of Hammes. However, by November in that year, 1484, Thomas still hadn't left for France and his writ was cancelled.

S. L. Thrupp, *The Merchant Class of Medieval London*

11th – A Knight of the Bath

Here is a letter of 1461 written by Thomas Playter in London to John Paston:

Please your mastership to know that the King [Edward IV], because of the siege about Carlisle, changed his day of coronation to be upon the Sunday next after St John the Baptist [i.e. on 28 June, see below], with the intent to speed northward in all haste and howbeit that he now has good tidings that Lord Montagu has broken the siege and slain 6,000 of the Scots, with two knights, of whom one is Lord Clifford's brother, yet notwithstanding he will still be crowned on the said Sunday.

And John Jenney informed me, and I have truly learned since, you are named to be made a knight [of the Bath] at this coronation. Whether you had understanding of this beforehand I know not, but if it pleases you to take the worship upon you, considering the comforting tidings aforesaid ... it is time that your necessary clothes for that should be provided for; also you should need to hasten to London, for I think the knights will be made the Saturday before the coronation. As much as may be provided for you secretly without cost I shall arrange for you to have, if necessary, before your arrival, trusting for the best; nevertheless, if you are agreeable, you need to send a man before in all haste, that nothing is left to be sought for ...

R. Virgoe, *The Illustrated Letters of the Paston Family*

Despite the honour being offered to him, John Paston refused it and had to pay a fine.

12th – Magdalen College, Oxford

Magdalen College, Oxford was founded on 12 June 1458 by William Waynflete, the Bishop of Winchester. His statutes included provision for a choral foundation of men and boys (a tradition that still continues today) and made reference to how the name of the college should be pronounced in English – 'Maudlin'. The college received another substantial endowment from the estate of Sir John Falstolf of Caister Castle in Norfolk (1380–1459), a friend of the Paston family.

13th – Treaty of London

A treaty of alliance was signed in London on 1373 by King Edward III and the Portuguese ambassadors on behalf of King Ferdinand of Portugal. This Treaty of London is the oldest treaty in the world that still remains in force today.

14th – The Revolt of the Commons

14 June 1381 saw the climax of what is known today as the Peasants' Revolt, but at the time it was referred to as the Revolt of the Commons, i.e. the common people. Technically, in England there was no such thing as a peasant. The term comes from the French *paysans,* meaning those who live in the countryside, and was used as an insult by English soldiers in France to describe the locals.

The commoners of England had had enough – their wages were being kept low by law and now a new poll tax had been levied on them, a flat rate to be paid by everyone over the age of fourteen, whether they were a labourer or a lord. It wasn't fair and the ordinary folk of Essex and Kent marched on London in protest. King Richard II was just a teenager but, while his counsellors hid in fear of their lives, he rode out to Smithfield, just to the north-west of the city walls, accompanied by the Lord Mayor and aldermen, to confront the rebels. The lords had been astounded at how well organised the commons were, coordinating precisely their two-pronged attack on the capital, sending letters and information across the River Thames.

Having crossed London Bridge with the connivance of the Londoners, the rebels went on the rampage. At first, their intension was to destroy all the legal paperwork used by the tax gatherers but soon they were releasing prisoners from gaols and attacking lawyers. Their actions became ever more drastic as they stormed the Tower of London and executed the Chancellor and the Treasurer of England who had both taken refuge there – those whom they saw as the instigators of the poll tax. They burned the luxurious palace of the Savoy in the Strand, the home of the king's unpopular uncle, John of Gaunt. Fortunately, he wasn't at home, or they would probably have killed him too.

When the king and the rebels met at Smithfield, the king listened to their grievances, as stated by their leader, Wat Tyler, and promised redress of their complaints, if they went home peaceably. The *Anonimalle Chronicle* provides a detailed account of what happened – historians believe the author was an eyewitness:

Wat Tyler of Maidstone approached the king mounted on a small horse … He dismounted, holding in his hand a dagger … he half bent his knee and took the king by the hand, shaking his arm forcefully and roughly, saying to him. 'Brother, be joyful, for you shall have in a fortnight, 40,000 more [men] than you have at present'.

The king said to Tyler, 'Why will you not go back home?' He replied that neither he nor his fellows would leave until they had got their charter as they wished to have it. The king asked him what were these points which he wished considered.

Wat Tyler asked that no lord shall have lordship in future, but that land should be divided among all men. He also asked that the goods of the Holy Church should not remain in the hands of the parsons and vicars and other churchmen ... that their goods should be divided among the people of the parish. And he demanded that there should be only one bishop in England and that all the lands and possessions should be taken from the Church and divided among the commons. And he demanded that there should be no more serfs in England and that all men should be free.

At this point, there was an altercation – the details are unclear in the sources – but the result was that the Lord Mayor, William Walworth, ran Tyler through with his sword. Tyler was taken into the hospital of St Bartholomew nearby but he died the next day. The rebels saw their leader fall, which could have been the start of further mayhem, but the young king held his nerve and told the mob that *he* would be their leader. The rebels dispersed and went home. The king knighted and rewarded the mayor with £100 and a grant of land. He had no intention of honouring any of his promises to the commons, but the crisis had passed.

15th – The *Magna Carta*

King John had a talent for upsetting people, especially his long-suffering barons whom he had taxed without mercy to pay for his disastrous wars in France. He had ignored all their rights as his vassals, treated them viciously whenever he felt like it and done nothing to compensate them for their huge losses when his mercenaries had been allowed to go on the rampage. From the barons' point of view, the king could do exactly as he pleased and their only option was to take up arms against him – this was civil war, bloody and messy. In an attempt to restore order, a charter was drawn up by Archbishop Langton and the rebelling barons. At the time it was just a list of demands which the barons wanted John to abide by, restoring their privileges as his vassals and limiting his freedom to ignore them – it was a peace treaty, nothing more. Though the king, famously, set his seal to the document – he never signed it – at Runnymede, not far from Windsor Castle on 15 June 1215 in the presence of Langton, the barons with their contingents of well-armed knights and representatives of the London citizens, he had no intention of keeping it.

Almost before the seal was fixed on the parchment, John was appealing to the Pope, asking him to annul the charter. By early September, the papal letters arrived, excommunicating the rebels, including the Londoners and nine barons, and declaring the charter illegal; John argued he should not be bound by the agreement because he had sealed it under duress – note all the armed knights who had attended at Runnymede. The Pope agreed: the *Magna Carta* was repudiated, the barons and citizens excommunicated. Everything was just the same as before and this was the signal for the resumption of civil war. Stephen Langton, far from being given any credit for his efforts to make peace, was suspended from his Church duties for refusing to excommunicate King John's enemies. Bitter, he contemplated resigning his archbishopric and becoming a hermit.

16th – The Battle of Stoke Field

The last major engagement of the Wars of the Roses took place at the Battle of Stoke Field on 16 June 1487, near the town of Newark in Nottinghamshire, beside the River Trent. Although the last Yorkist king, Richard III, had been killed at the Battle of Bosworth (see 22 August) two years earlier, the victorious Lancastrian king Henry VII's grip on the crown remained shaky.

Hoping to reverse the outcome of Bosworth was King Richard's nephew, John de la Pole, the Earl of Lincoln, who had arrived in England at the head of a mainly mercenary army recruited from Germany, Switzerland and Ireland. At Lincoln's side was Francis, Viscount Lovell,

King Richard's Lord Chamberlain, and a young lad who had been crowned King Edward of England in Dublin just a few weeks earlier. The identity of this lad has always been a mystery. King Henry gave out the story that he was Lambert Simnel, the son of an Oxford baker, and that the Yorkists were trying to pass him off as Edward, Earl of Warwick, another of King Richard's nephews. Henry proved the lad couldn't be young Warwick since he was Henry's prisoner in the Tower of London, but then Henry was alone in claiming that this was what the Yorkists were saying. The boy's coronation in Christchurch Cathedral, Dublin, had been organised by Lincoln and Lovell and was well attended by the Irish lords who consistently supported the Yorkist cause. It was never explained why Lincoln, himself designated Richard III's heir, and so many nobles besides would have had a baker's boy anointed King of England – an appalling insult to both God and the English people. Also, it was again only King Henry who said the lad had been crowned 'Edward VI'. In fact, no regnal number was given out for this King Edward, but it may be significant that the official documents that he signed were sealed with the seal of Edward V – the elder of the little 'Princes in the Tower', supposedly disposed of by their uncle, King Richard.

Despite the misinformation given out by King Henry, he was as much mystified as to the true identity of Edward as we are today and he gave orders that, if it came to battle, Lincoln, Lovell and their 'king' were to be taken alive so he could interrogate them and unravel the intrigue.

On 16 June 1487 the 8,000 strong Yorkist force took up position on Rampire Hill, to the south-west of the village of East Stoke, and there awaited the far larger royal army of Henry VII. By 9 a.m., the vanguard of the royal force under the command of the Bosworth veteran, John de Vere, Earl of Oxford, encountered the rebel army and deployed for battle. The Yorkists advanced to the attack. Only the royal vanguard was engaged and at first they came under considerable pressure. Although probably outnumbered, these were the crack troops of the royalist army, better equipped and far more experienced than most of their opponents, many of whom were Irish peasants armed with clubs and farming implements. As at Bosworth, the Earl of Oxford's troops took the pressure and then counter-attacked, first breaking the Yorkist army and then destroying them in the rout, although the Swiss and German mercenaries under Martin Swartz, put up an incredible fight, the possibility of retreat barred by the River Trent. The battle raged for three hours, and when the Yorkist ranks finally did break, they were pursued down a ravine, known today as the Bloody Gutter, by the king's troops and put to the sword.

Despite King Henry's order to the contrary, Lincoln was slain in the fight and Lovell managed to escape by swimming his horse across the Trent – both man and beast in full armour. Unlikely as that feat seems, the viscount's name appears in Scottish documents a year later, so we know he survived. With most of the Yorkist commanders killed in the battle and only a lad called Lambert Simnel in custody, the mystery remained unsolved. Was Lambert the same lad as the one who had been crowned in Dublin? It seems unlikely because Henry let him go to work in the royal kitchens and later become a falconer, but the king crowned in Dublin vanished from history; perhaps he too had died in battle. Either way, the future of King Henry's rule and that of his Tudor dynasty was all but secured.

17th – Edward Longshanks

The future King Edward I was born at Westminster in 1239, the first son of Henry III and Eleanor of Provence. Being unusually tall, he was also known as Edward Longshanks and, in later years, as the Hammer of the Scots (Latin: *Malleus Scotorum*). He had a drooping eyelid, a trait he inherited from his father. Edward was King of England from 1272 to 1307. The Lord Edward, as the young man was known, had been named after his father's favourite saint, King Edward the Confessor, but must have been a disappointment to his parent when he became involved as a youth in the political intrigues of his father's reign. These included an outright rebellion by the English barons, led by Simon de Montfort, the young man's uncle by marriage.

In 1259, aged twenty, Edward briefly sided with the baronial reform movement, supporting the Provisions of Oxford, but after a reconciliation with his father, he remained loyal throughout the subsequent conflict, known as the Second Barons' War – in fact he proved to be his father's best military commander. After the Battle of Lewes in 1263, Edward was taken hostage by the barons, but managed to escape after a few months and rejoin the fight against Simon de Montfort. De Montfort was defeated at the battle of Evesham in 1265, mainly due to Edward having learned from earlier strategic mistakes he had made at Lewes, and the rebellion was over. With England at peace, Edward joined the Ninth Crusade to the Holy Land. The crusade achieved nothing, but Edward was wounded, stabbed with a poisoned dagger, so the story goes. Poisoned or not, his was a long, slow recovery, aided by his wife, Eleanor of Castile. They were on their way home in 1272 when they learned that his father had died and he was now King of England. He didn't hurry his return – perhaps he was still unwell – and finally reached England in 1274, being crowned at Westminster on 19 August.

18th – Explosions in the Sky

Five monks at Canterbury claimed to have seen an explosion on the moon in 1178. No other records corroborate this, so were the brothers incredibly observant in seeing a possible meteor strike on the lunar surface or had they been over generous with the communion wine?

19th – Churching

The following entry is recorded in the Suffolk coroner's rolls for 19 June 1378:

Alice, wife of Bartholomew Sley, was forty years old when her last child was born in June 1378. She underwent the process of purification [churching] soon after the birth of her child, however, on the tenth day after delivery, she was gripped by an infirmity and suddenly died.

S. M. Butler, *Forensic Medicine and Death Investigation in Medieval England*

The ceremony of 'churching' a woman who had given birth, allowing her to take part in religious and social events once more, didn't usually take place until her post-partum bleeding had ceased – any time from about four to six weeks after the birth. The office involved thanksgiving for her safe delivery, purification and blessing of the woman. Why Alice was churched so soon after the birth isn't stated and, if her sudden infirmity was caused by some obstetric complications, the thanksgiving was sadly premature in her case.

20th – The Seeds of the Terrible Pestilence

In this year, 1348, in Melcombe in the county of Dorset, a little before the feast of St John the Baptist [24 June], two ships, one of them from Bristol, came alongside. One of the sailors had brought with him from Gascony the seeds of the terrible pestilence and through him the men of that town of Melcombe were the first in England to be infected.

Grey Friars' Chronicle, Lynn

By the autumn, the plague had reached London; by the summer of 1349 it had covered the entire country. More recent research into the lives of lesser folk, rather than just the better-documented landowning minority, means that estimates of mortality have risen – it may be that almost half the population died. The following was written at the time by Henry Knighton, a canon at the abbey of St Mary of the Meadows, Leicester:

In this year there was a general mortality among men throughout the world ... The dreadful pestilence penetrated the sea coast by Southampton and came to Bristol, and there almost the whole population of the town perished, as if it had been seized by sudden death; for few kept their beds more than two or three days, or even half a day. Then this cruel death spread everywhere around ... And there died at Leicester in the small parish of St. Leonard more than 380 persons, in the parish of Holy Cross, 400; in the parish of St. Margaret's, Leicester, 700; and so in every parish, a great multitude. Then the Bishop of London sent word throughout his whole diocese giving general power to each and every priest, regular as well as secular, to hear confessions and to give absolution to all persons with full Episcopal authority ... Likewise the Pope granted full remission of all sins to anyone receiving absolution when in danger of death, and granted that this power should last until Easter next following, and that everyone might choose whatever confessor he pleased.

In the same year there was a great murrain of sheep everywhere in the kingdom, so that in one place in a single pasture more than 5,000 sheep died; and they putrefied so that neither bird nor beast would touch them. Everything was low in price because of the fear of death, for very few people took any care of riches or property of any kind. A man could have a horse that had been worth 40s for half a mark (6s 8d), a fat ox for 4s, a cow for 12d, a heifer for 6d, a fat wether [ram] for 4d, a sheep for 3d, a lamb for 2d, a large pig for 5d; a stone of wool [14 lbs] was worth 9d. Sheep and cattle ran at large through the fields and among the crops, and there was none to drive them off or herd them; for lack of care they perished in ditches and hedges in incalculable numbers ... and none knew what to do ... In the following autumn a reaper was not to be had for a lower wage than 8d, with his meals; a mower for not less than 10d, with meals. Wherefore many crops wasted in the fields for lack of harvesters. But in the year of the pestilence, there was so great an abundance of every type of grain that almost no one cared for it.

Master Thomas of Bradwardine was consecrated by the Pope [as] Archbishop of Canterbury, and when he returned to England he came to London, but within two days was dead ...

Meanwhile the King sent proclamations into all the counties that reapers and other labourers should not take [in wages] more than they had been accustomed to take, under the penalty appointed by statute. But the labourers were so obstinate ... if anyone wished to have them he had to give them what they wanted, and either lose his fruit and crops, or satisfy the covetous wishes of the workmen. And when it was known to the King that they had not observed his command and had given greater wages to the labourers, he levied heavy fines upon abbots, priors, knights, greater and lesser, and other great folk and small folk of the realm, of some 100s, of some 40s, of some 20s, from each according to what he could give. And afterwards the king had many labourers arrested, and sent them to prison ... And in like manner was done with the other craftsmen in the boroughs and villages ... After the aforesaid pestilence, many buildings, great and small, fell into ruins in every city, borough, and village for lack of inhabitants, likewise many villages and hamlets became desolate, not a house being left in them, all having died who dwelt there; and it was probable that many such villages would never be inhabited.

E. Rickert, C. C. Olson and M. M. Crow (eds),
Chaucer's World

21st – Rose-Honey

Here is a medicinal recipe for mel-roset or rose-honey; thought to be good for the throat:

Roses, before the leaves [petals] be fully sprung out, shall be gathered and of the red leaves, shredded small, and of honey is made mel-roset. To a pound [weight] of roses thou shall take eight pounds of honey; the roses shall be shredded small and seethed with the honey gently on an easy fire of charcoal, till the honey have both the savour and colour of roses.

W. R. Dawson, *A Leechbook of the Fifteenth Century*

22nd – Richard of Bordeaux

On this day in 1377, Richard of Bordeaux, ten-year-old son of the late Black Prince (see 8 June), succeeded his grandfather, Edward III, as King of England. As Richard II, he would not have an easy reign. Had this been foretold when he lost a shoe and his spur as he left Westminster Abbey after his coronation on 16 July 1377? Those who believed in ill omens thought it had.

*

Also, on this day in 1485, two women were in trouble with the authorities in Chester:

Memorandum that [on] 22 day of June the second year of the reign of king Richard the third since the conquest of England, Marion, wife of Richard Hoghton, servant to Richard Oldone [Oldham], Abbot of the monastery of St Werburg of Chester and Bishop of Sodor, at Chester and in Northgate Street, beside the convent of St Werburg and within the liberty of the said city, made an assault on Elizabeth Tame, servant to Cecily, the late wife [widow] of Henry Wermyncham, goldsmith, and then and there struck the said Elizabeth on the head with [her] right fist, and dragged [her] by her hair, and scratched [her] in the face, making it bleed profusely, and with force and arms, and against the peace of our present lord the king. And concerning this John Savage senior, knight of the body of the Lord King, mayor of the city aforesaid, by virtue of his office, ordered John Norres and Hugh Hulton sheriffs of the said city, and each of them, that they attach [arrest] the said Elizabeth and Marion, and deliver them to the custody of Oliver Hepay, keeper of Northgate gaol … handing over and keeping them there until they sufficiently secure the peace of the lord king between each other and all the subjects of the lord King. And the said sheriffs, as each was ordered by the said mayor, did and fulfilled [everything], and the said Elizabeth and Marion, namely on 22 day of June in the year above said, namely on the Thursday before the vigil of the nativity of St John, having been taken, were delivered to Oliver Hepay at 'le Northegate' aforesaid, etc.

By kind permission of Randolph Jones and
Dr Heather Falvey (translator)

Dr Falvey also noted the following:

The medieval bishopric of Sodor [yes, the same place as Thomas the Tank Engine!] on the Isle of Man was not originally part of a province of the Church in England. By act of Parliament in 1542 (33 Henr. VIII, c. 31) it was included in the province of York.

E. B. Fryde, et al. (eds), *Handbook of British Chronology*

23rd – Prisoner of War

A letter was sent on 23 June 1487 from Henry Percy, Earl of Northumberland, to Sir Robert Plumpton as bailiff of Knaresborough and custodian of the castle there, under the earl's authority, concerning some prisoners, taken at the Battle of Stoke Field (see 16 June) in rebellion against King Henry VII:

To my right trusty and wellbeloved cousin Sir Robart Plompton, kt.

Cousin Sir Robart, I commend me unto you; and wher it is so that diverse gentlemen and other commoners, being within your office [custody] at this tyme, hath rebelled against the king, as well in ther being at this last felde [battle], as in releving [supporting] of them that were against the Kings highness, I therefore on the kings behalfe strictly charg you ... that ye ... take all such persones as be within your office, which this tyme hath offended agaynst the king, and in especiall John Pullen and Richard Knaresborough, and that ye keepe them in the castell of Knaresborough in suer [sure] keepeing, to the tyme be ye know the kings pleasure in that behalfe ... Se that ye faile not, as ye love me, within the time, and as ever ye thinke to have me your good lord, and as ever I may trust you. Your Cousin, Hen. Northumberland.

Written at Richmound [Yorks], the xxiii Juyn.

T. Stapleton (ed.), *The Plumpton Correspondence*

24th – Midsummer Solstice

On this day in 1314, Edward II's English army was routed and humiliated by the Scots at the Battle of Bannockburn.

*

On a more cheerful note, the midsummer solstice was one of the pagan festivals taken over by the early Christian Church and renamed as the feast of St John the Baptist on 24 June. In the medieval period, the celebrations had developed as a boisterous combination of both Christian and pagan ideas.

Fire was always a central element: people lit bonfires, feasted, drank and danced around them. In the countryside, fires were lit on the windward side of crops and animals so that the smoke would blow over them; in some places, it was traditional to drive the animals through the cooling embers. Various benefits, such as protection against disease or against witches, who were particularly active at the midsummer solstice, were believed to derive from this exposure to fire. The fear of witches was also evident in the ritual of decorating houses or wreathing livestock with garlands of particular plants and birch branches were hung on signposts.

St John's wort, with its dazzling golden flowers blooming in this season, was associated with the sun and, with its religious connotation, was thought that its red-flecked leaves represented the blood of the martyred saint. Trefoil was considered another protective plant because its three-part leaves suggested the Holy Trinity; White Madonna lilies were associated with the Virgin Mary, as their name implies.

Apart from the religious and magical aspects, the occasion also involved socialising and money matters. Wealthy folk might provide ale and flavoured breads for their poorer neighbours, occasionally bequeathing money in their wills for this end. But the midsummer highlight in medieval towns was the torchlit procession after dark: the Marching Watch. In London on one such occasion the spectacular parade included 4,000 people marching through the streets, with Morris dancers, giants and elaborate pageants. Although a little out of our time frame, Katharine Edgar gives us this description of the continuing processions in the sixteenth century:

In 1521, the Lord Mayor's Guild in London put on five pageants: The Castle of War, The Story of Jesse, St John the Evangelist, St George and Pluto. They were all carried on platforms and the Pluto pageant included a serpent that spat fireballs. There was also a model giant called Lord Marlinspikes, not to mention Morris dancers and naked boys dyed black to represent devils. Giants were popular, as were dragons and pyrotechnics. In 1541 the Drapers' Guild procession including a dragon that burned aqua vitae in its mouth and in Chester there were unicorns, camels (model ones, we assume), hobbyhorses and sixteen naked boys.

1. January – Drinking, Calendar Page. (Courtesy British Library, Add 21114 f. 1)

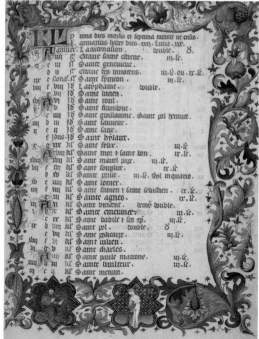

2. January – Calendar Page, *The Hours of René d'Anjou*; *c.* 1420. (Courtesy British Library, Egerton 1070 f. 6)

3. 6 January – Adoration of the Magi, *The Hours of René d'Anjou*; *c.* 1420. (Courtesy British Library, Egerton 1070 f. 34v)

4. 14 January – Marriage of Henry III and Eleanor of Provence. (Courtesy British Library, 14 Royal 14 C VII f. 124v)

Right: 5. 19 January – Two men talking, Sumptuary Laws; *c.* 1475, Bruges. (Courtesy of British Library, Royal 15 E IV f. 14)

Below: 6. 25 January – Edward II deposed, Queen Isabella and her army. (Courtesy of British Library, Royal 15 E IV f. 316v)

Above: 7. March – Calendar Page (*the Golf Book) Book of Hours, Use of Rome*; workshop of Simon Bening, *c.* 1540, Bruges. (Courtesy of British Library, Add 24098, f. 20v)

Below: 8. February – Men burning firewood, Calendar Page. (Courtesy of British Library, Yates Thompson 3 f. 2)

9. 18 March – Court Rolls. (Courtesy of Essex Record Office)

10. 24 March – Men working in a vineyard. (Courtesy of British Library, Yates Thompson 3 f. 3)

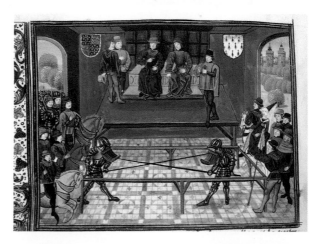

11. 20 April – Tournament before the Earl of Buckingham and the Duke of Brittany. (Courtesy of British Library, Royal 18 E I f. 139)

12. 23 April – John of Lancaster, Duke of Bedford, before St George, *Bedford Book of Hours*; *c.* 1410–30, Paris. (Courtesy of British Library, Add MS 18850, f. 256v)

13. May – Henry II and Eleanor of Aquitaine holding court, *Aliénor et Henri II écoutent, l'histoire de Lancelot du Lac*; *c.* 1100s. (Courtesy of Bib Paris, ms. fr. 123 fol. 229)

14. 23 May – Manorial Records. (Courtesy Warks County Records Office)

Above: 15. 14 June – Peasants' revolt, Blackheath. (Courtesy of British Library, Royal 18 E I f. 165v)

Right: 16. 1 June – 'Sumer is icumen in'; *c.* 1275–1300, England. (Courtesy of British Library, Harley 978 f. 11v)

Left: 17. 29 June – Edward IV coronation roll. (Courtesy of Philadelphia Free Library)

Below: 18. 15 June – Death of Wat Tyler. (Courtesy of British Library, Royal 18 E I f. 175)

Right: 19. 8 July – License to Export to Calais, Master of the London Wavrin; England. (Courtesy of British Library Royal 15 E IV f. 24v)

Below: 20. 16 July – Coronation of Richard II. (Courtesy of British Library, Royal 20 C VII f. 192v)

teur ſes ondes viuans.

Above and below: 21. 16 July – Fourteenth-century sugar cane factory; Cyprus (© G. Horne)

22. 25 July – St Christopher, Westminster psalter. (Courtesy of British Library, Royal 2 A XXII)

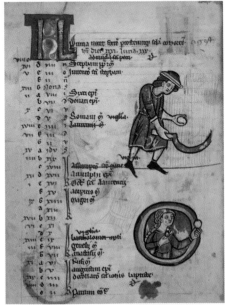

23. August – Harvesting, Calendar Page. (Courtesy of British Library, Add 21114 f. 4v)

Above: 24. August – Threshing, Calendar Page; *c.* 1500, Bruges. (Courtesy of British Library, King's 9 ff. 9 v–10)

Below: 25. September – Calendar Page *(the Golf Book) Book of Hours, Use of Rome*; workshop of Simon Bening, *c.* 1540, Bruges. (Courtesy of British Library, Add 24098, f 20v)

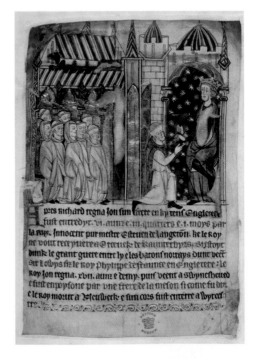

26. 4 September – Fifteenth-century will from prerogative court, Canterbury.

27. 19 October – King John poisoned. (Courtesy of British Library, Cotton Vitellius A XIII, f. 5v)

28. 11 November – Martinmas. (Courtesy of British Library, Add 21114 f. 6)

29. 28 October – Coronation of Kings Henry II, Richard I, John and Henry II, inset centre shows Henry the Young King; Matthew Paris, *Chronica Majora*. (Courtesy of British Library, Royal C vii f. 9r)

Right: 30. December – Slaughtering a pig, Calendar Page *(the Golf Book) Book of Hours, Use of Rome*; workshop of Simon Bening, *c.* 1540, Bruges. (Courtesy of British Library, Add 24098, f 29v.)

Below: 31. 18 November – A taverner greeting a guest; William Caxton, *The Game and Playe of the Chesse*; *c.* 1474. (Courtesy of Stephen Porter)

Above: 32. 20 December – Comet arrives, Astronomy and geometry. (Courtesy of British Library, Royal 20 B XX f. 3)

Below: 33. 29 December – Murder of the archbishop of Canterbury. (Courtesy of British Library, Royal 18 E f. 172)

It was, of course, expensive. But at times of political tension, gathering so many people together (some of them presumably drunk) could also lead authorities to fear civil unrest. In 1539 Henry VIII banned the London Midsummer Watch on the pretext of saving money, and it did not return until 1548. We can only imagine how people felt about that ...

http://katharineedgar.com/2014/06/21/its-all-about-st-john-the-baptist-or-how-the-tudors-celebrated-the-midsummer-solstice/

On a more mundane note, 24 June was one of the financial quarter days, along with Christmas, Lady Day (25 March) and Michaelmas (29 September), when quarterly rents were due, debts, tithes and taxes collected.

25th – Midday Eclipse

A midday eclipse was recorded on 25 June 1191.

26th – King Richard III

On this day in 1483, Richard, Duke of Gloucester, Lord Protector of England and sole surviving brother of the late King Edward IV, was presented with a petition by the lords and commons at Baynard's Castle in the city of London. The petition set out his precise entitlement to the throne which they humbly requested he should accept. He gave his formal acceptance and was escorted to Westminster Hall where, in the time-honoured tradition, he sat in the marble chair of King's Bench and addressed the assembly. The reign of King Richard III had begun:

The lord protectour took possescyon at wetsmynstyr in the grete halle, where he beyng sett in the kyngys cheyer or place where alle kyngys take ffyrst possescion. The duke of Norffolk syttyng upon his rigth hand that beffore dayes [previously] was callid lord

Howard, and upon his lyffth hand the duke of Suffolk, he [Richard] callid beffore hym the Jugys, commaundyng theym in rigth streygth [straight] maner that they justly and duly shuld mynystir his lawe withowth delay or ffavour. Afftyr which commandement soo to theym govyn and othyr ceremonyes there ffynysshide, he than good [go-ed, i.e. went] in to the abbay [Westminster], where at the chirch dore he was mett wyth procescion, and by the abbot or his depute there delyverd to hym the Ceptre of Seynt Edward, he then yood [yo-ed, i.e. went] unto the shrine [of St Edward the Confessor] and there offyrd ...

Great Chronicle of London

27th – A 'Female Liar'

On 27 June 1378, a case was brought to the Borough Court of London. It was claimed that on this date Alice Godrich, wife of Robert Godrich, maliciously aggrieved and scandalised Alderman William Walworth (he who would be mayor at the time of the Peasants' Revolt in 1381; see 14 June). Alice had come to William's house in Crooked Lane in St Michael's parish in the city and raised a hue and cry against him alleging he was a thief. She called him a false man and further claimed that he had disinherited her of land worth £20 a year. He had also falsely imprisoned her husband, Robert, simply because he had the power to do so and to prevent Robert from fighting Alice's case.

William demanded that Alice should be chastised as a scold and a 'female liar' for having slandered his reputation. Alice was summoned to court in July 1379 and asked if she wanted a lawyer to speak for her. She refused counsel, saying she was in no way guilty of slander; all that she had said of William Walworth was true, she averred. Not surprisingly, the jurors – all men of standing like William – found Alice guilty. She and her husband were ordered to pay William damages of £40 and Alice was to stand in the pillory – 'called the thewe, provided for such women' – for an hour a day with a whetstone hung around her neck. William, perhaps suffering a pang of conscience, asked that the punishment be remitted, that the £40 be 'put in respite' so long as Alice behaved herself in future, and that she should be released from prison. Since William was an alderman, his wishes carried weight and Alice Godrich was released at his request.

P. J. P Goldberg, *Women in England, c. 1275–1525*

28th – Edward IV's Coronation

Edward Plantagenet, 4th Duke of York and 7th Earl of March, was born on 28 April 1442 at Rouen in Normandy, the son of Richard, 3rd Duke of York, and Cecily Neville. Edward had been declared King of England after defeating the Lancastrian forces at the Battle of Towton on 29 March 1461 and deposing the incapable Lancastrian king, Henry VI. After putting down further risings in the north, Edward had made his triumphal state entry into London on Friday 26 June, riding from Lambeth to the Tower of London. He was formally received at the city gate by the Lord Mayor, Richard Lee, with the aldermen in their scarlet robes and 400 of the most worthy and prominent citizens of London.

The sumptuous procession made its way through the streets, giving people the chance to cheer and get a good look at their new monarch. Edward was perfect for the part: just nineteen years old, well over six feet tall, victorious in battle and described as 'the handsomest prince in Christendom'. He was a huge hit with the ladies, too – such a contrast to the middle-aged, shabby-looking, dull-witted king that he had displaced. Here was a man capable of putting an end to the strife of the previous decade. On the next day, Saturday, at the Tower of London, Edward created thirty-two new Knights of the Bath, as was the custom on the eve of a coronation.

On Sunday 28 June 1461, he was crowned King Edward IV in Westminster Abbey. This was noted in the contemporary *Croyland Chronicle*:

King Edward, after the festivities of Easter, which he celebrated with great splendour at York, having placed garrisons throughout the whole country in whom he could fully rely, returned, as conqueror, to London. Here he immediately assembled the Parliament, and was crowned at Westminster by the venerable father Thomas, archbishop of Canterbury, and solemnly graced with the diadem of sovereignty.

As the Chronicle records, Edward was crowned by Thomas Bourchier, the Archbishop of Canterbury, assisted by William Booth, Archbishop of York. After the ceremony, during the traditional banquet, Sir Thomas Dymoke, the hereditary King's Champion, rode into the hall in full armour, flung down his gauntlet, and challenged anyone who disputed Edward's right to do battle with him. No one accepted the challenge.

A gorgeous manuscript, a vellum roll almost twenty feet long, was commissioned to celebrate Edward IV's coronation. Images of the roll and more information can be viewed at: http://libwww.library.phila.gov/medievalman/Detail.cfm?imagetoZoom=mca2010001

29th – A Child on St Peter's Day

In a letter to her husband, John, written in early July 1444, Margaret Paston tells him of some of the local gossip around Norwich:

Heydon's wife had a child on St Peter's Day. I heard say that her husband will have nothing to do with her nor with her child that she had last neither. I heard say that he said that if she came in his presence to make her excuse, he would cut off her nose to make her be known for what she is; and if her child come in his presence he said he would kill it. He will not be entreated to have her again in no wise, as I heard say.

R. Virgoe (ed.), *The Illustrated Letters of the Paston Family*

Having your nose cut off was the traditional – but, fortunately, very rarely enacted – punishment for prostitution, so you can guess what Heydon thought his wife had been getting up to.

30th – A Weaver's Will

John Kendale, a weaver in York, compiled his will on 30 June 1492, making provision for his nephew to continue weaving wool on the loom and for his apprentice to complete the terms of his indenture, learning the craft of linen weaving from John's widow, Agnes:

I wit [will] to Petir Bolton, my suster['s] son a wollen lome. Also I wit to Roger myn apprentice and servant a lynnen [linen] lome uppon this condicion soe that he be lawly [humble] and gentill to my wife and for to abide with hir his terme as it specifys in his indentour and serve hir. And she for to content hym al maner of duetes [responsibilities] according to his indentours with the letter.

H. Falvey, et al. (eds), *English Wills proved in the Prerogative Court of York, 1477–99*

JULY

1st – A Shameful Marriage

In July of 1469, the Paston family were still trying to thwart the marriage between daughter Margery and Richard Calle, their steward, their union having been made without her mother's and brothers' approval (her father was deceased) (see 3 May and 3 October). Margaret Paston, as matriarch of the family, had the couple summoned to appear before the Bishop of Norwich to explain themselves. They were examined separately and the bishop seemed to believe that Margery might be the easier to persuade that her marriage was invalid. He reminded her of the shame her marriage to a man of lesser standing brought upon her family, the disapproval of her friends and relatives: was she certain that the words she had spoken in her private pledge to Richard were sufficiently binding that their union could not be in doubt?

Margery replied that 'if those words made it not sure, she would make it sure ere she went from thence, for she thought in her conscience she was bound [to Richard] whatsoever the words were'. When questioned, Richard's story confirmed Margery's. The bishop didn't want to upset the influential Paston family but could see no way to escape the issue, so he said he would make his decision and let them know the week after Michaelmas (29 September). In the meantime, he sent Margery home.

However, her mother, worrying over the outcome of the couple's interviews with the bishop, had already made her decision. She sent a messenger to intercept Margery, telling her that her mother would never again have her under her roof, nor would her mother's friends have anything to do with her. Margery returned to Norwich and begged the bishop's aid. He found safe lodgings for her.

H. S. Bennett, *The Pastons and their England*

2nd – John's French Campaign

In 1214 King John began his final campaign to reclaim Normandy from King Philip of France. John was optimistic, having built up alliances with the Emperor Otto, Renaud of Boulogne and Count Ferdinand of Flanders; he was also in the Pope's good books and, for once, had substantial funds to pay for his mercenary army. When John left England for Poitou in February 1214, many of his barons had refused to do their duty and provide military service; hence the mercenary knights to fill the gaps, but their experience should have proved an advantage. John planned to split Philip's French forces by pushing north-east from Poitou towards Paris, whilst Otto, Renaud and Ferdinand, supported by John's illegitimate half-brother, William Longespée, marched south-west from Flanders. The first part of the campaign went well, with John outmanoeuvring the forces under the command of the French Dauphin, Prince Louis, and retaking the county of Anjou by the end of June. John then besieged the castle of Roche-au-Moine, a key stronghold, hoping to force Prince Louis to engage John's larger army. Having waited at Chinon for a fortnight for instructions from his father, King Philip, Louis moved south to La Roche, sending a herald to King John with a very public message of defiance. Following such an insult, John was eager to do battle against what he believed was a much smaller force. However, at this point the local Angevin nobles refused to advance with the king. Finding his army now depleted and at a disadvantage, John attempted to retreat back to La Rochelle.

The *Histoire des ducs de Normandie* reports that on this day a major battle was fought at La Roche-aux-Moins between King John's army and the forces of Prince Louis. So great was the panic in the English king's camp, so the French chroniclers recount, that not only was John forced to abandon his own tents and supplies but a large number of his troops perished in crossing the River Loire on 2 July.

3rd – Strawberry Season

This is the season for strawberries. In medieval times, strawberries were planted in garden plots but produced fruits just the size of a fingernail, like wild strawberries but very sweet. They were often eaten fresh from the plant because they didn't keep for long. Medieval doctors seemed to think strawberries were very bad for you, perhaps because the brief glut of fruit meant folk ate far too many in such a short time, leading to stomach upsets. The fruit was blamed for this ill, rather than human greed. Here is a fifteenth-century recipe using strawberries:

Take strawberries and wash them at this time of year in good red wine, then strain them through a cloth and put them in a pot with good almond milk. A-lay it with amyndoun [wheat flour] or rice flour and boil until it thickens. Add raisins of coraunce [currants], saffron, pepper, plenty of sugar, powdered ginger, canel [cinnamon], galingale, point it with [a dash of] vinegar and a little white grease, colour it with alkanet and drop it about, plant it with grains of pomegranate and then serve it forth.

T. Austin, *Two Fifteenth-Century
Cookery-Books c. 1430–1450*

I am slightly mystified by the instructions concerning saffron and 'point it with … a little white grease, colour it with alkanet …' Medieval diners loved brightly coloured food, and this dish should have been a bold red but saffron would have turned it more orange (or 'tawny' as they would have said). Alkanet was a herb used for blue colouring, so you can imagine its addition would produce a muddy colour instead – not very attractive at all. The instructions are none too clear, so I wonder if it was the 'white grease' only that was meant to be dyed blue and used as little cubes to dot about the dish. Personally, I would leave out the grease altogether and use the bright blue alkanet flowers – also in season at this time – along with the jewel-like pomegranate seeds to decorate this summertime dish.

4th – The Third Crusade

On this day in 1190, Richard I of England and Philip II of France set out together from Vézelay in France on the Third Crusade to the Holy Land. To ensure none of the men should sully the event with any kind of sexual adventure, the crusade would be for males only – no women allowed. But then some practical fellow realised this would mean the men would have to do their own laundry! So the kings and their religious advisors made an exception 'for washerwomen who will not be a burden nor an occasion for sin'.

5th – Murdered by a Mare

The Sussex coroner recorded on 5 July 1490 that:

When a cart belonging to John Brownyng, yeoman ... stood in Shopton Lane in the king's highway in Sutton, Margaret, wife of Ralph Derbye, labourer, came on a grey mare belonging to her husband. Wishing to hurry on her business to Petworth market, she put caution to one side and forced the mare to pass by the near wheel of the cart where an embankment about four feet high had been erected, upon which the mare raised its front hoofs so that ... Margaret was thrown from its back and fell to the ground on her neck, receiving a large wound on the neck of which she immediately died; and so the mare murdered her. It is deodand [forfeit] and worth no more than 5s. It remains with Ralph for the king's use.

P. J. P. Goldberg, *Women in England, c. 1275–1525*

6th – Richard III's Coronation

William Trumpour fornicated with Joan de Gyldsum: both appear on this date [before the Dean and Chapter of York Minster in 1363]. She confessed the article [charge] and abjured the sin on penalty of six whippings. She has three whippings for her confession. The woman said that the man [Trumpour] betrothed her and promised to marry her as his wife. The man denied this on oath and immediately after promised on oath that if he should henceforth know her carnally, he would thereafter have her and hold her as his wife. The woman likewise promised that if hereafter she should allow him to know her carnally, she would have him as her husband.

P. J. P. Goldberg, *Women in England c. 1275–1525*

*

In 1483, on the same date and on a more illustrious note, Richard III was crowned king at Westminster Abbey in the most well attended coronation up to that time. Alice Claver, a London silkwoman, supplied the great lace mantle and silk tassels for the king's gloves for the occasion.

7th – Longshanks' Death

On this date, 7 July 1307, King Edward I of England was on his way north to fight the Scots, yet again. He was ill with dysentery and could ride no further. He died at Burgh-by-Sands, near Carlisle. Also known as 'Longshanks' because he was so tall, as well as being nicknamed the 'Hammer of the Scots', Edward had been born on 17 June 1239 at Westminster, the eldest son of Henry III and Eleanor of Provence. He ascended to the throne on 20 November 1272, aged thirty-three, but was actually away from England on Crusade at the time; he was recovering from a knife wound, inflicted by a would-be assassin, so was unable to hurry home. Therefore, the coronation was delayed until 19 August 1274, when it was conducted in Westminster Abbey.

In 1254, Edward had married his beloved wife, Eleanor of Castile, but she died in 1290. He took Margaret, daughter of Philip III of France, as his second wife in 1299. By his two wives, he fathered seventeen children, although many of them died in infancy. When Edward died he was sixty-eight years old and had ruled for well over thirty-four years – a reign that was dominated by warfare. It was said that as he lay dying he asked for his heart to be taken to the Holy Land and for the flesh to be boiled from his body so that his bones could lead the English army in battle against the Scots. Neither request was carried out by his son and successor, Edward II, but he was given a fine burial. His body was buried in royal purple robes in Westminster Abbey. The Latin inscription on his tomb, reads *Edwardus Primus Scottorum Malleus hic est, 1308. Pactum Serva* – 'Here is Edward I, Hammer of the Scots, 1308. Keep Faith.'

In his youth, Edward had led the royal forces against Simon de Montfort, Earl of Leicester, in the Barons' War of 1264–67, long before he became king. His father wasn't much of a warrior so the Lord Edward, to give him his proper title at the time, filled the king's place and learned the warrior's art so well. As king, he established English rule over all of Wales in 1282–84, and secured recognition of his overlordship from the Scottish king, although the Scots under Sir William Wallace and Robert the Bruce (later Robert I) fiercely resisted. His reign saw Parliament move towards its modern form with the Model Parliament of 1295. Edward kept Wales under control by building a system of castles, including Conway, Caernarfon, Beaumaris and Harlech castles.

http://www.educationscotland.gov.uk/scotlandshistory/
warsofindependence/deathofedwardi/index.asp

8th – The Calais Garrison

Richard III wrote this letter dated 8 July 1484 from Scarborough Castle. There was ongoing trouble with the French and he was provisioning the Calais garrison, in readiness, should the French besiege this outpost of England:

To all mayors, sheriffs, bailiffs, customs controllers, searchers, keepers of our ports and passages and all our other officers, true liegemen and subjects, on this side [of] the sea as at our town of Calais ... These our letters let you know that we ... have licensed ... our trusty and well beloved squire Richard Forthey, one of the marshals of our hall, that he, by himself, his factors or attorneys, shall move, purvey and buy in this our realm, two hundred beefs, two hundred muttons and two hundred hogs, and ship and convey the same, at one time or at diverse times to our said town and marches [surrounding area] of Calais and to the parties of Picardy or Flanders. Any act, ordinance, statute, proclamation or restraint made to the contrary thereof notwithstanding, wherefore we will and charge you all and every [one] of you to permit and suffer [allow] the said Richard, his factors or attorneys to use and enjoy the effect of our licence without any molestation, perturbance or impediment as you will eschew our grievous indignation at your peril, provided always that the customs and subsidies which shall grow [become] due unto us in this behalve, we be truly answered [paid] as right requireth.

R. Horrox and P. W. Hammon (eds), *British Library, Harleian Manuscript 433*, vol. 2

As with all official royal letters and legal documents, it was a case of never use just one word if half a dozen could be used as well. It would be interesting to know how long the meat supplies were supposed to last the garrison. Keeping the meat fresh wouldn't be an issue: the animals would be shipped live, put out to pasture for as long as possible and slaughtered as needed.

9th – The Sin of Adultery

The Archdeacon's Court at Hartwell, Buckinghamshire heard this case in 1485:

Agnes Chardesley is accused with Edmund Bampton of the sin of adultery. She appeared and denies the article [charge]. She appeared with Marion Hikkes, Christine Hare, Alice Smewyn and Alice Cowper and lawfully purged herself and is dismissed.

P. J. P. Goldberg, *Women in England, c. 1275–1525*

The other women may have been character witnesses to swear to Agnes' otherwise good reputation, or more likely they were similarly accused. This isn't clear from the wording.

10th – The Great Fire of Southwark

On this day in 1212, a Sunday, the Great Fire of Southwark began, which destroyed the area to the south of London Bridge. St Mary Overy (now Southwark Cathedral) was gutted, along with much of Borough High Street and the houses on London Bridge. The cause of the fire was not recorded, but its devastating effects were noted. The following entries come from the *Liber de Antiquis Legibus (Book on Ancient Laws)*, composed in 1274 and now the oldest book preserved among the records of the City of London. On its third page, this document tells us:

In this year [1212] was the terrible fire of Southwark and it burned the church of St Mary and the Bridge with the chapel and the great part of the city.

According to a later edition, numerous casualties resulted when a crowd of Londoners rushed onto the bridge:

An exceeding great multitude of people passing the Bridge, either to extinguish or quench it, or else to gaze at and behold it, suddenly the north part, by blowing of the south wind, was also set on fire, and the people which were even now passing the Bridge, perceiving the same, would have returned, but were stopped by the fire.

Some estimates state that 3,000 people were killed by the fire but no reliable evidence survives to allow an accurate estimate of casualties in the city out of a population of 40,000 to 50,000. However, it is certain that the damage done to London Bridge was such that it remained in ruins and only partially usable for years afterwards.

*

Also on this day in 1460, the Battle of Northampton took place as yet another in the series of confrontations that we call the Wars of the Roses, fought between the houses of York and Lancaster. It took place in the grounds of Delapre Abbey, close to where the Lancastrian army of King Henry VI had set up camp in a meadow, between Hardingstone village and the abbey. They dug deep ditches and built a palisade of sharp stakes around their camp and blocked the London Road with cannon. Despite this, they weren't in a good defensive position: the River Nene had flooded after heavy rain and was difficult to cross, should they need to escape. It didn't matter: the Lancastrians were confident of victory.

The Earl of Warwick was in charge of the Yorkist army that arrived on the morning of 10 July. After the attempts at negotiation, led by the Archbishop of Canterbury, had failed, battle began. Warwick gave orders to kill Lancastrian nobles but not to kill the king or 'ordinary men', especially the men of Lord Grey of Ruthin – a Lancastrian who switched to the Yorkist side. The battle was short – over in half an hour – and a resounding victory for Warwick. The marshy conditions of the Nene meant that many Lancastrians died trying to escape across the river after the battle. In all, 300 Lancastrians died, including many lords who were killed trying to protect the king, the Duke of Buckingham among them. King Henry was captured by Henry Mountfort, a Yorkist archer. Directly after the battle, Edward, Earl of March (the future King Edward IV) knelt and paid homage to Henry VI. The Yorkist nobles told Henry they only wanted a 'stable and just government'. However, a few months later, Edward's father, Richard, Duke of York – who had been in Ireland when the battle of Northampton was fought – made a formal claim to the throne. York was persuaded to wait until after Henry died, according to an Act of Settlement (see 31 October) but was killed at the Battle of Wakefield a few months later (see 30 December), leaving Edward, Earl of March as the Yorkist claimant. Henry's wife, Queen Margaret, refused to accept an agreement that disinherited her son and the civil war inevitably rumbled on.

http://www.northamptonshiretimeline.com/
scene/1460-war-of-the-roses/
and http://www.battlefieldstrust.com/resource-centre/
warsoftheroses/battleview.asp?BattleFieldId=33

11th – The Birth of Robert Bruce

On 11 July 1274, Robert Bruce, the future King of Scots, was born at Turnberry Castle. His grandfather, also Robert Bruce, attempted to claim the Scottish throne in 1290–92 but failed. His mother, Marjorie,

Countess of Carrick, was a formidable woman: when his father, Lord of Annandale – inevitably named Robert – returned from crusade, Marjorie took him prisoner and wouldn't release him until he agreed to marry her. So Robert came of high born and determined stock.

In 1296, he became Earl of Carrick, inheriting his mother's title. He was a man convinced that his family had a right to the Scottish crown. Both he and his father supported Edward I's invasion of Scotland that year, hoping they would be rewarded with the crown. When Edward kept the title for himself, they were hugely disappointed; they raised their own private rebellion, rather than join the more successful cause of William Wallace. The Bruce revolt came to nothing and in 1298 father and son again turned to King Edward in hope of a crown. In 1304, his father died and, when the Scots gave in to the English, Robert took the chance to seek allies for his own cause.

On 11 February 1306, Robert met another claimant to the Scottish throne, John Comyn, at Grey Friars Kirk in Dumfries. They argued, drew their weapons and Robert stabbed Comyn with his sword, killing him before the high altar. Although Comyn's death wasn't premeditated, Bruce was outlawed by the State and excommunicated by the Church. But not for long: on 25 March he was crowned Robert I, King of Scots, and would rule until 1329, a reign that would see the Scots defeat the English at the Battle of Loudoun Hill in May 1307 and his ultimate victory over the old enemy at Bannockburn on 24 June 1314.

http://www.bbc.co.uk/scotland/history/articles/robert_the_bruce/

12th – The Capture of Jack Cade

The new Sheriff of Kent, Alexander Iden, pursued the rebel Jack Cade (see 8 May) and caught him on 12 July 1450 at a little hamlet near Heathfield in Sussex. The hamlet is now known as Cade Street. There, Cade was mortally injured and died on his way back to London. His corpse was hanged, drawn and quartered and his head – as was the tradition – placed on a pole on London Bridge to deter others who might contemplate rebellion.

*

Also on this day in 1483, the Mayor of York, John Newton, and the aldermen decided to send a delegation to Middleham Castle in North Yorkshire. They were to take their best wishes and gifts to the young son of the new king, Richard III, who was living at Middleham. The boy, Edward, was the designate Prince of Wales, so it was as well for the citizens of York to curry favour with him and his father:

At the which day it was agreed that my lord the mayor with William Snawsell, John Tong, John Fereby and Robert Amyas, aldermen, and Thomas Asper, gentleman, and as many of the twenty-four [aldermen] as will, shall ride to Middleham to my lord the prince with a present ... that is to say with [blank] pennyworth of payn mayn [the finest white bread], ij [2] barrel of wine, one red, another white, vj [6] cygnets [young swans], vj heronshews [young herons], ij dozen rabbits, and that they shall ride upon chamber cost [i.e. the mayor's chamber would pay their expenses for the journey].

L. C. Attreed, *York House Books*, vol. I

Thomas Asper, the gentleman mentioned who wasn't one of the aldermen, was paid 13s 4d on 19 July as a reward for his part in the visit to Middleham, so perhaps he set up and organised the event.

13th – An Abusive Relationship

Around this date in 1467 – he couldn't recall the exact day – William Saunder told the court that he'd seen Alexander Brownyng, dagger in hand, chasing his wife, Eleanor, by St Bartholomew's Hospital. Eleanor was in her undergarments, her hair streaming loose and uncovered as she ran, terrified, to Master Burgoyn's house, where her sister was. Her sister let her in and closed the door. Outside, Alexander was shouting and swearing that he would kill Eleanor the next time he saw her, but the sister and Master Burgoyn kept her safe. William said Eleanor would have been mutilated or killed if she hadn't reached the house.

Subsequently on a later date, William had been at the Sun Tavern in Lombard Street when he'd witnessed Alexander threatening Eleanor once again with his dagger. She only escaped the weapon by jumping 'at least the distance of four men long', as William had seen 'with his own eyes'.

S. McSheffrey, *Marriage, Sex and Civic Culture in Late Medieval London*

Eleanor Brownyng was suing for divorce from her husband on the grounds of cruelty. Divorce as we know it wasn't possible in medieval times. Either a marriage could be annulled, as though it had never happened, in the scenarios that the couple were too closely related, already married to someone else, not old enough, forced in to it or unable to consummate it; or the couple could be granted a legal separation 'from bed and board'. This meant the partners no longer had to share a bed or eat at the same table, i.e. they could live apart, but neither of them could marry someone else unless the partner died.

14th – Fyssher's Bequest

On 14 July 1485 John Fyssher, a citizen of London mercer, merchant of the Staple and one-time alderman of the city, drew up his will. In a very detailed document he bequeathed money to numerous religious foundations, including all four orders of friars, to various parish churches around the city, and to the church of Godmanchester in Huntingdon where his parents were buried; he also made provision for the usual charitable donations to poor maidens, and for the repair of highways and bridges, including Rochester Bridge in Kent, where the Watling Street from London to Dover crossed the River Medway.

John bequeathed to his wife, Margaret 'all her array, apparel, girdles, rings, beads and brooches to her body belonging for her own proper wearing'. In other words, he left to her all her own clothes and jewellery – a reminder that a wife's possessions were actually her husband's property. Here are some of his more personal monetary bequests:

To my sister Johanne of Godmachestre and to heir children to be dyvided betwene heir and them by the discretion of my seid wiff, xl li [£40]. To my broder Thomas Crawforth, xx li [£20]. I bequeth to everich of myn men servants and apprenticez beyng in service with me the day of my deceese v mark [5 marks]. I bequeath to Anne Lilie x mark [10 marks]. Whereas Rande oweth me certeyn money, as yt apperith in my boke of detours, I pardon and forgeve to the same Rande all the duete that he oweth me and over that I bequeth to the same Rande xl s [40s] to pray for my soule.

L. Boatwright, et al. (eds), *Logge Register of PCC Wills*

He also left money to his wife, his five sons and two daughters over and above what was due to them as his heirs. John Fissher was evidently very wealthy but also generous.

15th – Rosemary

In medieval times, so the story goes, the Countess of Hainault sent her daughter Queen Philippa, wife of Edward III of England, a copy of a book about the herb rosemary along with a cutting of the plant. Rosemary was tricky to grow but soon became incredibly popular, not only for flavouring food and drink, but for scenting clothes, strewing on the floor and burning as incense in churches. The powdered flowers and stems were used as toothpaste, a scalp treatment and a face wash. Consumed as a herbal tea, rosemary was calming and cleansed the body within. Sprigs of rosemary were buried with the dead – rosemary for remembrance, as Ophelia says in Shakespeare's *Hamlet* – to show they would not be forgotten. Bees loved its pale blue flowers and people loved the scented honey they made – and still do.

Rosemary had religious symbolism in that it never grew taller than Christ, nor exceeded his age of thirty-three years; it healed with Christ's compassion and purified like his holy grace.

T. McLean, *Medieval English Gardens*

16th – Start of the Sweet Tooth

Medieval Europeans had probably first seen and tasted sugar while on the First Crusade in 1096. It was in Syria that the method of cultivating sugar cane had developed and the process of extracting the juice, concentrating it by heating and then drying it slowly into crystals was discovered. Damascus was then the centre of the Arab sugar trade but, having swiftly developed a sweet tooth, Europeans were soon planting sugar cane in Spain and Sicily, places with a suitable climate and, at the time, a high proportion of Arabs in their population. The standard sugar loaf had to be 'white, dry and a well-compacted paste', its conical shape formed as the liquid sugar dripped slowly from the spout of the pot in which it had been heated and solidified. Sicily became the centre of the European trade, exporting brown sugar, molasses and the most luxurious powdered sugars, often flavoured with aromatic spices.

M. W. Labarge, *Mistress, Maids and Men*

Here is a very upmarket early Tudor recipe, using sugar, for little cakes called 'Manus Christi' or hand of Christ:

Take five spoonfuls of rose water and grains of ambergris [used in perfumery] and four grains of pearl beaten very fine. Put these things in a small dish and cover it close. Let it stand covered one hour. Then take four ounces of very fine sugar and beat it small and sieve it through a fine sieve. Then take a little earthen pot, glazed, and put into it a spoonful of sugar and a quarter of a spoonful of rose water and let the sugar and rose water boil together softly till it do rise and fall again three times. Then take fine rice flour and sift on a smooth board. And with a spoon take of the sugar and rose water and first make it all into a round cake and then into little cakes. When they be half cold, wet them over with some rose water and then lay on your gold [leaf]. And so shall you make very good Manus Christi.

T. Dawson, *The Good Housewife's Jewel*

17th – Feigned Amity

In a dispute of 1433 a young landowner in Clapham, Robert Weston, claimed that William Wetenhale, a wealthy Londoner, had tried to ingratiate himself with Robert, hoping to buy a manor from him at the knock-down price of 300 marks, instead of the 500 marks it was truly worth:

Wetenhale feigned to be of amity, ready to do all he could for the boy, for his mother's sake, called him 'cosyn', invited him often to come to London to dine with him, and so with fair promise and gay deceiving language had the said manor.

S. Thrupp, *The Merchant Class of Medieval London*

Robert's family were attempting to redress the matter.

18th – Eleanor de Montfort's Cat

In 1265 Eleanor de Montfort, Countess of Leicester, bought a cat for her chamber at Dover Castle. It may have been a pet, or simply to hunt mice – perhaps it served both purposes – but it only cost her a few pence. There had been a note back in February that year of Eleanor paying for milk for a cat and pet dogs in her chamber at Odiham Castle in Hampshire.

Cats were worth far more in Ireland, where a cat that could both purr and catch mice was valued at the price of three cows (without the ability to kill mice, a cat was only worth one and a half cows). A Welsh mouser was worth 4d. In Scotland and England, the generic name for a cat was 'Gib' or 'Gybbe', as in this Scottish poem:

> Where when the two mice are on table-topy:
> Scantlie had thay drunkin anis [once] or twyse
> Quhen [when] in come Gib Hunter oure cat.

Or:

> Gybbe, owre grey catt …

K. Walker-Meikle, *Medieval Pets*

19th – Shopping List

On this date in 1480, Harold Stawnton wrote to George Cely, the son of a London wool merchant in Bruges in Flanders, sending him a shopping list:

Master Cely, I pray you let your man do so much for me as to go to the sign of the Star next to Fleming's Dame where daggers be made and let him receive a dagger off him [the bladesmith] and pay 2*s* 6*d* by the same [for which] I paid him 6*d* [already]. Also I pray you that he may go to the cap-maker next beyond William Kennett's on the same side towards Fleming's Dame and let him receive off him six bonnets of diverse colours as I bespake for [ordered] and I pray you let him be paid for them … Sir, you may say you have a homely fellow of me, for you have done so much for me that it lies not in me to deserve it, but you shall have my services and that God knows … by your own to my power, H. Stawnton.

A. Hanham (ed.), *The Cely Letters 1472–1488*

How difficult it must have been in those days before house numbers were invented to identify a particular address.

20th – The Death of Roger Bacon

Sometime around this date at Oxford in 1292, the English scholar Friar Roger Bacon died. As a philosopher, he believed the study of nature was paramount in furthering knowledge, both in religion and what we would now call science – medieval folk called it natural philosophy. Roger Bacon was born in Ilchester in Somerset, England, possibly in 1213 or 1214. He studied at Oxford and became a master there, lecturing on Aristotle. Sometime between 1237 and 1245, he began lecturing at the University of Paris; around 1256 he became a friar in the Franciscan Order and no longer held a teaching post in the universities. After 1260, his activities were restricted by a Franciscan rule that banned friars from publishing books or pamphlets without prior approval, but Bacon carried on. At a time when unicorns and dragons were thought to be as real as lions and eagles, some of the friar's writings would have been unbelievable, but these are a few of his ideas about the future:

Ships may be made to move without oars or rowers, so that large vessels might be driven on the sea by a single man more swiftly than if they were strongly manned. Chariots can be built which can move without any draught animal at incalculable speed. Flying machines might be made ... And very many things of this sort might be made: bridges which cross rivers without pier or prop whatsoever, and unheard-of machines and engines.

I. Mortimer, *The Time Travellers' Guide to Medieval England*

21st – The Battle of Shrewsbury

When Henry Bolingbroke had usurped the throne of England from his cousin Richard II in 1399, thereby becoming King Henry IV, he did it with the assistance of the powerful Percy family, including Henry Percy, 1st Earl of Northumberland. But the Percies and the king fell out. By 1403, the Percies were demanding payment from the king of debts outstanding from 1399, amounting to the incredible sum of £20,000. Added to this was their annoyance that the king was keeping the Scottish nobles, captured at the battle of Homildon Hill the previous year, as prisoners, instead of insisting their ransoms be paid. To Northumberland, who had led the victorious English, this was depriving him of his just reward. But it seems King Henry wasn't deliberately withholding payment of his debts: he was simply broke; as were the Scots who couldn't afford to pay any ransoms.

King Henry had given Northumberland's son, the fiery tempered Henry 'Hotspur' Percy, high office in Wales, where he was successful against the rebellious Owain Glyndwr in 1401 and 1402. But Hotspur hadn't been paid either, having to use his own money to finance the campaigns. Tired of the king's failure to reimburse them, the Percies now formed an alliance with Glyndwr and Edward Mortimer. Mortimer was brother-in-law to Hotspur and son-in-law to Glyndwr, as well as being uncle to the Earl of March – a young lad still in his minority, but Richard

II's rightful heir. To gain support and justify their actions, the Percies now claimed that they had only supported Henry Bolingbroke in 1399 on the understanding that he was trying to reclaim his confiscated lands as Duke of Lancaster, and they had no idea he'd intended to usurp the throne. They also accused Henry of starving his cousin, King Richard II, to death in the castle at Pontefract, so the Percies now supported the Earl of March as rightful heir to the throne.

Marching to join his would-be allies on the Welsh border, by the time he reached the town of Shrewsbury in Shropshire, Hotspur's army had grown to around 14,000 men, including the formidable and skilled Cheshire archers. Shrewsbury was garrisoned by the king's eldest son, Harry of Monmouth (later Henry V), but his small contingent of men was unlikely to withstand an attack from the combined rebel forces. Meanwhile, learning of the plot against him, the king headed north-west to intercept Hotspur before he could join forces with Glyndwr. The race for Shrewsbury was won by the king, who reached the town shortly before Hotspur on the 20 July. Hotspur was now isolated on the north side of the town, with the River Severn and the king's army between him and reinforcements from Wales. Withdrawing from the town, Percy spent the night in a village three miles north-west of Shrewsbury. The following morning, with no sign of Glyndwr and with the king's forces marching towards him from Shrewsbury, Hotspur advanced.

When negotiations for compromise failed, the battle began a few hours before dusk on 21 July 1403. For the first time on English soil, massed divisions of archers faced each other across the field, to demonstrate – if there lingered any doubt – the deadly abilities of the longbow. As the mounted knights then closed with their opponents, Hotspur was killed, apparently shot in the face when he opened his visor to get a breath of air. He should have known better: it was such a basic mistake, but he had probably taken to heart a soothsayer's prediction that he would die in battle after having slept at Berwick. Hotspur was familiar with the frequently fought-over Scottish border town of Berwick-upon-Tweed, and must have believed he was safe that day. Perhaps he hadn't known that the name of the little village where he had spent the previous night was Berwick. The rebels' resolve withered away with the death of their leader and the battle was over, but not without other casualties.

To quash rumours that he had survived the battle, the king had Hotspur's body quartered and put on display in various corners of the country, with his head impaled on the city of York's north gateway. But Prince Harry had received an arrow shot in the face. An incredible feat of battlefield surgery was performed by one of the king's surgeons, John Bradmore, and the prince lived to fight another day. However, he had learned a brutal lesson of just how effective the English longbow could be; a lesson he would put to deadly use as King Henry V, just a few years later on the battlefields of France (see 25 October).

http://www.battlefieldstrust.com/resource-centre/medieval/
battleview.asp?BattleFieldId=39

http://www.historic-uk.com/HistoryMagazine/DestinationsUK/
The-Battle-of-Shrewsbury/

22nd – Arbitration

On this day in 1476, the feast day of St Mary Magdalene, two men of York agreed to arbitration in their disputes. Unfortunately, the cause of the dispute isn't recorded:

Dyer John Wetewod and merchant Thomas Spicer, both of York, bound themselves for £40 well and faithfully to obey and carry out the arbitration and ordinance of Nicholas Pereson, Richard Croklyn, Thomas Juddson and William Pikard, arbiters impartially chosen to judge all disputes, debates, complaints, crimes and demands had, moved or hanging between Wetewod on the one side and litster [a dyer] Thomas Watson and merchant Richard Scott on the other side, from the beginning of the world to the present day. The judgement is to be given by the feast of the Assumption of the Blessed Virgin Mary next coming. If the arbiters are unable to agree then they are to elect an umpire, and Wetewod should faithfully obey the judgement of the umpire as well.

L. C. Attreed, *York House Books*, vol. I

The record isn't specific but it seems Thomas Spicer wasn't involved in the actual dispute, so probably he was the one who put up the bond money of £40 for Wetewod.

23rd – The Medieval Physician

Around this date in 1400, John Mirfield, a priest and physician at St Bartholomew's Hospital, wrote these instructions for his fellow doctors, in order that they might determine whether a patient was going to live or die:

Take the name of the patient, the name of the messenger sent to summon you and the name of the day upon which the messenger first came to you; join all their letters together, and if an even number result, the patient will not escape [death]; if the number be odd, he will recover.

I. Mortimer, *The Time Traveller's Guide to Medieval England*

It was important for a physician to know the outcome before he agreed to treat the patient; after all, a dead patient would dent his reputation and might even result in legal action for negligence by the family. However, Mirfield's method could be problematic: how did the patient and the messenger spell their names? Was it John, Johan or Jack; Henry, Harry, Herry or Hal? Should you include their surnames? And what of the day? Perhaps it was a Tuesday or a Tewesday or even the Eve of the Vigil of the Feast of St James the Great ...

24th – Richard III's Household

On 24 July 1484, King Richard III drew up an ordinance for the running of his household in the north. His son and heir, Edward of Middleham, had died the previous spring; the household concerned here was that of the king's nephew and designated heir, John de la Pole, Earl of Lincoln, the eldest son of the king's sister Elizabeth. With the assistance of a Council appointed by the king, John was to govern the north of England. The household also included other noble children, among them the king's illegitimate son, John of Pontefract, and Elizabeth of York, daughter of King Edward IV, and possibly others of his nephews and nieces. The household was most often based at Sheriff Hutton Castle, near York. Here are some excerpts:

First that the hours of God's service, diet, going to bed and rising and the shutting of the gates to be at reasonable times and hours convenient.

Item. That monthly the Treasurer and Comptroller show the expenses to one or two of the Council, the which shall appoint themselves monthly through the year.

Item. That if any person offend in breaking of any of the said ordinance ... the Council to punish or expel the Offenders after their discretion, out of the said house according to their demerits.

Item. My lord of Lincoln and my lord Morley to be at one breakfast, the Children together at one breakfast & such as be present of the Council at one breakfast. And also that the household go to dinner at the farrest [latest] by eleven of the Clock ...

Item. The Treasurer to have the keys of the gates from the time of the dinner and supper begin til the end of the same.

Item. The costs of my lord of Lincoln when he rideth to Sessions [i.e. on official business] or to any meeting appointed by the Council, the Treasurer to pay for meat and drink.

Item. At all other ridings, huntings and disports my said lord to bear his own costs and charges. ...

R. Horrox and P. W. Hammond (eds), *British Library*
Harleian Manuscript, vol. 3

25th – Feast Day of St James the Greater and St Christopher

The shrine of St James, one of Christ's original apostles, at Compostella in northern Spain, was a popular place of pilgrimage for medieval people. However, James shares his feast day with another popular saint, Christopher. Making a pilgrimage to Spain might be a once-in-a-lifetime event, but in everyday life Christopher seems to have been of far greater importance to ordinary folk as they went about their daily work. He was the patron saint of travellers, seamen, ferrymen and boatmen, archers, soldiers, market carriers and carters, bookbinders, fruit dealers, gardeners and epileptics. As well as giving protection against lightning, floods, storms, pestilence and toothache, most importantly St Christopher ensured a holy death by warding off a sudden, accidental fatality.

For this reason many churches placed wall paintings, images or statues of him, usually opposite the south door so he could be easily seen, in the belief that a quick look at Christopher's likeness first thing in the morning was sufficient to keep the viewer safe for the rest of the day. He is usually shown as a huge man, larger than life-size, with a child on his shoulder and a staff in one hand. In England, there are more wall paintings of St Christopher than of any other saint: in 1904, a Mrs Collier, writing for the British Archaeological Association, reported 183 paintings, statues and other representations of the saint, outnumbering all others except for the Virgin Mary. Even today, medallions with St Christopher's name and image are commonly worn as pendants, especially by travellers to request his blessing. In France, a common phrase for such medals is *Regarde St Christophe et va-t-en rassuré* (Look at St Christopher and go on reassured, i.e. go your way in safety); and in Spain medals have the phrase *Si en San Cristóbal confías, de accidente no morirás* (If you trust St Christopher, you won't die in an accident).

A sudden death, without the time to make confession, receive absolution and the last rites, was a terrifying possibility for medieval people as it meant they had little chance of ever making it to heaven. An eternity in hell would be the outcome for them on the Day of Judgement. No wonder that, even if they didn't attend mass every day, a quick peek through the church door at the image of St Christopher was probably an early morning ritual for many Christians to ensure they were safe from death, at least until tomorrow.

26th – Struck by Lightning

A coroner noted in a record of 26 July 1270 that:

About midday, Amice, daughter of William le Lorimer of Bedford, went into Wilputtesburne in Cardington field by Cardington wood to gather corn. Thunder and lightning came on and she was struck and fell and died instantly. Maud, daughter of Nicholas de Augul first found her.

P. J. P. Goldberg, *Women in England, c. 1275–1525*

Perhaps the unfortunate Amice had forgotten to take her early morning glance at St Christopher (see above).

27th – A Season of Good Health

The medical instructions for living a healthy life have this to say about the month of July:

Hold thee from women [i.e. no sex], for thy brain beginneth to gather its humors. And let thee not blood. Two days there be of peril, the fifteenth and the nineteenth day.

W. R. Dawson, *A Leechbook of the Fifteenth Century*

28th – Remedy for the Palsy

Here is a fifteenth-century remedy, a 'sovereign medicine', for the palsy – paralysis or tremors:

Take a loaf of dough and a handful of sage and mix the sage in the midst of the dough and let it bake. And then draw it forth and take the hot loaf and break it all into morsels into an earthen pot and mingle ... a gallon of white wine with the bread and sage and stop the pot fast with a lid and stop the chinks fast about [seal] with dough that the breath [steam] pass not out. And heat the oven again somewhat hot and put in that pot and let it bake well, and then draw forth the pot and let it cool.

And then take every day at morn, fasting, two spoonfuls thereof or three. And if thou hast not that evil [palsy], thou shall never have it. And if thou hast it, this medicine shall sovereignly help thee. And use to eat much mustard and take aqua vitae and anoint thy temples and under thy mouth. And take sage water and anoint the palms of thy hands, and also wash thy pulse [at the wrist] and lay thereto pounded sage and bind thereto night and day.

W. R. Dawson, *A Leechbook of the Fifteenth Century*

29th – Dame Frances' Will

Probate was granted on this day in 1483 for the will of a widow, Dame Frances Skulle of Worcester. Her husband, Sir Walter Skulle, had been a lawyer and MP for Worcestershire, as well as Keeper of the King's Wardrobe and Treasurer of the Royal Household in 1460. He had died in 1482. Frances wrote her will during the very brief reign of the boy-king Edward V on 14 June 1483. As the widow of a royal servant, it seems Frances had quite a nice wardrobe too, if nowhere near that of royalty, for in her will she bequeaths:

To Alice my doughter ij [2] rynges of gold, oon with a diamound, with a gowne of myn owne wering russete colour furred with martrons [the fur of a pine marten] and my best gyrdell of gold. Also, I bequeth to Anne Williams my doughter a gowne of rede crymesyn [crimson], ij rynges of gold.

L. Boatwright, et al. (eds), *The Logge Register of PCC Wills, 1479–86*, vol. I

30th – Harvesting Grain

With harvest time approaching, here are the instructions to a steward as regards harvesting grain:

And you ought to know that five men can easily reap and bind two acres of any kind of corn in a day ... And in places where four men take each 1½d a day and the fifth, because he is the binder, 2d, one ought to give 4d per acre ... But you should engage the reapers as a team, that is to say five men or women, whichever you wish, and whom you term 'men', make one team.

P. J. P. Goldberg, _Women in England, c. 1275–1525_

This may sound like early gender equality but, whether they were termed 'men' or not, women were always paid less, and so were more cost effective.

31st – Clothed in Scarlet

On this day [31 July 1483] it was agreed that the mayor, John Newton, and all the aldermen of the city of York, should be clothed in scarlet and ride out to meet their sovereign lord the king [Richard III] at Brekles Mylnys on horseback.

L. C. Attreed, _York House Books,_ vol. I

Having been recently crowned (see 6 July), Richard was eager to celebrate with the citizens of his favourite northern city. The scarlet robes to be worn by Newton and the aldermen were not necessarily going to be red in colour – 'scarlet' was the finest quality woollen cloth, often dyed with the most expensive red dye, but it could be any colour. During King Edward IV's reign, on one occasion the aldermen of London were described as wearing scarlet cloth of violet colour when they greeted him. Over time, because it was so frequently a bright red, 'scarlet' came to denote the colour, as well as the cloth, until this type of fabric was eventually forgotten.

AUGUST

1st – The Southampton Plot

This day is Lammas Day (Anglo-Saxon for *hlaf-mas*, or loaf-mass), the festival of the wheat harvest – the first harvest festival of the year. On this day it was customary to bring to church a loaf made from the new grain which had been reaped, threshed, milled into flour and made into bread. The loaf was then blessed; a book of Anglo-Saxon charms directed that the lammas bread be broken into four pieces to be placed at the four corners of the barn, to protect the grain.

In many parts of England, tenants were required to present freshly harvested wheat to their landlords on 1 August. The day was also known as 'the feast of first fruits' when other harvested produce was blessed.

*

On this day in 1415, a plot to assassinate King Henry V – known as the Southampton or the Cambridge Plot – was thwarted. The bungled attempt on the king's life was led by Richard, Earl of Cambridge, who planned to put Edmund Mortimer, Earl of March, on the throne. Other major conspirators included Henry, Lord Scrope of Masham and Sir Thomas Grey of Heton.

The Earl of March had been the heir presumptive of the childless king, Richard II. In 1399 Richard was forced to abdicate in favour of Henry

IV, and for the next few decades Mortimer served as a focal point for conspiracies aimed at removing Henry and his heirs from the throne. In 1405 Henry Percy, Earl of Northumberland, tried unsuccessfully to oust Henry IV and place Mortimer on the throne. In 1415 the Earl of Cambridge and his friends were ready to try again.

In 1414, Henry V had raised his cousin, Richard, second son of the Duke of York, to the earldom of Cambridge but granted him no lands or estates to befit the title. Seven years prior to the plot, Richard had married Lady Anne Mortimer and they had a son who would become Richard, Duke of York. In financial difficulties, Cambridge struggled to raise the men and equipment needed to accompany Henry V to France and conspired with Lord Scrope, Henry's trusted advisor and Lord Treasurer, and Sir Thomas Grey, a commoner, to unseat Henry and put Cambridge's late wife's brother, Edmund Mortimer, on the throne.

The conspirators planned to kill the king and his three brothers, the dukes of Clarence, Bedford and Gloucester, as they boarded a ship to France at Southampton. This would be the signal for a general uprising. Messengers galloped off with secret orders to the conspirators' agents throughout the country. It remained only to tell Edmund Mortimer of their plans to place him on the throne that should rightfully be his. More than one meeting was held with Mortimer in Southampton; the plotters were assured that he would cooperate with them.

However, it wasn't until the last day of July that Mortimer reached his decision. That night, unknown to Cambridge and the others, he went to the king and told him everything. It was on the following day – 1 August and the day fixed for the king's assassination – that Henry called his council to Portsmouth. Among its members were the three unsuspecting leaders of the conspiracy, still intent on carrying out their treacherous purpose. Henry now informed the council that he had received a report of a plot against his life, and asked their advice as to what steps he should take.

The guilty men realised it was over. Without waiting to be accused, they stood up and confessed. All three were arrested and taken to Southampton Castle. Two days later, a commission consisting of two judges, ten lords and a jury of twelve local men heard the case at the Red Lion Inn in Southampton. In his defence, Scrope claimed he hadn't known that the plot involved the king's assassination, and that all along he had intended to reveal the conspiracy. Cambridge and Grey made full confessions of their guilt: Grey, as a commoner, was sentenced to death, being hanged on 3 August. Despite pleas for clemency, Cambridge and Scrope were executed outside Bargate, on Southampton Green, on 5 August.

Mortimer was fortunate to come through unscathed, for it seems likely that he had, however briefly, considered joining the conspiracy. But Henry was satisfied with disposing of the leaders and took no further action against others who might have been implicated in the plot.

Just over a week later, he set sail on what would become known as the Agincourt campaign. After the 'Southampton Plot', there were no other treasonous conspiracies against the victorious hero, Henry V.

Ironically, Richard, Duke of York, the Earl of Cambridge's son, opposed and took up arms against the son of Henry V, and two of York's sons would become kings as Edward IV and Richard III.

http://www.hampshire-history.com/the-southampton-plot/
http://www.lookandlearn.com/blog/13727/henry-v-foils-the-southampton-plot-of-1415/

2nd – Rufus' Hunt

King William II, known as Rufus, was an immoral, vain and ill-tempered man, the second son of William the Conqueror. He came to the throne in 1087 and on 2 August 1100 was hunting in the New Forest. The chronicler, Orderic Vitalis, gave an account of that fateful day. Rufus was in a good mood and dined with the hunting party, including his youngest brother, Henry, the de Clare brothers and Walter Tirel. While preparing for the hunt, a fletcher presented Rufus with six arrows. The king kept four for himself and gave the other two to Tirel, saying that it was only right that the sharpest arrows went to the man who knew how to inflict the deadliest shots. Before the party set off, a letter arrived, warning of a monk's vision of the king's death. Rufus dismissed it, saying he wasn't interested in the 'dreams of snoring monks'.

In the forest, the party separated, leaving Rufus and Walter Tirel together. Tirel took a shot at a stag coming towards them but his arrow missed and struck the king in the chest. Rufus was dead within minutes, and Tirel fled to France. Rufus' younger brother, Henry, galloped to Winchester to secure the crown, while Rufus was carried away by his servants 'like a wild boar' from the hunt.

Was the king's death an accident? Rufus had already lost his elder brother and one of his cousins to similar accidental arrow-shots in the New Forest, but his younger brother Henry, gained the English throne and, once he had been crowned was extremely generous to the de Clare family. Was this a reward for helping him to murder Rufus?

Contemporary writers believed that Rufus' death was an act of divine punishment. He had been an evil king: he had mocked the Church and so paid the ultimate price. Whether it was an accident, intentional murder or act of God, Rufus' death remains a most intriguing medieval mystery.

http://www.historyinanhour.com/2010/08/02/who-killed-william-rufus-a-great-medieval-mystery/#sthash.33rd1hS0.dpuf

*

Also on this day in 1133, an eclipse of the sun was seen in northern England and Scotland.

3rd – A Stabbing in Self-Defence

A 1367 coroner's account recorded the following:

Henry Bailiff; John, son of Juliana; and Alice, wife of the said John, were gathered together in a field at Stanton-under-Bardon (Leicestershire) when a dispute arose over a loan that had not been repaid.

Henry had borrowed money from John and Alice and had failed to repay it. Alice told him, 'You have 12*d* that belongs to us'. Henry became angry, shouting, 'I curse you', and brandishing an axe. Fearing for his wife's safety, John cried out, 'Henry wishes to kill my wife', took out his knife and stabbed Henry. Henry died of his wound there and then, without any chance of receiving the last rites.

The coroner found the case to be self-defence on John's part.

S. M. Butler, *Forensic Medicine and Death Investigation in Medieval England*

4th – An Earthquake Hits England

On this day in 1133, an eye-witness account by the chronicler, William of Malmesbury, tells of an earthquake affecting many parts of England.

*

Also on this day in 1265, the Battle of Evesham was fought in Worcestershire. It was the second of the two main battles of the Second Barons' War (see 14 May), and saw the defeat of Simon de Montfort, Earl of Leicester, and the rebellious barons by the Lord Edward (later King Edward I) who commanded the forces of his father, Henry III.

De Montfort was in Evesham, awaiting the arrival of the forces of his son Simon before engaging the royal army which he knew was on the way. Unknown to de Montfort, the younger Simon had already been overwhelmed by the Lord Edward at Kenilworth in Warwickshire. Edward had confiscated Simon's banners and the elder de Montfort, seeing his son's colours approaching, believed his reinforcements had arrived. Slow to realise the truth of the deception, Edward trapped de Montfort and his small force in a loop of the River Avon, blocking off the only bridge and forcing the rebels to fight, outnumbered. De Montfort supposedly said: 'May the Lord have mercy upon our souls, as our bodies are theirs.'

Despite being outnumbered more than three to one, de Montfort rode out to engage the enemy. Just north of the town, he encountered the royal forces deployed in three divisions. He made a bold cavalry attack and, at first, some of the royal forces retreated; but soon they counter-attacked. De Montfort and his knights were surrounded. Unusually, no quarter was to be given and de Montfort and most of his main supporters were cut down as their infantry was routed. The rebel forces were pursed back into the town, the killing continuing through the streets and into Evesham Abbey. The Battle of Evesham had completely broken the rebellion, for almost all of its major supporters had been slaughtered on the field.

http://www.battlefieldstrust.com/resource-centre/
medieval/battleview.asp?BattleFieldId=14

5th – Gloucester's Scots Campaign

On 5 August 1482, the mayor of York, Richard Yorke, and the aldermen of the city agreed the following:

That for as much as the soldiers of this city now being with my Lord of Gloucester in Scotland, being desolate of money, that a tax shall be raised [from] the parishioners of this city for seven days wages ...

L. C. Attreed, *York House Books,* vol. 1

As so often in history, the Crown was slow in sending money to its commanders in time of war. In this case, Edward IV was not yet forthcoming with the cash to fight the Scots. His brother, Richard, Duke of Gloucester (the future King Richard III), was trying to finance the campaign from his own coffers. He was quite wealthy but couldn't keep up the wages bill for the army.

Nevertheless, he made a good job of the conquest of southern Scotland which saw the citizens of Edinburgh open the gates to him. In Edinburgh Castle, Gloucester discovered 'the King [of Scots] with other chief lords of the kingdom ... shut up and nowise thinking of arms, of war, of resistance ...' King Edward was delighted and on 25 August wrote to the Pope, telling him of his brother's achievements.

P. W. Hammond and A. F. Sutton,
Richard III – The Road to Bosworth Field

6th – Pets at Table

In medieval times, as now, it was considered bad manners to have cats and dogs at the table, or to pet them or feed them from your plate, although it was common to let the dogs into the hall after the meal to eat up any morsels that had fallen to the floor. This is what a courtesy book has to say:

> If thine own dog thou scrape or claw [pat and stroke]
> That is holden a vice among men knawe [of knowledge]
> Where e'er thou sit at meat at board [table]
> Avoid the cat sat on bare wood
> For if thou stroke cat or dog
> Thou art like an ape together with a clog [wooden shoe].

K. Walker-Meikle, Medieval Pets

7th – Landing at Milford Haven

The pretender to the English throne, Henry Tudor, landed at Milford Haven on 7 August 1485. King Richard III's intelligence network had informed him to expect Tudor's arrival at Milford but hadn't been explicit in the detail. Richard dispatched his Lord Chamberlain, Francis, Viscount Lovell, with a contingent of troops to repel Tudor when he should attempt a landing at Milford-on-Sea, on the south coast between Bournemouth and Southampton. In the event, the invader was able to land, unopposed, in Milford Haven, south Wales (see 22 August).

8th – De Sasiola's Oration

On this day in 1483, Richard III received an ingratiating letter and verbal 'oration' via de Sasiola, an ambassador from the Queen of Castile. Here is the gist of the message:

The Queen of Castile was turned in her heart from England in time past for the unkindness which she took against the king last deceased [Edward IV], whom God pardon, for his refusing of her and taking to his wife a widow of England [Elizabeth Woodville]. And therefore she moved for this cause against her nature, which was ever to love and favour England, she took the French king's part and made considerations with him.

Now the king is dead that showed her this unkindness and the French king hath broken four principal articles concluded and sealed between him and her. Wherefore she now, returning to her natural kind disposition, desireth such things to be appointed and concluded betwixt these two realms, England and Spain.

And as an additional incentive, de Sasiola says:

The most serene lady, the Queen, my supreme mistress, promises that if the said lord King of England chooses to wage war against King Louis of France for the recovery of his lands, lordships and possessions which appertain to the crown of England, the Queen will give to the said king, his people and his captains the use of all her sea ports, victuals and arms at a low cost, and her ships at sea armed for reasonable wages; and on land, knights and cavalrymen, strong and well armed, and infantrymen of the like kind, competent and in sufficient numbers at fair wages – paid by the said lord king.

R. Horrox and P. Hammond (eds), *British Library, Harleian Manuscript 433*

Yes, there had to be a catch to all this good will …

9th – A Strike to the Head

The coroners' rolls of Bedfordshire recorded the following on 9 August 1270:

Late in the night, Simon and Richard, sons of Hugh the Fisher of Radwell, came from the house of Alice, Hugh's daughter, towards that of their father in Ashwell. They crossed the courtyard of Robert Ball of Radwell, in which Simon, son of Agnes of Radwell, and Juliana, daughter of Walter the Fisher of Radwell, were lying under a haystack. Simon [son of Agnes] immediately got up and struck Simon the Fisher on the top of his head to the brain, apparently with an axe, so that he instantly died. Richard, on seeing this, raised the hue and cry. Simon the felon fled and Juliana with him.

P. J. P. Goldberg, *Women in England c. 1275–1525*

10th – The Feast of St Lawrence

On this day in 1103, it was recorded that on the morning of the mass day of St Lawrence, strong winds did more damage in England than anyone could remember.

*

In 1435, in Southampton, the borough court heard the following case:

To this court comes Katherine … which was the wife of Andrew Payn, formerly burgess of Southampton, now in her lawful widowhood … She declared that she was seventeen years [old] at the feast of St Lawrence and asks that she be allowed to prove her age according to the custom of the town. This was granted to her …

And then the men [twelve burgesses], sworn to speak the truth, say on their oath that the aforesaid Katherine was seventeen on the feast of St Lawrence the martyr last, that she was born on the feast of St Lawrence in the fourth year of King Henry V [1416], father of the lord king, and was baptised in the parish church of Holy Cross in Southampton on that feast day by Thomas Haughton, lately vicar there. Her godfather was Walter Fetplace and her godmothers were Isabel, widow of William Soper, and Katherine, widow of William Nycoll, and each of the twelve burgesses was then living in the aforesaid town.

P. J. P. Goldberg, *Women in England, c. 1275–1525*

In a time before birth certificates and parish registers, the only way to prove your age was to call upon respected witnesses who could recall the day you were born. In this case, Katherine must have needed to prove how old she was – she was actually nineteen. Perhaps the legality of her marriage to Andrew, now deceased, was being questioned by someone hoping to deny her the widow's dower due to her. For her marriage to be valid, a girl had to be twelve years of age when wed.

11th – Murder at the Abbey

This story began on 3 April 1367 at the Battle of Najera, in Spain. The Black Prince became involved in a civil war in Castile as two brothers squabbled over who should be king. During the fighting, two English squires, Robert Hauley and John Shakel, had captured Alphonso, Count of Denia. The ransom demanded by the English was huge and, while the money was raised, Alphonso offered his eldest son and heir, also named Alphonso, as hostage in his place, as was the chivalrous custom. The Black Prince took responsibility for the welfare of young Alphonso and would receive the ransom, if and when it was paid.

A decade later, in 1375, when he became ill, the Black Prince signed over his rights to the ransom money for Alphonso to Hauley and Shakel themselves, making them now responsible for his welfare. As the prospect of payment and the return of the hostage seemed imminent, Hauley and Shakel looked forward to being made rich. But others in London were envious.

By 1377, their benefactor, the Black Prince, had died and ten-year-old Richard II had ascended the throne. Rival claims on the ransom were made against Hauley and Shakel, and fearing for his safety, it was decided that Alphonso should be removed from their custody. Appalled, Hauley and Shakel attempted to hide Alphonso – a diplomatic incident that jeopardised the country, for which Hauley and Shakel found themselves imprisoned in the Tower of London. They appealed to young Richard II but nothing came of it. Desperate after almost a year's incarceration, Hauley and Shakel escaped from the Tower and sought sanctuary in Westminster Abbey.

Letters were written to the abbot of Westminster from the Tower, demanding that the prisoners be returned, but Abbot Litlyngton refused on the grounds that their forty days of sanctuary had not ended yet. Having failed by peaceful means, the Constable of the Tower, Sir Alan de Buxhall, resorted to more violent means. On 11 August 1378, he and fifty armed men broke into the abbey during High Mass. John Shakel surrendered without fuss, but Robert Hauley tried to resist them. He was cut down and died of his wounds in the church. A monk named Richard was also injured and later died from his wounds. Entering the church with weapons broke the rules of sanctuary, but by spilling blood, de Buxhall and his men had desecrated the church. Pope Gregory XI immediately excommunicated de Buxhall and his armed retinue.

Hauley was buried in the south transept of the abbey, in what is now known as Poets' Corner. Shakel spent another year in the Tower but, once released, he managed to regain the rights to the ransom of Alphonso. However, after yet more legal disputes, Alphonso was allowed to go home to Spain; Shakel received not a penny. The Constable, Alan de Buxhall, was able to reverse his excommunication – for a substantial fee – and Westminster Abbey was reconsecrated four months after the murder of Robert Hauley and the monk named Richard.

https://tourguidegirl.wordpress.com/2014/04/25/
murder-at-the-abbey/

12th – A Benefactor to Shoreham

On this day in 1485, probate was granted on the will of Katherine Mason, a London widow. Her husband's family came from Suffolk, but Katherine seems to have had connections with Shoreham in Kent and made these bequests there to benefit her soul:

I bequeath to the werkes [repairs] of the brigge of Shorham in the counte of Kent iijs iiijd [3*s* 4*d*]. Also I bequeath to be destributed among the poure people inhabitant in Shorham aforseid having most yong children vjs viijd [6*s* 8*d*]. Also I bequeath to the chirch werkes of Shorham aforseid vjs viijd [6*s* 8*d*].

L. Boatwright, et al. (eds), *The Logge Register of PCC Wills*, vol. 2

13th – Plague Victims

During this month alone in 1349, it was recorded that the Cistercian Abbey of Meaux, near Beverley in East Yorkshire, lost thirty-two monks and seven novices to the Plague.

14th – A Low-Status Marriage

In London, around this date in 1472, Robert Smyth sued Rose Langtoft through the Consistory Court (a church court), claiming she had consented to marry him 'in the present tense', i.e. now, and therefore was his wife. He brought to court Thomas and Alice Hynkley as his witnesses to the marriage that had taken place one August afternoon in Alice's bedchamber. Rose insisted she hadn't been at the Hynkleys' house that day and, although she admitted telling Robert on other occasions that she would marry him, it had always been on the condition that her parents approved – which they didn't. Robert then brought three other people, including Rose's employer, Thomas Howden, who, although they hadn't witnessed the event, could testify to it being 'common knowledge' in the parish of St Mary Abchurch that Robert and Rose were contracted in marriage.

Rose's parents were richer than Robert's family. She worked for a tailor – a far higher status job than Robert's, as he was a lowly sherman, a man who sheared the excess knap off woollen cloth. The Langtofts could hardly approve of such a match for their daughter, so a countersuit was brought against Robert. Once again, Thomas Howden was called as a witness, this time to testify to the tasks he had set Rose to do on that same afternoon, in order to attest that she couldn't possibly have been at the Hynkleys' house. Besides, he said, Rose had been wearing an old gown of murrey (mulberry colour) all day, not the fine red gown Alice Hynkley said she'd worn for the occasion. Two of the tailor's apprentices, William Taylbos and Ralph Nowell, and Howden's kitchen maid, Alice Calcote, all swore on oath that Rose never left the house that day. So was Robert after her money and looking to improve his social standing?

After all that, in January 1473 Rose again came before the court. In Robert's presence, she now admitted that she had been at the Hynkleys' home on that August afternoon and had contracted a marriage with

Robert, there and then, with the Hynkleys as witnesses. They were truly man and wife; her employer had perjured himself and persuaded his apprentices and servant to do the same. The suspicion is that the Langtofts may have offered bribes in the hope of saving their daughter from a low-status marriage.

S. McSheffrey, *Marriage, Sex and Culture in Late Medieval London*

15th – The Feast of the Assumption of the Blessed Virgin Mary

This date was celebrated in medieval times as the feast of the Assumption of the Blessed Virgin Mary. It was believed that when Christ's mother died, because she had been born and lived her life entirely without sin, her body, uncorrupted, was taken straight to heaven, leaving a scattering of lilies – to represent her purity – and roses – to represent her love – in her otherwise empty tomb. Therefore, as with other feast days of the Virgin Mary (see 1 May), churches were decked with flowers in celebration.

A churchyard was not just the last resting place for parishioners; it was also a proper garden, growing flowers to decorate or 'garnish' the church. The church of St Mary-at-Hill in London, near the Tower, owned gardens throughout the city, many of which had been left to the church in people's wills. St Mary's rented out most of these gardens to Londoners for a few shillings a year but was always short of greenery and blossoms for garnishing on special occasions and so had to buy in extra.

St Mary's accounts show that in the summer of 1479 the churchwardens paid 4s 7d for 'flags, garlands and torches' for Corpus Christi, St Barnabas (11 June) and other festivals. St Barnabas' Day seems to have required plenty of floral decoration: in 1487, St Mary's bought thirty garlands of roses at a cost of 8½d. Rushes to strew upon the floor were another expense. In 1493, rushes cost St Mary's 3d and, although these accounts don't mention buying them, herbs were often mixed with the rushes to sweeten the air. It may be that the church grew its own herbs – fennel, rosemary and meadowsweet being favourite strewing herbs – their perfume much appreciated by the sweaty, crowded congregation in the days before deodorants.

T. McLean, *Medieval English Gardens*

16th – A Mother's Reproach

In August 1477, Margaret Paston sent a sternly worded letter to her eldest son Sir John, concerning money:

I must leave you in no doubt that I will never pay him [Cokett] from my own purse a penny of what is due to him, even though he sue me for it, for I will not be compelled to pay your debts against my will, and even if I would I cannot ...

I marvel that you have dealt so foolishly with Sporle, considering that you and your friends had so much to do to recover it previously ... It grieves me to think upon your behaviour, considering the great property you have had ... since the death of your father, whom God assoil, and how foolishly it has been spent ...

And as for your brother, William, I wish you to provide for his upkeep, for as I told you the last time, I will no longer find for him at my cost and charge. His board and school charges are owing ... and he has great need of gowns and other gear necessary for him to have in haste. I would that you should remember and provide for them, for I will not.

I think you set but little by my blessing and, if you did, you would have asked me for it when you wrote to me.

R. Virgoe, *The Illustrated Paston Letters*

That sounds harsh, but Sir John had inherited considerable wealth from his father and was wasting it, running up debts, having a good time with his friends and forgetting about William at school. He even forgot to ask his mother's blessing.

17th – Fine Bread

With the harvest well underway, there would be plenty of flour for making bread. This is an early Tudor recipe for 'fine bread', believe it or not, although it sounds more like cake:

Take half a pound of fine sugar, well beaten, and half a pound of flour. Take four egg whites, being very well beaten, and put thereto. You must mingle them with aniseeds [a herb rather like sweet Cecily], bruised, and being all beaten together, put into your mould, melting the sauce over first with a little butter [I think it means grease the mould] and set it in the oven and turn it twice or thrice in the baking.

T. Dawson, *The Good Housewife's Jewel*

18th – An African Elephant

An African elephant arrived in England in 1254, a gift from the King of France, Louis IX, to Henry III of England. The elephant had been acquired by Louis during a crusade to the Holy Land. Henry ordered the Sheriff of Kent 'with John Gouch, to provide for bringing the King's elephant from Whitsand to Dover, and if possible to London by water'.

There had been a royal menagerie at the Tower of London since 1235, when Henry had received a wedding gift of three leopards from Frederick III, the Holy Roman Emperor; in 1246, Henry was given a bear by the Mayor of Northampton. A Norwegian polar bear joined the menagerie in 1252. It was kept muzzled and chained but was allowed to catch salmon in the Thames when secured by a strong rope. In 1255, Henry ordered elaborate arrangements to be made for his new elephant's accommodation at the Tower of London. 'We command you,' he wrote to the Sheriff of London, 'that ye cause without delay, to be built at our Tower of London, one house of forty feet long and twenty feet deep for our elephant.'

Matthew Paris, a Benedictine monk at St Albans Abbey, said of the beast, 'We believe that this was the only elephant ever seen in England.' He drew the animal twice and was evidently pretty accurate, so it seems he had visited the menagerie at some time.

In 1258, after just three years at the Tower, the elephant died, apparently because it had been given too much red wine to drink. The chilly English climate and cramped quarters probably hadn't helped.

Unlike Matthew's correct illustrations, a bestiary book of the same period was sometimes quite wide of the mark in its description of an elephant's habits:

There is an animal called an elephant; his nose is called a trunk because he uses it to put food in his mouth; the trunk is like a snake and is protected by a rampart of ivory. Elephants have a lively intelligence and memory. They move about in herds, flee from mice and mate with their backs to each other. They live for three hundred years; pregnancy lasts for two years, nor do they give birth more than once and never to several young but to only one. They have no desire to mate. If, however, they want to have offspring, they go to the east, near the earthly paradise where a tree called mandragora grows. The elephant's mate picks a fruit from the tree and gives it to him. After they have both eaten it, she seduces him, they mate and she at once conceives. When the time comes for her to give birth, she goes to a pond and the water comes up to her udder. The male elephant guards her while she gives birth because the dragon is the enemy of the elephant.

R. Barber, *Bestiary*

19th – King Edward Crowned

King Edward I was crowned on 19 August 1274. He had been king since the death of his father, Henry III, in November 1272, but had been abroad on his way home from the Crusades. England was at peace for once. No one disputed Edward's right to be king, so he didn't hurry home – hence the belated coronation.

*

However, on this day in 1388, things were far less peaceful. The Scots defeated the English at the Battle of Otterburn, in Northumberland. (Although some sources say it was fought on 5 August, and others give 19 August.)

In the troubled reign of Richard II, a truce had recently expired between England and Scotland, and the Scots decided to take advantage of the power struggle that existed between King Richard and his nobles by mounting a series of major cross-border raids. In the summer of 1388 James, Earl of Douglas led an excursion of around 6,000 men across the border into England, invading as far south as Durham, burning and looting along the way.

The Earl of Northumberland sent his son, Henry 'Hotspur' Percy (see 21 July), to intercept the marauding Scots as they returned north. During a preliminary skirmish, Hotspur and Douglas met face to face in combat; in the ensuing encounter Hotspur's silk banner was captured by Douglas – a blow to Percy dignity. Heading back to the border with his trophy and the ill-gotten gains of his marauding campaign, Douglas paused to lay siege to the castle at Otterburn. But Hotspur, true to his name, was galloping up behind. One chivalric version of the story says that Douglas paused on purpose to allow Hotspur the chance to regain his colours; another has it that Douglas simply thought the matter was already settled. In either case, Hotspur's arrival at Otterburn in the early evening took the Scots by surprise. However, the Scots quickly organised themselves and launched a counter-attack. The fierce fighting continued through the night and, eventually, the Scots won a decisive victory; but the victory came at a high price – Douglas was killed in the fighting. Although Hotspur and twenty-one other knights were captured by the Scots, his reputation as a valiant hero and leader survived.

20th – Easing Gout

This was the time of year to prepare a noble medicine to ease a man of gout, according to a fifteenth-century leechbook:

Take ripe elderberries and ripe berries of walwort [the European dwarf elder] and take an earthen pot and strew salt therein. And strew of either berries three handfuls and let it stand a day or two and it will go all to water, and keep that pot in the earth always cold that no heat may come thereto. And when though hast ache of gout, anoint the ache by the fire and afterwards shall the ache soon slacken ... These berries must be gathered in harvest between St Mary's days – the feast of the Assumption, 15 August, and the Nativity of the Virgin, 8 September.

W. R. Dawson, *A Leechbook of the Fifteenth-Century*

21st – A Royal Visit

The king, Edward IV, wrote to the Mayor of York on 21 August 1479 concerning a forthcoming visit from the King of Scots' sister:

To our trusty and well beloved the mayor and his brethren of our city of York, we greet you well, letting you witt [know] how it is agreed betwixt us and our dearest cousin and brother, the king of Scots that our right dear cousin his sister shall in all goodly haste arrive in this our realm for to come towards our town of Nottingham for her marriage, so that with God's mercy she shall be at our city of York upon Saturday the ninth day of October next coming, for which cause we desire you and pray you that with the worshipful persons of our said city are ready to meet and receive her into the same, and that for the time of her being there you will make her and all other in her company such loving and hearty cheer, as we therefore may have cause to give unto you our right especial thanks. Given under our signet at our town of Guildford the twenty-first day of August.

L. C. Attreed, *York House Books*, vol. 1

22nd – Minutes of Regicide

As noted in the minutes of a York City Council meeting in 1485:

On this day, at Redemore near Leicester there was fought a battle between our Lord King Richard III and others of his nobles on the one part, and Harry [Henry Tudor], Earl of Richmond, and others of his followers on the other part. In this battle the foresaid King Richard, in the third year of his reign, John, Duke of Norfolk, Thomas [*sic*], Earl of Lincoln, Thomas, Earl of Surrey, son of the aforesaid duke, Francis, Viscount Lovell … Sir Richard Ratcliff and Sir Robert Brackenbury … with many other knight, squires and gentlemen were killed.

The council hadn't got all its facts right: John (not Thomas), Earl of Lincoln, Thomas, Earl of Surrey, and Francis, Viscount Lovell (King Richard's Lord Chamberlain), all survived to fight another day. The council then included this epitaph to King Richard in its minutes:

It was shown that ... King Richard, late mercifully reigning upon us, was, through great treason ... piteously slain and murdered, to the great heaviness of this city ...

P. W. Hammond and A. F. Sutton (eds),
Richard III – The road to Bosworth Field

23rd – The Trial of William Wallace

The famous Scotsman, William Wallace, had become the hated enemy of King Edward I. Edward put a price on his head and ordered the Scots nobles to deliver Wallace to him.

Wallace joined Sir John Comyn and Sir Simon Fraser as they defeated three English armies in a single day at the Battle of Rosslyn on 24 February 1303.

On 3 August 1305, Wallace was captured just north of Glasgow. He was taken prisoner by the underhanded actions of Sir John Menteith, who had been made Sheriff of Dumbarton by King Edward. Wallace was escorted south to Carlisle and then paraded, bound hand and foot, the length of England to London. Wallace was tried in Westminster Hall on 23 August 1305. A list of his crimes, including murder and treason, was read out. Wallace denied he was guilty of treason – after all, he had never sworn allegiance to Edward – but the verdict and the punishment were decided even before the trial proceedings began. Wallace would suffer a traitor's death, being hanged, drawn and quartered. Wallace was tied to a wooden hurdle and dragged though the streets of London to Smithfield, just outside the city walls. There he was hanged from the gallows but cut down while he still lived. He was then disemboweled before his head was struck off and his body cut into pieces. The quarters of Wallace's body were sent to Berwick,

Newcastle-upon-Tyne, Stirling and Perth – a stark warning to other would-be rebels of the price to be paid for treason. Wallace's head was hoisted on a spike above London Bridge.

If Edward thought this would be the end of the matter – that Wallace would be forgotten – he was wrong. The people of Scotland told tales of their hero, recalling his deeds for future generations.

http://www.educationscotland.gov.uk/scotlandshistory/
warsofindependence/executionofwallace/index.asp

24th – Ela, Countess of Salisbury

On this day in 1261, Ela, Countess of Salisbury died at Lacock Abbey in Wiltshire. She had been born at Amesbury, Wiltshire, in 1187. She was a wealthy English heiress and Countess of Salisbury in her own right, succeeding to the title in 1196 when her father, William FitzPatrick, Earl of Salisbury, died. That same year, despite being only nine years old, she was married to William Longespée [or Longspear], an illegitimate half-brother of kings Richard I and John of England. William took the title Earl of Salisbury by right of his marriage to Ela.

There is a story that, shortly after her father's death but prior to her marriage, Ela was imprisoned in a castle in Normandy by her father's brother, who wanted her title, lands and wealth. She was supposedly rescued by William Talbot, a knight who sang ballads beneath castle windows across Normandy, until Ela heard him and joined him in song. If this really happened, it may be the reason for her hasty wedding, so her husband could ensure her safety from covetous relations.

Her husband, William Longespée, was an illegitimate son of King Henry II of England by his mistress Ida de Tosny. He and Ela had eight or possibly nine children. In 1225, William was shipwrecked off the coast of Brittany and spent months recovering at a monastery in France. He eventually returned home to England, but perhaps the journey proved too much for him because he died shortly thereafter at Salisbury Castle on 7 March 1226. Following his death, Ela held the post of Sheriff of Wiltshire for two years, taking on her husband's duties.

In 1238, Ela entered Lacock Abbey in Wiltshire as a nun. She had founded the abbey for sisters of the Augustinian order in 1229 and became abbess there in 1240. She kept the post of abbess until 1257 when she retired. Ela died on 24 August 1261, aged seventy-four, and was buried in the abbey.

Her numerous descendants included the English kings Edward IV and Richard III, Mary, Queen of Scots, and Sir Winston Churchill.

https://en.wikipedia.org/wiki/
Ela_of_Salisbury,_3rd_Countess_of_Salisbury

25th – York's Proclamation of Allegiance

Having realised their beloved king, Richard III, was no more (see 22 August), just a day or two later, the city of York thought to reconcile itself with the new regime; hence, the mayor ordered this proclamation to read out across the city:

That the mayor [Nicholas Lancaster] and others shall ride unto the king's grace, Henry the seventh, on behalf of the city, beseeching his grace to be a good and gracious lord unto this city, as his noble progenitors have been before, and to confirm of his most abundant grace all the liberties, freedoms, etc. that they granted …

L. C. Attreed, *York House Books,* vol. 2

26th – The Hundred Years War

On 26 August 1346, the first major engagement of the Hundred Years War took place in northern France. King Edward III and the English army had just crossed the River Somme and, knowing the forces of King Philip of France were fast approaching, had taken up position on a ridge between the villages of Crécy and Wadicourt. Edward made his headquarters at a windmill on the highest point of the ridge.

Edward, Prince of Wales, otherwise known as the Black Prince, commanded the right division of the English army, assisted by the earls of Oxford and Warwick and Sir John Chandos. The left division was commanded by the Earl of Northampton. Each division had spearmen in the rear, dismounted knights and men-at-arms in the centre and, in the front line, archers with their longbows. Edward had yet to show the French what the English bowmen – men of humble birth – could do against King Philip's finest. The English reserves were based at the windmill, commanded by King Edward.

Philip's army began to arrive at the Crécy–Wadicourt ridge at around midday on 26 August. A party of French knights reconnoitred the English position and advised Philip that the army should make camp and be fresh to fight the next day. Philip agreed but many of his arrogant nobles wanted to deal with the upstart English army, with its low-born archers, immediately. The French king was forced to allow the attack to go ahead that afternoon.

The Genoese formed the vanguard and the Duke d'Alençon led the following division of knights and men-at-arms; among them was the blind King John of Bohemia with two of his knights, their horses strapped either side of the old monarch's mount, the King of the Romans and the so-called King of Majorca – a ruler without a throne. The Duke of Lorraine and the Count of Blois commanded the next division, while King Philip led the rearguard.

Around 4 o'clock, the French began to move, having to march uphill on the narrow track that led to the English position. As they advanced, there was a cloudburst – rain soaked the two armies. The English archers removed their bowstrings, protecting them inside their jackets or under their hats; the Genoese crossbowmen couldn't take the same precautions with their weapons.

As the French advanced, the chronicler, Jean Froissart, describes the Genoese as whooping and shouting. Once the English were within crossbow range, the Genoese discharged their bolts, but the rain had loosened the strings of their weapons and the shots fell short. Froissart then writes: 'The English archers each stepped forth one pace, drew the bowstring to his ear, and let their arrows fly; so wholly and so thick that it seemed as snow.' The arrow storm inflicted terrible casualties on the Genoese, forcing them to retreat, much to the contempt of the French knights behind. These knights – still on horseback, unlike the English knights who dismounted to fight – rode down the Genoese, calling them cowards.

The clash of the retreating Genoese against the advancing cavalry threw the French into chaos. The following divisions of knights and men-at-arms found they were unable to move forward under the rain of English arrows. They were sitting targets for the archers.

A messenger arrived at King Edward's post by the windmill, asking for support for the Black Prince's division which was bearing the worst of the French assault. Edward is reputed to have asked whether his son was dead or wounded and, on being reassured, said 'Then I am confident he will repel the enemy without my help. Let the boy win his spurs.'

The French cavalry made repeated attempts to charge up the slope, only to come to grief, piling on top of wounded men and horses already brought down by the barrage of arrows. King Edward's five cannon trundled forward and added their fire from the flank of the English position – the first time we know of their use on a battlefield.

In the course of the battle, the aforementioned John, the blind king, was struck down with his accompanying knights riding to attack the Black Prince's position. The fight continued into the night. At around midnight, King Philip abandoned the field. The battle ended soon after, the surviving French knights and men-at-arms fleeing into the darkness while the English army remained in position for the rest of the night.

In the morning, the Welsh and Irish spearmen moved across the battlefield murdering and pillaging the wounded, sparing only those that seemed worth a ransom. English casualties were few; their opponents are said to have lost about 30,000 men, including the kings of Bohemia and Majorca, the Duke of Lorraine, the Count of Flanders, the Count of Blois, eight other counts and three archbishops. Meanwhile, King Edward marched his army north to Calais and besieged the town. Although it would take a year before the town surrendered, the French king was unable to help the townsfolk of Calais, his army so depleted after the confrontation at Crécy.

After the battle the Black Prince, according to tradition, adopted the emblem of the King of Bohemia, the three white feathers and his motto 'Ich Dien' (I serve). This is still the emblem of the Prince of Wales today.

As a further aside, Raoul, Count of Eu, the Constable of France, spent several years in captivity in England, taking part enthusiastically in activities at the English royal court, especially the tournaments and jousting. Word got back to the French king concerning Raoul's enjoyment, and upon his return to France he was tried for treason and beheaded.

http://www.britishbattles.com/100-years-war/crecy.htm

27th – Two Indictments

The court at Lincoln indicted two women on 27 August 1351: one for theft, the other for receiving stolen property:

They say that Alice, the daughter of Robert Skynnere, on the Monday after the feast of St Bartholomew, entered the house of Cecily Skynnere in the parish of St Botolph in the suburbs of Lincoln by night and secretly took and carried away a purse with twenty-eight shillings from one John de Shaftesbury sleeping in the aforesaid house.

Also, they say the aforesaid Alice went to the home of one Emma de Sleford ... with the twenty-eight shillings stolen in this way and gave them to the said Emma to receive, Emma knowing of the theft.

P. J. P. Goldberg, *Women in England, c. 1275–1525*

28th – Liverpool's Charter

On this day in 1207, King John granted the little town of Liverpool, located on the River Mersey, a charter, giving it borough status and the right to elect a mayor and aldermen.

29th – The Treaty of Picquigny

The peace treaty of Picquigny was negotiated between King Edward IV of England and Louis XI of France on 29 August 1475. Edward had invaded France in cooperation with Charles the Bold, Duke of Burgundy, landing with a force of around 16,000 troops in June. The plan was to march through Burgundian territory to Rheims. However, Charles failed to turn up and refused to allow the English to enter towns under Burgundian control. No help was forthcoming from Edward's other ally, Francis, Duke of Brittany, either. So when King Louis sent Edward word that he was willing to sign a peace treaty that offered the most generous terms to the English, Edward was eager to negotiate. The two kings met on a specially made bridge with a wooden grill between them at Picquigny, just outside Amiens.

The monarchs agreed to a seven-year truce and free trade between their countries. Louis would pay Edward 75,000 crowns immediately – basically, to bribe him to go home. After that, Louis would give him an annual pension of 50,000 crowns with pensions for many of his lords as well. The Chancellor, Thomas Rotherham, would receive 1,000 crowns a year and William Hastings, Edward's Lord Chamberlain, would have 2,000 crowns a year. There were various other provisions: Louis was to ransom the deposed Queen Margaret of Anjou, who was in Edward's custody, with 50,000 crowns, and Edward's daughter, Elizabeth of York, was to marry the Dauphin Charles when she came of age.

The chronicler, Philippe de Commines, noted that Richard, Duke of Gloucester (later Richard III), was opposed to the treaty, considering it dishonourable, and refused to participate in the negotiations. The blatant bribery led both English and French commentators to consider it unchivalrous. Louis de Bretaylle, the English envoy to Spain, complained that, in a single act, Edward had destroyed his reputation and the honour of all his previous victories.

30th – The Bishop of Ely's Woman

It was unusual but the Bishop of Ely had a woman, Juliana, in charge of his gardens at Little Downham, around 1345. Juliana kept her labourers busy, planting beans, peas and leeks and harvesting apples, pears, cherries, plums, nuts and vegetables: enough for the manor kitchens and a surplus to sell for profit. The work was hard, the soil so heavy that her workers broke their spades and had to be given better, stouter tools. Juliana was too busy ever to marry but leased meadows and a fishery from the manor, in her own right. Unfortunately, the wage she was paid by the bishop isn't recorded.

T. McLean, *Medieval English Gardens*

31st – The Death of Henry V

On the last day of August in 1422, the hero of Agincourt, Henry V, died at the Château de Vincennes, in France. He was apparently suffering from dysentery, contracted during the siege of Meaux. He was just thirty-five years old. His son and successor, Henry VI, was still a baby, just nine months old; his reign would see endless trouble for England.

SEPTEMBER

1st – The English Pope

Nicholas Breakspear(e), the only Englishman ever to be Pope, known as Adrian IV, died on 1 September 1159 at Anagni, near Rome, after just five years in power (see 4 December).

2nd – An Orphan's Inheritance

Around this date in 1462, the mayor and aldermen of London were worried that an elderly physician, Haymen Voet, who had applied to them for permission to marry a city orphan, might already have a wife. In medieval times, the city authorities acted as guardians for orphans – but these youngsters weren't necessarily orphans in the modern sense of having lost both parents: if their father died they qualified as orphans; mothers didn't count, hence the phrase 'widows and orphans'.

In this case, Alice Heydon, the bride-to-be, had inherited a legacy and the authorities feared that Voet might simply want her money. Added to this, there was the unresolved doubt that he may be married to someone else. So although the mayor did grant a licence for Voet to wed Alice, he was obliged to give securities before they handed him her inheritance, in case a church court, at a later date, found he had married her bigamously and annulled their union. If this were to happen, Voet was obliged to return her legacy to the chamberlain.

The doubts about his marital status may have been exacerbated because Voet was a foreigner, perhaps Dutch, who may or may not have had a wife back home.

S. McSheffrey, *Marriage, Sex and Culture in Late Medieval London*

3rd – The Coronation of Richard the Lionheart

On this day in 1189, Richard the Lionheart was crowned at Westminster. In the ceremony, the king took the crown from the altar and handed it to the archbishop to place on his head. This wasn't how it was usually done. Despite it being midday, a bat, disturbed from its roost in a dark corner of Westminster Abbey, fluttered around Richard's head as he was crowned and continued to annoy the king on his throne. The appearance of this creature of the darkness seemed to have immediate repercussions. A group of wealthy Jews came with a gift for the king, but the crowds around the abbey, already afire with the new monarch's crusading zeal, determined to get the crusade off to a flying start by killing the Jews. As the Jewish community in London was decimated, word spread northwards and a wave of fanaticism took hold. Jews were slaughtered in towns all along the Great North Road, culminating months later in a massacre and mass suicide in York.

*

Also on this day in 1323, Roesia (Rose), the daughter of a wealthy London merchant, Thomas Romayn, married her father's business partner, John de Burford (Bureford), a pepperer, i.e. a grocer, and Sheriff of London in 1303–04. Rose was actively engaged in her husband's spice trade, as well as running her own business as a wool merchant, exporting English wool to France and Flanders.

Among their main customers was the Royal Wardrobe, a state office that supervised expenses of the king's household. Queen Isabella, wife of Edward II, had commissioned a cloak from Roesia, to be decorated with coral as a gift for the Pope. Husband John had lent money to Edward II for his failed war efforts against the Scots; when John died in

1322, the debt was still outstanding. As her husband's executrix, Roesia was obliged to collect payment, petitioning the Royal Wardrobe and the Exchequer on at least five occasions without success. Knowing the royal coffers were probably empty, Roesia asked the king if she could offset the money he owed against the taxes due on her wool exports – the cash-strapped monarch agreed, saying 'Make it so'.

Roesia also took on the management of her husband's spice business and acquired extensive properties in Kent, Surrey and Sussex which were inherited by her son James, after her death. But business didn't always run smoothly for Roesia, as noted in the Calendar of Pleas and Memoranda Rolls, p.3:

Letter from the mayor, aldermen and commonality of London to the mayor, barons and bailiffs of Dover on behalf of Roesia, widow of John de Boreford of London, whose goods have been arrested in Dover for the payment of £9. They are requested to notify the cause of this arrest by the bearer.

4th – Rotten Fish

On this day in 1372, the Saturday after the feast of St Giles, Margery Hore, a London fishwife, was brought before the mayor and aldermen, accused of selling 'fish called soles [that were] stinking, rotten and unwholesome for the use of man'. Margery admitted her guilt and it was ordered that:

She should have the punishment of the pillory ordained for women called the 'thewe' for her aforesaid fraud and deceit, and that the said fish should there be burnt etc., and the cause of her punishment be proclaimed there.

P. J. P. Goldberg, *Women in England, c. 1275–1525*

*

Also on this day in 1483, Thomas Wombwell of Northfleet in Kent wrote his will. Apart from leaving money to his parish church of

St Botolph, his testament – a will dealt with estates; a testament dealt with more personal possessions – bequeathed mostly barley and cattle. Four quarters of barley each were to be given to Thomas Raynold, Thomas Hyllis, John Hilles and to both his kinswomen, Alice Wombwell and Alice Pegot. John Wombwell was to have two cattle of three years in age and Agnes Clerk was to have a two-year-old bullock.

L. Boatwright, et al. (eds), *The Logge Register of PCC Wills*

5th – Canterbury Cathedral Fire

On 5 September 1174, a terrible fire destroyed much of Canterbury Cathedral. The conflagration was interpreted as an act of divine displeasure – if somewhat delayed – at the murder of Archbishop Thomas Becket more than four years earlier (see 29 December).

*

Also on this day in 1441, an indenture was drawn up at Stafford Castle between Humphrey, Earl of Buckingham, and Sir John Maynwarynge. Sir John was to receive £10 a year, the money coming from the revenues of Rothwell in Northamptonshire, half to be paid at Easter, half at Michaelmas, for the rest of his life. In return, Sir John would in time of peace serve the earl in his household, attending whenever summoned.

In time of war, whether at home or overseas, Sir John had to be ready – with reasonable warning – to bring men-at-arms and archers, wages to be paid by the king or his captain (i.e. commander-in-chief) for the duration. If Sir John should take any 'prisoners, prizes and winnings, gotten by way of fortune or adventure of war', the Earl of Buckingham was to be awarded one-third of the ransom or booty.

A. C. Reeves, *Some of Humphrey Stafford's Military Indentures*

6th – Alms for the Poor

On this day in 1464, probate was granted for the will of William Rotheley of Dartford in Kent. He gave money for repairs to no less than ten local churches, including his own parish church in Dartford where he wished to be buried in the Lady Chapel, beside his wife.

William was especially generous in his alms for the poor:

At the day of my burying, every man, woman and child thereto coming, taking alms [i.e. in need of charity] every creature [to have] 1*d*. To thirteen poor men and women for to be clothed all new, that is to say in shirts, breeches, smocks [women's undershifts], hosen, shoes, gowns, kirtles and hoods and in such cloth as is most profitable to [suitable for] them, after the discretion of my executors, and that they have meat and drink at my month's mind.

No. 5 in the *Godyn Register of PCC Wills*, Canterbury.

A month's mind was an occasion held a month after a death. At a time when bodies couldn't be kept in cold storage, a funeral was held as soon as possible. This meant that relatives and friends couldn't always be informed in time to attend the service and burial itself, but they could come to the month's mind instead to pay their respects and give the deceased a good send-off.

7th – John the Gardener's Practical Guide

In the fourteenth century, John the Gardener of Kent wrote a practical guide to gardening in English – thought to be the first such handbook – in poetical form. These are his instructions for planting saffron-crocus, *Crocus sativus,* corms or bulbs, a task best done on this day or next week:

Saffron will have without lesying [lying]
Beds y-made well with dyng [dung]
Forsooth, if they shall bear [flower]
They should be set in the month of September,

Three days before St Mary day nativity [8 September]
Or the next week thereafter; so must it be.
With a dibble you shall him set.
That the dibble before be blunt and great:
Three hands deep they must be set.

T. McLean, *Medieval English Gardens*

Saffron, despite being home-grown, was more expensive than any of the exotic spices from faraway lands. This was because each saffron-crocus flower only produces one central stigma and it took – according to one expert – 4,320 stigmas to produce just one ounce of the precious spice. Every stigma had to be picked by hand. The town of Saffron Walden in Essex must, at one time, have specialised in growing these pretty little flowers and, in medieval times, English saffron was considered to be of the highest quality.

Not only was saffron used to flavour and colour food, it could be used as a yellow dye. The illuminators of medieval manuscripts would mix a dash of saffron with egg-white and apply it as a golden glaze to enhance their miniatures or illustrations. It was also believed to have medicinal properties and was added to cordials as a tonic for the heart.

Here is a delicious late summer or autumnal recipe from King Richard II's chef: gourd soup. Two courgettes (zucchini), a small pumpkin or a large butternut squash could be used in this 'gourdes in potage':

Take young gourds. Pare them and carve them into pieces. Cast them into good broth [stock], adding a good portion of minced onions. Take cooked pork, grind it and mix it with egg yolks [the egg yolks are omitted from the modern version but would have added to the colour and thickened the soup]. Add saffron and salt and serve it forth with sweet powder.

L. J. Sass, *To the King's Taste*

Sweet powder, or *poudre douce* as it was often called, can be made by mixing ½ teaspoon of ginger, ¼ teaspoon of cinnamon, a dash of nutmeg and a tablespoon of brown sugar.

8th – Richard the Lionheart's Birth

On this day in 1157, the future king, known as Richard the Lionheart, was born into one of the most ambitious and quarrelsome families in the land – the Plantagenets – but Richard would hold his own. He was the third surviving child of Henry II, one of the most formidable of English kings, who ruled more land in France than the French king. Henry's domains stretched from the Scottish border to the Pyrenees. His father was twenty-four when Richard was born and his mother, the beautiful, accomplished and self-confident Eleanor, Duchess of Aquitaine was about thirty-five. Neither of his parents spoke English. Their first son, William, had died as a baby. Their second son, Henry, later known as the Young King, was two when Richard was born, and their daughter Matilda was one. There would be two more daughters and two more sons.

Richard was born in Oxford, close to the site of Worcester College today, at Beaumont Palace, built by his grandfather, Henry I. Richard became his mother's favourite, but he probably saw little of his parents when he was small. After his birth, he was given into the care of a wet-nurse called Hodierna, who brought him up with her own son, born the same day. His name was Alexander of Neckham and he grew up to be a great scholar. When Richard became king, he made sure Hodierna was well provided for.

As he grew older, Richard saw more of his parents. Aged seven, his mother took him and his sister Matilda to join their father in Normandy; at nine he was in Anjou with his father. He received an excellent intellectual education and a thorough training in the art of war. A splendid horseman, he enjoyed hunting and took pleasure in the legend that his family was descended from the Devil, which he used to say explained their behaviour.

Eleanor was determined Richard should be Duke of Aquitaine, succeeding to her title when the time came. She governed her domains of Poitou and Aquitaine from 1168, with Richard at her side, and he learned the lessons well. At the age of twelve, he was invested as Count of Poitou and two years later as Duke of Aquitaine. He revelled in the troubadour culture of southern France and wrote poetry and songs and loved music, conducting the choir in his chapel so they should 'sing good and loud'.

Richard was tall, perhaps 6 feet 5 inches, with reddish-auburn hair and piercing blue eyes. He had a sense of humour and, according to a disapproving clerical chronicler, could keep his companions in fits of laughter. He could be kind, charming and generous, and alternatively ruthlessly cruel; like all his family he had a terrible temper. Daring and brave, he would become an inspiring leader of men and one of the best generals of his time.

Family quarrels gave Richard his first experience of war. In 1173 he, the Young King and their younger brother, Geoffrey, backed by their mother, took up arms against their father in a war that lasted eighteen months, until Henry II fought them to a standstill and was reconciled with his sons. Richard was just seventeen. He and his brothers began fighting each other but, when he was twenty-five, his situation changed with the unexpected death of the Young King. Richard was now heir to the throne of England (see 3 September).

http://www.historytoday.com/richard-cavendish/birth-richard-lionheart#sthash.rFkLEihK.dpuf

9th – Trade Dispute

Christopher Bell, a tiler of York, had been involved in a quarrel with other citizens: William Garland, a spurrier (spur maker), Thomas Rede and Thomas Tod, both tilers like Christopher, John Spynke, a cordwainer (shoemaker), John Forster, a barber, Thomas Watson, a dyer, and William Miller, a miller. Thomas Saxton and John Stokesley had been appointed as arbiters between Christopher and the others, to sort out the problem.

On 9 September 1476, the mayor and council decided that both parties:

Shall from henceforth be full friends to each other ... as though there had never been any variance [disagreement] between them. The arbiters ordain and adjudge that from henceforth if either party trespass against the other in word or deed beyond what is reasonable, then he that trespasses shall forfeit and pay £10 without delay – half to the common use [i.e. the city coffers] without any pardon [excuse] and half to St Peter's [York Minster].

L. C. Attreed, *York House Books,* vol. I

10th – Autumn Hastens

Here is a passage from the anonymous fourteenth-century English poem, *Sir Gawain and the Green Knight,* about autumn:

But then Autumn hastens and immediately puts heart into the crops and orders them to ripen fully ... a fierce wind from the sky struggles with the sun, the leaves fall from the lime-tree and land on the ground, and all the grass which was previously green grows faded; then everything that has grown in the beginning ripens and rots, and so the year runs past in many a yesterday, and winter returns, as nature requires.

M. Collins and V. Davis, *A Medieval Book of Seasons*

11th – The Battle of Stirling Bridge

During Scotland's wars against King Edward I of England, a significant battle was fought on this day in 1297 at Stirling Bridge on the River Forth, when the forces of Andrew Moray and William Wallace defeated the combined English forces of John de Warenne, Earl of Surrey, and Hugh de Cressingham, the hated Treasurer of Scotland, appointed by King Edward. The English commanders planned that the army should cross the River Forth at Stirling. The wooden bridge was the safest place to cross as the river widened to the east and the marshland of Flanders Moss lay to the west, but it was very narrow.

William Wallace and Andrew Moray, the Scottish leaders, had arrived north of Stirling before the English army. They watched from the hilltop as the English force, which included Welsh and Scots knights, bowmen and foot soldiers, made camp south of the river. The English had between 200 and 300 cavalry and 10,000 foot soldiers, compared to the Scots' thirty-six horsemen and 8,000 on foot.

John de Warrene gave orders for the English army to cross Stirling Bridge to face the Scots the next morning. At dawn, the English began to cross the bridge, but John de Warrene was still in bed in Stirling Castle. He arrived late and recalled his men. Two Dominican friars were sent to negotiate the surrender of the Scots with Wallace and Moray. They were told by Wallace to return to de Warrene and:

Tell your commander that we are not here to make peace but to do battle, defend ourselves and liberate our kingdom. Let them come on, and we shall prove this in their very beards.

John de Warrene called a council of war but ignored the advice of a Scottish knight, Richard Lundie, who said 'My Lords, if we go on to the bridge we are dead men'. Hugh de Cressingham urged de Warrene to cross quickly and finish the Scots. Over the next few hours, the English cavalry, led by Hugh de Cressingham, slowly made their way over the wooden bridge and waited in the loop of the River Forth. Wallace and Moray watched, prepared their men for battle and seized the opportunity to send their spearmen to attack, cutting off the escape route back across the bridge. The English knights were trapped, their horses floundering in the marshy ground as the Scots forced them back to the river. In an hour, the Scots had slaughtered them, although a few English knights managed to fight their way back across the bridge. A small number of foot soldiers swam to safety on the south bank, but the rest were cut down.

John de Warrene had the wooden bridge set on fire and demolished to keep the Scots from following as he retreated to Berwick. Hugh de Cressingham, detested by the Scots, was flayed alive; legend says that Wallace had his skin fashioned into a sword-belt. Andrew Moray was seriously wounded during the battle. He never recovered, dying two months later. The Scottish knight, Richard Lundie, switched sides after the battle of Stirling Bridge, joining Wallace in the fight against King Edward.

http://www.educationscotland.gov.uk/scotlandshistory/
warsofindependence/battleofstirlingbridge/

12th – Murder by Drowning

On this day – although the year isn't given – Elizabeth Taillour and Alice Rolff, two London silkwomen, waylaid a rival, Elizabeth Knollys. Grabbing the unfortunate victim, Taillour and Rolff drowned her in a tub and then tried to conceal the murder by burning the body and then throwing the charred remains into a latrine pit. The corpse must have gone undiscovered for weeks because the inquest wasn't held until November. Taillour confessed and was sentenced to hang but Rolff said she was pregnant. The death sentence would then be delayed until after the birth but, in this case, a jury of midwives proved that Rolff was lying about her condition. Both women were hanged.

B. Holsinger, 'Sin City' in *Medieval Life*

13th – Quince Recipe

Here is a recipe using quinces:

Quynade. Take quinces and peel them clean, cast them in a pot and cast thereto rosewater. Do it over the fire and cover. Let it boil a good while until they [the fruit] be soft; and if they will not be soft, crush them small in a mortar, pass them through a strainer. Take good almond milk and caste it in a pot and boil it. Take white wine and vinegar and caste thereto the milk and let it stand a while. Then take a clean cloth and pour the milk upon it and with a platter, strike it off the cloth, into the pot. Gather up the quinces and add to the cream and heat it over the fire. Take a portion of cloves, ginger and grains of Paradise [a kind of pepper] of equal amounts; take enough sugar, a little salt and saffron and mix all together. When you dress it forth 'plant it' with foil of silver.

T. Austin, *Two Fifteenth-Century Cookery-Books, c. 1430–50*

14th – Beeswax and Honey

Around this time of year, Brother John of Beaulieu Abbey would tend to the beehives in the monastery's kitchen garden. He would collect the wax and the honey. The honey would be sold but the beeswax was far more valuable to the monks for making the highest quality church candles.

T. McLean, *Medieval English Gardens*

15th – Continence in the Streets

On this day in September 1413, on the Feast of the Exaltation of the Cross, the mayor, Henry Holeway, the aldermen and bailiffs of Southampton, ordained:

That all prostitutes holding the common lodging in East Street be entirely removed from the said street, and that neither they nor any other women of their kind of life be admitted to live in or hold from anyone else any tenement or cottage in the same street, and especially on account of the continence of those passing through the said street or setting out from home to the churches of St Mary, Holy Trinity and St Andrews.

So that the above ordinance be held and observed in perpetuity they had it enrolled in the Black Book of the said town.

P. J. P. Goldberg, *Women in England c. 1275–1525*

In this case, as often in medieval writing, the word 'continence' could refer to sexual matters as well as bowel control. Therefore, it seems the prostitutes had been tempting the local menfolk to sin, even on their way to church, and too many had been incontinent and given in to the temptations of sex.

16th – Wedding Gifts

Around this date in 1497, Christopher Kechyn gave his intended bride, Margaret Broke, a ruby and sapphire ring and an emerald ring. In return,

Margaret's employer, as her guardian, gave Christopher 20 marks in gold as her dowry. Rather morbidly, Christopher later gave Margaret his deceased wife's wedding gown of violet ingrained with grey, more jewellery, lengths of cloth to make more gowns with various furs to trim them, a silver-gilt cup, a gold belt with a silver buckle and a pendant. She gave him a bittern's foot mounted with silver and gold and a waistcoat of fine wool trimmed with white lamb and a silk lace to fasten it.

S. McSheffrey, *Marriage, Sex and Culture in Late Medieval London*

17th – To Autumnal Good Health

According to a fifteenth-century medical text, here are the instructions for keeping healthy this month:

In September, all fruit that is ripe is good to eat, and blood is good to let [phlebotomy]. For whoso letteth him blood on the 17th day for the dropsy, neither the frenzy [insanity] or the falling-evil [epilepsy] that year he shall have, no doubt.

W. R. Dawson, *A Leechbook of the Fifteenth Century*

18th – Crab Recipe

To dress a crab. Take out all the crab-meat and lay it in a little vinegar, take and put a little wine thereto and strain all through a sieve. Take powdered ginger, cinnamon and sugar and mix them all together [with the crab-meat] and put it in the shell. Set it on the fire until it is boiled. Cast powdered cinnamon and sugar upon it and serve it forth.

G. A. J. Hodgett, *Stere htt Well*

Perhaps not to our modern tastes – fish with sugar – but sugar and sweet spices, like cinnamon, went with just about anything and everything, to suit the medieval palate.

19th – The Battle of Poitiers

Edward the Black Prince, son and heir to King Edward III, with English troops under Sir John Chandos and with Gascon troops under the Captal de Buch – less than 7,000 men in all – was carrying out raids from Bordeaux into central France in September 1356. He was turning south-westwards from the Loire valley, being pursued by the superior forces of King John II of France. The two armies met just east of Poitiers on 17 September, but a truce was agreed for 18 September because it was a Sunday. This day's delay allowed the English to secure themselves a position near Nouaillé, south of Poitiers, where thickets and marshes surrounded the confluence of the Miosson and Clain rivers.

Forgetful of the lessons of Crécy (see 26 August), fought a decade earlier, the French launched a series of assaults in which their knights, bogged down, became easy targets for the Black Prince's archers with their longbows. King John II himself led the last French charge and was taken prisoner, along with thousands of his knights. These losses left France open to brutal raids by its enemies and set off numerous uprisings by disgruntled French peasants. The French government, unable to restore order, was forced to sign over nearly one-third of France to the English – including the provinces of Béarn, Gascony, Poitou and Rouergue – according to the Treaty of Brétigny, signed later that year (1360). Raising the huge ransom for John II upset the peasants still further because of the taxation forced upon them.

http://www.britannica.com/event/
Battle-of-Poitiers-French-history-1356

20th – Fornicating with Priests

At the London Borough Court, this case was heard on 20 September 1422:

They say that Alice, wife of John Cheyney, and Isabel Cobham on 20 September and on many other occasions, committed fornication with two priests and afterwards with various other unknown men, and that they are common whores.

P. J. P. Goldberg, *Women in England, c. 1275–1525*

21st – The Birth of Richard Plantagenet

On 21 September 1411, Richard Plantagenet was born, the only son of Richard of Conisburgh, Earl of Cambridge, the second son of Edmund of Langley, Duke of York and Isabella of Castile. Edmund of Langley was the fourth surviving son of King Edward III. Richard's mother was Anne Mortimer, sister to King Richard II's heir, Edmund Mortimer, but she died giving birth to him. Richard had an elder sister, Isabel, who would marry the Earl of Essex.

When Richard was not yet four years old, his father was executed by Henry V (see 5 August) in 1415, for plotting to place his brother-in-law, Edmund Mortimer, on the throne. However, after the death of his father's brother, Edward, Duke of York at the battle of Agincourt, Richard succeeded to his vast estates and the title. His wardship was granted to Ralph Neville, Earl of Westmorland, who in 1424 betrothed Richard, aged thirteen, to his nine-year-old daughter, Cecily.

In 1436, York lead an expedition to France, where he acquitted himself so well that he was appointed Lieutenant of France in 1440, taking on the role previously occupied by John, Duke of Bedford, the brother of Henry V. Cecily accompanied him, and three of their children – Edward, Edmund and Elizabeth – were born there.

In 1443, John Beaufort, Duke of Somerset, grandson of John of Gaunt's illicit union with Katherine Swynford, was sent to France to relieve Gascony, being given all the money and resources being denied to York to maintain the borders of Normandy. This led to much ill-feeling on York's part, since he was attempting to finance the protection of Normandy from his own purse, never receiving the promised reimbursements from the coffers of King Henry VI.

Despite full royal backing at every turn, Somerset's mission was a failure and he died on his return to England in disgrace – rumours suggested he may have committed suicide. Against York's advice, peace was negotiated with the French and York returned to England in 1445, attaching himself to the pro-war party, headed by the king's paternal uncle, Humphrey, Duke of Gloucester, in opposition to the policies of Cardinal Henry Beaufort. The lieutenancy of France was given to Somerset's younger brother and successor, Edmund Beaufort, 2nd Earl of Somerset, which exacerbated York's resentment of the Beaufort family.

The death in suspicious circumstances of Humphrey, Duke of Gloucester in 1447 made Richard of York the first Prince of the Blood and the premier descendant of Lionel of Antwerp, Duke of Clarence, Edward III's second son. By the strict laws of primogeniture, this made Richard the heir of Edward III, giving him a slightly better claim to the throne than Henry VI, who was descended from Edward's third son, John of Gaunt, Duke of Lancaster. Concerned by York's increasingly powerful influence, the king appointed him as Lord Lieutenant of Ireland in 1448, a convenient means of keeping him out of the country while the Beaufort faction was high in royal favour.

In 1450 rebellion broke out against Henry VI's rule in Kent and Sussex, led by Jack Cade (see 8 May). York landed at Beaumaris on Anglesey and, resisting attempts to waylay him, marched on London. Although he insisted on his loyalty to the king, York demanded better government and that those responsible for the loss of Normandy, which had recently fallen to the French, face punishment. Parliament elected York's chamberlain, Sir William Oldhall, as speaker and Somerset was placed in the Tower for his own protection. In 1452, York advanced on London from Ludlow and demanded recognition as the heir of Henry VI, he laid before the king a list of accusations against Somerset, but still swore fealty to the king. At a meeting at Dartford, a temporary agreement was reached.

After years of a barren marriage to the king, Margaret of Anjou announced she was pregnant in 1453, a crushing blow to York's hopes of one day inheriting the throne – this, despite York being ten years older than the king. But then, in August 1453, aged thirty-two, Henry VI began to exhibit signs of serious mental illness. By means of a 'sudden fright' he descended into a trance-like state and the political scene was transformed.

22nd – A Royal Feast

On this day in 1387, the royal cooks were preparing for a great feast the next day to be given by King Richard II and his uncle, John of Gaunt, Duke of Lancaster. The incredible shopping list for the event still exists but there is no indication of who the guests were to be or how many people were invited. The amount of meat was huge:

14 salted oxen

2 fresh oxen

120 sheeps' heads and their carcasses

12 boars

14 calves

140 pigs

300 marrow bones

Lard and grease – enough

3 tons of salted venison [this may mean 3 tuns which were large
    barrels, rather than ton weights]

3 does [?] of fresh venison

50 swans

210 geese

50 larded capons [castrated cock chickens]

96 other capons

720 hens

400 conies [adult rabbits]

4 pheasants

5 herons and bitterns

6 kids [young goats]

60 pullets for jelly

144 pullets to roast

1,200 pigeons

144 partridges

96 rabbits [baby rabbits]

144 curlews

12 cranes

Wild fowl – enough

120 gallons milk

12 gallons cream

11 gallons curds

12 bushels apples

11,000 eggs

L. J. Sass, *To the King's Taste*

What more can I say?

23rd – The Fishmongers' Last Accounts

Richard Darneton, a London fishmonger, made his will on 23 September 1485 – one of a number of citizen-fishmongers who had their wills granted probate consecutively at the Archbishop of Canterbury's Prerogative Court on 14 October 1485, at his palace at Knole in Kent. Richard Darneton wanted to be buried in the cloister of St Magnus' church where he was a parishioner. He left 10 marks and a quarter of his 'stuff of household' to his apprentice, John Pery, so long as he finished his term of apprenticeship with a fellow citizen-fishmonger, John Crouch. Another fishmonger, Philip Seman, was to have Richard's shop in Bridge Street. Among other fishmongers who drew up their wills that summer was Thomas Goldwell who had made his on 23 July, but there is no way of knowing the exact date when he died. He left money to the hospital of St Thomas in Southwark, to St Bartholomew's, St Mary's and to 'Elsing spetill', as well as to the prisoners in Newgate and Ludgate that they would pray for him. (Elsing Spital was founded in 1331 as a hospital for the blind, near Cripplegate.) Thomas wanted to be buried in St Margaret's church, Bridge Street, where he had his shop, but also bequeathed 3s 4d to the church of St Magnus by the Bridge for two priests there to say masses for his soul.

A third fishmonger, Stephen Long, made his will on 25 September, perhaps in a hurry as it is very short. Apart from leaving money to the same prisons as Thomas Goldwell and to four unnamed 'spetill houses' (hospitals), he left everything to his wife, Rose, making her his executrix, 'she to dispose for me as she wold I shuld do for her in like case'. He too asked to be buried in St Magnus churchyard beside London Bridge.

Should the authorities have been concerned at this sudden spate of deaths among the fishmongers of Bridge Street? Along with these three, a draper, John Bennett, made his will on 27 September, also wanting to be buried in the cloister of St Magnus' church, suggesting he too lived close by. Was there some nasty disease prevalent at the north end of London Bridge? Had these men been friends and dined together off some dubious food or caught a sickness from one another?

At least three out of the four deaths date to the opening weeks of the reign of Henry Tudor, after the Battle of Bosworth (see 22 August) and the dreaded sweating sickness was once thought to have arrived in England with his army. Modern medicine believes this was some virulent strain of influenza which could prove fatal in a few days, although it is doubtful the 'sweat' was introduced by Tudor's men because Lord Stanley had already used it as his excuse for not joining King Richard III at Nottingham, before the Tudor forces had even landed. London certainly suffered a severe outbreak of the sweating sickness just after the new king, Henry VII, arrived in the city on 7 September. Were Goldwell, Darneton, Long and Bennett among its victims, struck down in the middle of business?

T. Mount, *Everyday Life in Medieval London*

24th – Employing Women

On this day in 1461, the mayor of Bristol, William Canynges, the sheriff, Thomas Kempson, and the town council met in the Guildhall and passed the following ordinance:

That for as much as various persons of the weavers' craft ... employ and engage their wives daughters and maids, some to weave on their own looms and some to engage them to work with others of the craft, whereby many of the king's subjects, men liable to do the king service in his wars and in defence of this land and sufficiently skilled [in weaving], go vagrant and unemployed and may not work for their livelihood. Therefore, no [weavers] of Bristol from this day forward [may] put or engage his wife, daughter or maid to any such occupation of weaving at the loom upon pain of losing [the loom?] 6s 8d to be levied ... except that this act does not pertain to the wife of any [weaver] now living ... during the natural life of the said women ...

P. J. P. Goldberg, *Women in England c. 1275–1525*

Women were always paid less than men for a given job, thus employers often preferred to take on women. In time of war, when men were away, fighting, that was acceptable, but in peacetime, ordinances like this were necessary to force employers to take on men instead. Fortunately, wives were usually exempt, as in this case.

25th – The Battle of Stamford Bridge

When Edward the Confessor died in 1066, he left no direct heir (see 6 January) and the throne of England passed to Harold Godwinson, Earl of Wessex. Harold's younger brother, Tostig, who had once been the Earl of Northumbria but was now in exile in Norway, persuaded King Harald Hardrada of Norway to invade England, and to deny Tostig's brother the crown, since Hardrada insisted he too had a valid claim. Meanwhile, a second claimant to the throne of England, William the Bastard, Duke of Normandy, planned to launch his own invasion fleet. The Norwegians sailed across the North Sea by way of the Orkney Islands and landed at Riccall, near York, with a force numbering about 10,000 men. William of Normandy waited on events.

King Harold of England was well aware of both threats to his new kingdom, and he summoned his levies in July. These were free Anglo-Saxon men from the shires who owed two months of military service each year. Unfortunately, by September the two months were up and rations were low, so Harold reluctantly allowed his army to go home as they were eager to bring in the harvest. This left him with an elite force of about 3,000 mounted men known as housecarls. When the news came of the Norwegian landing, Harold galloped his men north.

The earls of Northumbria and Mercia, Morcar and Edwin, advanced their men from York and met Harald Hardrada at Fulford on 20 September. The experienced Norwegian king completely routed the earls. On the 25 September, the victorious Norsemen appointed Stamford Bridge as a meeting place for an exchange of hostages with the city of York. They were relaxing in the meadows surrounding the bridge at a crossroads twelve miles from York when they were shocked to see another Saxon army coming from the south. King Harold's men must have been exhausted: they had covered 180 miles in just four days – an incredible feat, but the Norsemen were caught completely off-guard, having discarded their chain-mail shirts and helmets in the hot sun.

A desperate delaying action by the Norwegian lookouts kept the Saxons from crossing the River Derwent while the main army frantically dressed and armed and took up position. One anonymous Norwegian held the bridge alone until he was stabbed from beneath the planks of the bridge with a long spear. The Norse army formed a triangular-shaped wall of shields to present a narrow front to the enemy but the Saxons battered the wall in fierce hand-to-hand combat which went on all day, until Harald Hardrada fell. Tostig tried vainly to rally the demoralised men, but Norse resistance crumbled with the loss of their charismatic leader; the battle became a rout in which Tostig was also slain.

The Vikings fled, pursued all the way back to their fleet at Riccall. Only twenty-four ships out of the original 200 or more were needed to return the survivors to Norway. Before the battle, King Harold had sworn that Hardrada would get 'only seven feet of English soil' for his trouble, a vow which he kept, though the man's remains were later taken back to Norway. Tostig, Harold's treacherous brother, was buried in York (see 28 September).

http://www.britainexpress.com/History/battles/
stamford-bridge.htm

26th – Ludshut Manor Court

The manor court of Ludshut (Ludshott, Hampshire) was held on this day in 1460:

John Bugenell, customary tenant, is in default [hasn't attended Court], fined 2*d*. Headley tenants of the Lord Bishop of Winchester have appropriated some of the Lord's land at Lithwodd [Lightwood], two furlongs by half a furlong. To be prosecuted by writ.

Thomas Benifold and John Farlee have not repaired their ruinous houses as ordered at last Court; ordered to repair them adequately before next Court, on pain of fine of 3*s* 4*d* each. John Hownesham and John Lenchmere have dug clay on the Lord's land at Bournes Water and turned the water there onto the land of the Lord of Bramshott. To be prosecuted by writ. The same John Lenchmere with his pigs grazed, trampled and consumed the rye and oats of the Lord's farm tenant there, to his grave loss. To be prosecuted by writ.

http://www.johnowensmith.co.uk/headley/
ludshott2rolls.htm

27th – The Feasts of St Cosmas and St Damian

For those who were unfortunate and fell ill in medieval times, there was the option, open not only to the patient but to those treating him, of addressing prayers to an appropriate patron saint. In this event, St Cosmas was a good choice as he was the patron saint of physicians. Conveniently, Cosmas's twin brother, St Damian, was the patron saint of surgeons, so between them they had medical practice sewn up. This was just as well, because their most famous miracle was performed when the saintly physician and his surgeon brother carried out the first ever limb transplant, assisted by angels. In an exquisite illuminated miniature, the operation is shown in progress but, unfortunately for the pale-skinned patient, his gangrenous leg is being replaced by that of an African – not a good colour match, but a miracle it certainly was.

Cosmas and Damian were early Christians whose feast day is celebrated on 27 September. They were born in Arabia and practised their healing arts in the seaport of Aegea in Asia Minor. They accepted no pay for their services and attracted the attention of the Roman authorities at a time when Christianity was outlawed. The brothers were arrested and tortured but, miraculously, suffered no injury from 'water, fire, air, nor on the cross'. Finally, they were beheaded with a sword on this day in AD 287. Their remains were buried in the city of Cyrus in Syria. More than two centuries later, the Emperor Justinian (AD 527–65) was cured of a serious illness after praying to the saints and, in gratitude for their aid, rebuilt and adorned their church at Constantinople, which became a celebrated place of pilgrimage in medieval times. In Rome, there is another church dedicated to Cosmas and Damian, which has the most beautiful mosaics and is still a place of pilgrimage today.

T. Mount, *Dragon's Blood & Willow Bark*

28th – The Norman Invasion

Just outside York, in 1066, the battle of Stamford Bridge ended the long years of Viking threat to England (see 25 September). Although it was a triumph for King Harold and the Saxons, their strength was depleted by the fight. On this day, the news Harold must have been dreading arrived in York: William the Bastard, Duke of Normandy, had landed on the south coast of England, at Pevensey in Sussex. The Norman had brought a huge invasion force: everything from horses and weapons and materials for raising pre-fabricated wooden castles, to a banner, blessed by the Pope, proclaiming William's right to the crown of England.

With barely time to recover from one battle, the weary Saxons now faced a worse enemy. They turned south once more and marched back, almost the length of the kingdom, as quickly as they had come (see 14 October).

*

Also on this day, in 1106 King Henry I of England defeated his eldest brother Robert, Duke of Normandy, at the battle of Tinchebrai (or Tinchebray) in the county of Mortain, in Normandy, France. When William the Conqueror had died in 1087, he had left the dukedom of Normandy to his eldest son, Robert Curthose, the kingdom of England to his second son, William Rufus, but nothing to his youngest son, Henry. Rufus had tried, unsuccessfully, to reunite England and Normandy but after his death in the New Forest (see 2 August), Henry became King of England in 1100. He was a far more able strategist and warrior than either Rufus or Robert and, after Tinchebrai, England and Normandy were again united, as they had been in the Conqueror's day.

29th – Michaelmas

More properly named the feast day of St Michael and All Angels, in medieval times this was an important date, more than just a Church festival. In England, it was one of the four quarter-days – along with Christmas, Lady Day (25 March) and St John's Day (24 June) – on which rents were due to be paid, as well as being the beginning of the Michaelmas term for both lawyers and the universities. On this day, magistrates and town counsellors were elected. The day was usually marked in England by eating a Michaelmas goose for dinner.

*

Also on this day in 1328, Joan Plantagenet, known to history as the Fair Maid of Kent, was born at the royal palace at Woodstock in Oxfordshire. She was the daughter of Edmund of Woodstock, 1st Earl of Kent, and Margaret Wake, Baroness Wake of Liddell. Edmund was a son of King Edward I and his second wife, Margaret of France, and he supported Queen Isabella and her lover, Roger Mortimer, Earl of March, against his half-brother, King Edward II. However, Edmund soon changed his mind about the haughty queen and the ambitious Mortimer. Being convinced that King Edward II, whose funeral had been held in 1327, was still alive, Edmund became involved in a conspiracy to restore him to the throne. The plot was discovered and Edmund was executed on 19 March 1330, when Joan was only two years old.

When King Edward III assumed power from his mother and Mortimer, the new queen, Philippa of Hainault, had Joan brought up at court where she became friendly with her cousin Edward the Black Prince. He was two years younger than Joan and called her his 'Jeanette'.

The French chronicler, Jean Froissart, called Joan 'the most beautiful woman in all the realm of England and the most loving'. In 1340, aged twelve, Joan secretly married Thomas Holland without the king's consent. The following year, while Thomas was abroad, Joan was forced by her family to marry William Montacute, heir of the Earl of Salisbury, when both were about thirteen years old. She later claimed that she never revealed her existing marriage with Thomas, afraid it might lead to his execution for treason.

Several years later, Holland returned and the truth came out, causing a scandal. Thomas confessed to King Edward and appealed to the Pope for his wife's return. William Montacute was unwilling to give up Joan and kept her a prisoner in her own home. It took Pope Clement VI eighteen months to decide the issue. In 1349, he finally annulled Joan's marriage to William and sent her back to Thomas with whom she lived for the next eleven years. They had five children, including Thomas, who became Earl of Kent, and John, who became, briefly, Duke of Exeter. In 1352, Joan had become 4th Countess of Kent and 5th Lady Wake of Liddell. In 1360, Thomas Holland was given the title of Earl of Kent but died shortly after.

Edward, the Black Prince, Edward III's heir and Joan's first cousin once removed, had loved her since childhood. Now she was widowed, he wanted to marry her; but the king and queen didn't want a union between their son and Joan because of her reputation. Incredibly, the lovers decided to repeat Joan's earlier indiscretion and married in secret. However, Edward's parents were persuaded and the couple had a second official wedding on 10 October 1361, at Windsor Castle, with the king and queen present.

In 1362, the Black Prince was invested as Duke of Aquitaine and the couple moved to Bordeaux in south-west France, to govern the English lands of Gascony, where they spent the next nine years in happy marriage. In a letter addressed to Joan in 1367, Edward called her 'my dearest and truest sweetheart and beloved companion'. When he returned to Bordeaux from Spain, Joan met him and they walked together, holding hands. They had two sons: Edward of Angoulême, born in 1365, who died aged six, and Richard of Bordeaux (the future Richard II), born in 1367 (see 6 January).

In 1367, Edward led an expedition to Spain to support Pedro of Castile, leading an army over the Pyrenees. On 3 April 1367, they won a brilliant victory at Najera. Edward then declared Pedro King of Castile. In gratitude, Pedro presented him with a huge pigeon's-blood ruby – still in the Imperial State Crown today, known as the Black Prince's Ruby.

Edward's army suffered badly during the Spanish campaign and the prince showed the first symptoms of a mortal disease – possibly dropsy. In 1371, Edward was very ill and returned to England on the advice of his physicians. His health declined; he realised that he was dying, so he spent time in prayer and charitable works. Edward asked his father to protect his son Richard. The Black Prince died at Westminster, aged forty-five (see 8 June). He was buried at Canterbury Cathedral.

On the death of Edward III in 1377, Richard became king. Joan was a good influence over the young king and acquired a reputation as a peacemaker, being especially popular with the common folk. On returning to London from a pilgrimage to Canterbury in 1381, during the Peasants' Revolt, she found the way barred by Wat Tyler and his rebels on Blackheath. When they recognised her, Joan was allowed to pass unharmed, saluted with kisses and given an escort for the rest of her journey.

In 1385, Joan's son, Sir John Holland, was campaigning in Scotland with his half-brother King Richard when a quarrel occurred between John and Ralph Stafford, son of the Earl of Stafford. Ralph was killed and

John sought sanctuary at the shrine of St John of Beverley. On the king's return, Holland was condemned to death. Joan pleaded with Richard for four days to spare his half-brother's life but, on the fifth day, she died, at Wallingford Castle. Richard relented and pardoned Holland.

Joan was buried as she requested in her will, not by her royal husband at Canterbury but at the Greyfriars at Stamford in Lincolnshire, beside her first husband, Thomas Holland. The Black Prince had built a chantry for her in the crypt of Canterbury Cathedral, with ceiling bosses of her face, but Thomas had been her first love.

http://www.englishmonarchs.co.uk/plantagenet_39.html

30th – Richard II's Abdication

On 30 September 1400 King Richard II was forced to abdicate the crown to his cousin, Henry Bolingbroke, Duke of Lancaster, as King Henry IV. Richard was deeply distressed at having to do this, believing God had appointed him to rule England, but perhaps the most upsetting act of betrayal came from an animal.

Richard's pet greyhound, Math, had always fawned on his royal master but chose this moment to desert him, ignore him and greet Henry instead. Henry saw this as a most auspicious sign since the greyhound was one of his heraldic badges. Henry let Math sleep on his bed; the royal pet obviously approving of the new monarch.

K. Walker-Meikle, *Medieval Pets*

OCTOBER

1st – Birth of Henry III

A future monarch of England, Henry III, King John's eldest legitimate son, was born on 1 October 1207. Henry became king just after his ninth birthday in 1216. He would have the longest reign of any English medieval king, ruling for fifty-six years until his death on 16 November 1272, at the age of sixty-five.

Henry's failures in wars against the French (in 1230 and 1242), his unsuitable choices of friends and advisors, together with the extortionate costs of his scheme to make his younger son, Edmund, King of Sicily and to aid the Pope against the Holy Roman Emperor, led to disputes with his barons and civil war.

Although Henry was extravagant and his tax demands were resented, his accounts show that he was very generous and made many charitable donations and payments for building works, including the rebuilding of Westminster Abbey, which began in 1245.

2nd – Birth of Richard III

The future king Richard III was born on this day in 1452, a Monday, at Fotheringhay Castle in Northamptonshire. His parents, Richard, Duke of York and Cecily Neville, had twelve children; Richard was the eleventh. However, not all the children survived infancy, as this near-contemporary anonymous poem, telling of Duchess Cecily's numerous pregnancies, reveals:

> Sir, aftir the tyme of longe bareynesse
> God first sent Anne, which signyfieth grace,
> In token that al her hertis hevynesse
> He, as for bareynesse, wold fro hem chace.
> Harry, Edward and Edmonde, each in his place
> Succeeded, and aftir tweyn doughtris came,
> Elizabeth and Margarete, and afterward William.
> John aftir William nexte borne was,
> Which bothe be passid to Godis grace.
> George was next, and aftir Thomas
> Borne was, which sone aftir did pace
> By the path of dethe to the hevenly place.
> Richard liveth yit; but the last of alle
> Was Ursula, to Hym whom God list calle.

P. W. Hammond and A. F. Sutton, *Richard III,
The Road to Bosworth Field*

In a recent book by Kennedy and Foxhall, *The Bones of a King – Richard III Rediscovered* (p.197), it is even suggested there was an earlier, short-lived, baby Henry, born before Anne. Of the boys, Edward, Edmund, George and Richard lived to adulthood, although Edmund died at the Battle of Wakefield in 1460 (see 30 December), aged just seventeen. Edward became King Edward IV, George was created Duke of Clarence – dying in that famous butt of malmsey wine at the Tower of London (see 18 February) – and Richard became the last Plantagenet King of England. All the girls grew up and married, with the exception of little Ursula. Anne became Duchess of Exeter, Elizabeth married the Duke of Suffolk and Margaret wed the Duke of Burgundy.

3rd – Love Letters

As we saw in earlier entries (3 May and 1 July), when Margery Paston fell in love with the family's steward, Richard Calle, her mother and brothers were duly horrified. But this was a true love match and the couple married in secret. Here is part of a love letter Richard wrote to Margery:

My own lady and mistress and, before God, very true wife, I with full sorrowful heart recommend me to you, as one that cannot be merry nor shall be, till it be otherwise with us ... It seems a thousand years ago since I spoke with you and I had rather be with you than possess all the goods in the world. Alas, alas, good lady, those that keep us asunder remember full little what they do ...I sent you a letter from London by my lad, and he told me he could not speak with you, as there was so careful a watch kept upon both him and you ... I suppose that they think we are not contracted together [married] ... for they are not well advised, remembering how plainly I spoke to my mistress [Margery's mother, Margaret Paston] at the beginning ...

I marvel much that they should take this matter so hard as I understand they do, considering it is such a case as cannot be remedied ... and there should be no obstacle against it ... I pray you let no creature see this letter. As soon as you have read it, let it be burned.

R. Virgoe, *The Illustrated Letters of the Paston Family*

Clearly, Margery couldn't bear to burn her lover's letter, else we would not know of it. The family did all they could to 'remedy' the case and undo the marriage.

Her mother, Margaret, had her daughter summoned to appear before the Bishop of Norwich to answer for her actions. Following their examination by the bishop, his verdict was promised for the week after Michaelmas, the 29 September. His judgement was that their marriage was valid and should stand. The head of the Paston family, Margery's elder brother, Sir John, demanded that it be annulled but, having calmed down, wanted a proper, official wedding to be conducted before Christmas. Margaret was far less forgiving and wrote to him:

I pray you and require you that ye take it not pensively, for I know well it goeth right near your heart, and so it doth to mine and to others. But remember you, and so do I, that we have lost of her but a worthless person, and ... if he [Calle] were dead at this hour, she should never be at my heart as she was.

H. S. Bennett, *The Pastons and their England*

So her mother now considered Margery 'a worthless person'. However, Richard Calle was far from worthless and remained as the Pastons' bailiff, serving the family loyally and honestly for years, but without being accepted as one of their number. Regarding Margery's relationship with her mother, little is known whether there was any kind of reconciliation or not. However, it seems that Margaret did at least acknowledge her daughter's children by Richard, leaving her eldest grandchild £20 in her will.

4th – The Watching Hour

When the medieval family went to bed, exhausted from their labours, soon after dusk, they would have slept soundly – the first sleep – until around midnight. In the monasteries, monks would have risen to say Matins, but lay folk could stay in bed and chat, say their prayers or maybe have sex. This period of wakefulness was called the 'watching' hour and coincided with a natural burst of brain activity in the middle of the night. For some, it was time for a snack and for the more wealthy 'a night livery' was provided and is often mentioned in lists of expenses for those travelling on business. The night livery was usually wine or ale, bread and cheese and/or cold meat, kept in a livery cupboard by the bed. For the humble citizen, it might have been a piece of bread and a sip of ale. For the literate, if they could afford to use candles, the watching hour was a good time for writing poetry, reading or, more boring, doing the accounts. After this interlude of activity, it was time for the second sleep (see 15 April), which lasted until first light.

T. Mount, *Everyday Life in Medieval London*

5th – The Edgcott Widow

Around this date in 1450, Joan Buckland, a widow from Edgcott, wrote her will. Although Joan lived on for another twelve years, dying in 1462, she wanted to make sure that whoever the women were who cared for her in her last days, they would be rewarded:

All my gowns and kirtles, that they be given to my women servants dwelling with me at my departure ... Also, to the woman that is by me at my departing, 100*s*, one silver bowl, two spoons and one gown furred with mink.

P. J. P. Goldberg, *Women in England c. 1275–1525*

6th – The Flooding of the Lincolnshire Fens

A chronicler-monk, Ingulph, recorded the following disaster of 1467:

Throughout the whole of this county and in Hoyland [near Spalding] especially, there was scarcely a house or building but what the streams of water made their way and flowed through it. Nor must you suppose that this happened hurriedly and in a cursory manner only: but continuously during a whole month the waters either stood there without flowing off, or else, being agitated by strong gusts of wind, swelled and increased still more and more, day after day. Nor did the embankments offer any effectual resistance, but on the contrary, though materials had been brought from other quarters for the purpose of strengthening them, they proved of very little service and however diligently the work might have been attended to in the daytime, as the waters swelled and rose, the spot under repair was completely laid bare during the night. Then was there grief and lamentation among all and outcries and tumult among the Hoylanders.

H. C. Darby, *The Medieval Fenland*

7th – His Master's Bath

Here are John Russell's instructions for a squire giving his master a bath, from *The Bebees' Book: Manners for the Young,* written around 1460:

If your lord wishes to bathe and wash his body clean, hang sheets round the roof, every one full of flowers and sweet green herbs, and have five or six sponges to sit upon, and a sheet over so that he may bathe there for a while, and have a sponge also for under his feet, if there be any to spare, and always be careful that the door is shut. Have a basin full of hot fresh herbs and wash his body with a soft sponge, rinse him with fair rose water, and throw it over him; then let him go to bed; but see that the bed be sweet and nice; and first put on his socks and slippers that he may go near the fire and stand on his foot-sheet, wipe him dry with a clean cloth, and take him to bed to cure his troubles.

8th – A Squire's Will

On this day in 1479, John Grene, a squire, drew up his brief will, although he would live for another six years. Having bequeathed his soul to God, Our Lady and the holy company of Heaven, he simply says he leaves the arrangements of his daughters' marriages in the hands of his wife, Kateryn. He wants Edmund Lichfield to have a silver-gilt cup and John Woode to have a plain silver one. His sister and her husband, Holgrave, John Thetford and 'my cosyn Wyndesore' are each to be given a token of remembrance at Kateryn's discretion. William Peckham is to receive a pair of sheets and a vestment, but not the best one which is to go to the church where John's first wife is buried. Everything else he possesses and his funeral arrangements are to be left to Kateryn.

L. Boatwright, et al [eds], *The Logge Register,* vol. 2

9th – The Banishment of the Jews

On 9 October 1290, all Jews – up to 16,000 of them – were officially banished from England by Edward I. The King of France had done the same a few years before; once they were banished, the Jews' possessions became the property of the Crown. England was short of money and Edward himself was deep in debt to the Jews who had been lending him huge sums to finance his wars in Wales and Scotland. Now, they became his scapegoats. He banned them from usury (money-lending at interest, forbidden for

Christians) in 1275. 1278 brought widespread arrests of Jewish men; many were hanged and 600 imprisoned in the Tower of London.

In 1290, seeing how the King of France had profited from the move, Edward banished the Jews outright. He issued writs to the sheriffs of every English county ordering them to enforce his Edict of Expulsion, a decree which required all Jews to be removed from England by All Saints' Day (1 November) that year. They were only allowed to take with them their portable belongings. Apart from a few exceptions, money, houses and properties were passed to the king. Edward's money problems were solved instantly – but not for long. Once he'd spent the money acquired from the Jews, where now could he borrow more? Hence the advent of the Italian bankers in London.

It wasn't until the seventeenth century that Oliver Cromwell allowed the Jews back to Britain.

10th – The Disappearing Tide

On this day in 1141, a strange phenomenon was recorded in London: the tide in the Thames went out and failed to flow in again for an entire twenty-four hours.

*

Also on this date in 1271, there was a fight at Great Barford in Bedfordshire when Simon, the son of Roger de Cainhoe, attacked and beat John of Britville. John's wife, Emma, raised the hue and cry against Simon, fearing her husband might not survive. The next day, the coroner, Ralph of Goldington, visited John in order to talk to him and inspect his injuries. Some weeks later, although it seems John survived, because of his terrible wounds it was Emma who took their appeal to Bedford county court. (The murder of her husband was usually the only event for which a wife could take a case to court, so John's life must have continued to hang in the balance.) This is Emma's detailed declaration made on oath:

When she and her husband were walking together in the king's highway in Great Barford, between Jordan Cappe's house and that formerly of John of Blunham at vespers on 10 October, Simon came there and pursued and assaulted her husband and struck him on the top of the head on the left side between the crown and the ear with a sword of iron and steel, giving him a great wound five inches long, three inches wide and as deep as the brain, whence thirteen pieces of bone issued. Simon struck John again with the sword on the little finger, called the auricular finger of the left hand on the inside of the hand, cutting the sinews of the finger and thus maiming him. And he struck him on the next finger, called the leech finger, breaking its bones, and so he [John] was maimed in both fingers. His [Simon's] malice did not stop there but he again struck John many bloodless blows with the flat of the sword on the right side of his head, so that the whole of his head was excoriated and swollen and he lost his hearing on the left side. Simon also robbed John of a cordwain purse worth 6*d* with 8*s* of new money inside it.

S. M. Butler, *Forensic Medicine and Death Investigation in Medieval England*

That purse of Spanish leather from Cordoba had caused John the worst headache imaginable.

11th – Eton College

The school at Eton was founded by Henry VI as 'Kynge's College of Our Ladye of Eton besyde Windesore' in 1440, to provide free education to seventy poor boys who would then go on to King's College, Cambridge, which the king established the following year.

When Henry founded the school he granted it many endowments, but when he was deposed by Edward IV in 1461, the new king removed most of its assets and treasures to St George's Chapel, Windsor, on the other side of the River Thames. Construction of the chapel at Eton, originally intended to be slightly more than twice its present length, was stopped; the chapel as it is today and the lower storeys of the cloisters, including College Hall, have since been completed.

With reduced funds, little further building took place until around 1517, when Provost Richard Lupton built the tower that now bears his name, together with the range of buildings which includes Election Hall and Election Chamber.

http://www.etoncollege.com/briefhistory.aspx

12th – Unpaid Bills

Robert Passeleive, a knight, was summoned on 12 October 1380 to answer a charge by Edmund Fraunceys, a citizen and grocer of London. The charge claimed he owed the grocer £6 for spices and other exotic goods – a bill he had failed to pay at Easter and at Pentecost. Robert had purchased the goods from Edmund at his shop in St Stephen's parish in Walbrook ward on various occasions and now refused to pay for the pepper, saffron, ginger, cloves, dates, almonds rice, saunders [sandalwood], powder of ginger, powder called 'pouder lumbard', powder of cinnamon, figs, raisins, myrrh and canvas for the said £6. Despite reminders, Sir Robert still would not pay.

Common Pleas, Plea Roll 487m. 438d.

13th – The Coronation of Henry IV

On this day in 1399, Henry IV was crowned in Westminster Abbey. The omens weren't all good during the ceremony: as the archbishop anointed the king's head with the holy oil, he found that Henry's hair was swarming with lice. This was a common problem in medieval times but the chroniclers don't remark on it for any other king's crowning. Perhaps Henry's infestation exceptional?

As part of the coronation ceremony, it was customary for the king to make an offering at the high altar, but Henry dropped the gold offertory coin and, despite the acolytes frantically scrabbling around on the floor, it couldn't be found. (I expect the cleaners found it later.) However, after the hiccups of the church service, at least the coronation feast went without upset, including this dish of 'conyng' or rabbit:

Take rabbits and boil them well in good broth. Take Greek wine and add it with a portion of vinegar and ground cinnamon, whole cloves, whole cubebs and other good spices with raisins, currants and minced, pared ginger. Take up the [cooked] rabbits and smite them into pieces and cast them into the syrup and boil them a little on the fire and serve it forth.

L. J. Sass, *To the King's Taste*

The modern recipe suggests cutting the rabbit into pieces first before coating it in seasoned flour and browning in a pan. In this case, the cloves and cubebs should be finely ground, not whole, unless you use them like a *bouquet garni* in a muslin bag and remove them. Once the rabbit and syrup are combined, the dish should be cooked on a gentle heat for 40 minutes, or until the rabbit is tender. Weights and measurements aren't given in the original recipe – they rarely are – but suggestions for the syrup ingredients are three cups of Muscatel, four tablespoons cider vinegar, ½ cup currants, ¼ cup raisins, ¼ teaspoon cinnamon, two teaspoons freshly minced ginger, twenty cubebs and ten cloves finely ground.

14th – The Battle of Hastings

On this morning in 1066, the English army, led by King Harold, deployed on Senlac hill, where the abbey and town of Battle now stand in East Sussex. Duke William of Normandy's army had marched north from Hastings, and it is possible that he engaged before Harold's troops were fully deployed.

Contemporary accounts suggest it was a close run thing. William attacked with cavalry as well as infantry, a tactic the English had never experienced. In contrast, Harold's well-trained housecarls – his elite fighting men – and ordinary soldiers all fought on foot as was traditional in England. Formed up behind a shield wall in an excellent defensive position, they proved formidable opponents for the Normans and the fighting continued for most of the day.

Finally, after reversals on both sides, William breached the shield wall. The collapse of the English defence may have been as a direct result of Harold himself being killed. Once their carefully organised formation was broken, the English were vulnerable, especially to William's cavalry attack – another unique manoeuvre they had never seen before. Despite a futile attempt to hold off the Norman pursuit with a rearguard action at a site described as 'Malfosse' (Bad hole or ditch), the English forces were routed, fleeing northward towards the woods of the Weald. Having lost their king and most of his housecarls, the English could never again mount a serious challenge against William. Victory at Hastings gave him a great prize and subjected the English people to the oppressive Norman aristocracy.

Battle Abbey was built by William, now calling himself 'the Conqueror', in recognition of his victory and in memory of those who had fallen in battle. The abbey was laid out on Senlac Hill, originally thought to have been the site of the battlefield, but this is now being questioned as the topography doesn't fit the contemporary accounts of the action. It is possible that Harold's army took up position on Caldbec Hill, a little to the north of Senlac, and it was there that he was slain. One reason for thinking this is, ironically, if the English shield wall had been at the summit of the much-steeper Senlac Hill, the Norman cavalry could never have succeeded in charging up such a steep incline.

http://www.battlefieldstrust.com/resource-centre/
viking/battleview.asp?BattleFieldId=17

15th – 'How to Live a Good Life'

Here is a short verse by the fifteenth-century poet, John Lydgate, entitled 'How to Live a Good Life':

> Arise early,
> Serve God devoutly,
> The world busily.
> Go your way steadfastly,
> Answer politely.
> Sit down hungrily
> And get up temperately.

Go to supper soberly
And to your bed merrily,
And be there cheerfully
And sleep securely.

J. Lydgate, *Table Manners for Children*

16th – A Last Act of Charity

On 16 October 1497 Beatrice Stoughton, a London widow, drew up her will. As an act of charity, Beatrice wanted 13s 4d spent on bread and meat to be given to the poor prisoners in Newgate and Ludgate gaols. On a sartorial note, she left a violet gown with a lined train, a murrey kirtle (a mulberry-coloured under-gown), six silver spoons with lions on the handles, a golden girdle [belt] and a gold ring, all to Beatrice Skerne. To Cicelle (Cecily) Skerne, she left a red harnessed (decorated) girdle with a dolphin pendant. Margaret Debet was to receive a black gown, trimmed with black lamb and a violet kirtle.

Beatrice noted that she had been born in Dartford, Kent, and owned land in the town and surrounding area. Her stepdaughter Joanna was a nun there, so 20s was to be given to the nuns of Dartford Priory to pray for her soul. Dartford's parish church was to be given her silver-gilt chalice. Beatrice's own daughter, Elizabeth, was a nun at Sion Abbey in Middlesex, and they were to be given £5 to pray for her.

PCC Wills, Horne 34

17th – Tornado!

A powerful tornado hit London on this Friday, the eve of St Luke's feast day in 1091. Two Londoners were killed, the wooden London Bridge was destroyed, and the roof of the church of St Mary-le-Bow was blown off. Four of the church's twenty-six-foot-long rafters (7.9 metres) were driven into the ground with such force that only four feet (1.2 metres) of their length was left above ground – the rest driven into the earth in the same order in which they had supported the roof. This was thought to be a miracle. Other London churches were completely demolished by the wind, along with more than 600 wooden houses. This is England's earliest recorded tornado.

Having studied contemporary accounts of the damage, modern meteorologists have assigned the 1091 tornado T8 (severely devastating) status on the tornado scale (which runs from T0 to T10). Wind speeds would have been up to 240mph (385km/h). If such a tornado were to hit London today we could expect to see cars hurled along the street, houses smashed and skyscrapers twisted. Luckily, T8 tornadoes are rare in the UK – and let's hope it stays that way.

http://www.theguardian.com/news/2011/oct/19/
weatherwatch-tornado-london-britain

*

Also on this date in 1285, a Wednesday, at Beverley Minster in Yorkshire:

After dinner, Brother Walter lay asleep on his bed in his chamber … and Richard the clerk, whom he much loved, lay very sick in the same chamber. And being by the sickness rendered frantic and mad, Richard rose from his bed, and by the instigation of the devil smote Walter on the head as he slept, first with a form [bench] and afterwards with a trestle, so that the brains came out. He then went to the men in the kitchen with blood and brains on his hands. And when they asked him what he had done, he said, laughing, 'I have killed my dear master, Brother Walter: come and see where he lies slain; he will never speak another word.' And he brought them to the slain man, saying, 'Do I not say true, he is slain?' So being mad he was taken and imprisoned, and still persists in his madness.

S. M. Butler, *Forensic Medicine and Death Investigation in Medieval England*

18th – Change and Mutability

Thomas Hoccleve was an early fifteenth-century poet who, feeling depressed at the thought of winter's inevitable approach, wrote this rather gloomy piece:

After Harvest had brought in its sheaves and brown Michaelmastide had come and robbed the trees of their leaves, which had been green and delightful in vigour, and had dyed them a yellowish colour and cast them underfoot, that transformation affected me to. the depths of my heart, for it reminded me once more that there is no stability in this world. There is nothing but change and mutability. The world is not going to last. Man must forego it. Death will thrust him down to the ground under his foot. That is everyone's end.

M. Collins and V. Davis, *A Medieval Book of Seasons*

19th – The Death of King John

It was possibly on this day in 1216 that King John died at Newark Castle, most probably from an attack of dysentery. Writing forty years later, Matthew Paris, monk and chronicler at St Albans Abbey, had this to say: 'Foul as it is, Hell itself is made fouler by the presence of John.'

The medieval chroniclers could not agree on the exact date that John died. Matthew Paris and his St Albans' predecessor, Roger of Wendover, plumped for 17 October. Ralph, Abbot of Coggeshall Abbey in Essex, said John had passed away on 18 October. Other chroniclers, writing at Tewkesbury, Winchester, Worcester and elsewhere, thought it was on 19 October. The anonymous chroniclers writing at Waverley Abbey and Southwark Priory, both in Surrey, agree with this date – they were writing in 1216, so most probably got it correct.

Earlier in his reign, King John had said that he wanted to be buried at the Cistercian abbey he had founded at Beaulieu, Hampshire, but in October 1216, Beaulieu lay in that part of England held by the rebel barons; John asked instead that he be buried at Worcester Cathedral, where his tomb can still be seen. The tomb was opened in 1797, to confirm whether it did contain John's body. Mr Sandford, a local surgeon, inspected the skeleton and reported that King John stood five foot six and a half inches tall (1.69 metres).

http://britishlibrary.typepad.co.uk/digitisedmanuscripts/2014/10/
the-death-of-king-john.html#sthash.fho0ikMG.dpuf

According to Ralph of Coggeshall, John's final illness was brought on by gluttony but rumours soon started to circulate that he had been poisoned by a monk of Swineshead Abbey in Lincolnshire, where he spent the night after losing much of his baggage train in the treacherous sands of the Wash as the tide turned.

*

Also on this date in 1485 at Linton in Kent, Marion Sponeley drew up her 'nuncupative' will. A nuncupative will allowed for wishes, as spoken by the dying, to be written down later if, on the point of death, it was impossible to find a literate person at short notice. However, although it states in the text that Marion 'declared her will nuncupatyve' in the presence of five witnesses, it doesn't seem that she was on her deathbed at all.

Marion doesn't mention that she had ever had a husband or children, naming only her cousin, Thomas Harry. Neither does she bequeath her lands, properties and goods to him. In fact, Thomas was required to pay her forty shillings for everything in two instalments: half at the feast of All Saints (1 November) and half at Christmas. Clearly, Marion wasn't expecting to die just yet if she hoped to collect payment from her cousin in the next two months; she also required him to attend to her needs for the rest of her life. So why the emergency nuncupative will? We shall never know.

L. Boatwright, et al. (eds), *The Logge Register,* vol. 1

Nuncupative wills were made invalid in 1837, excepting those on active military service, because they often resulted in disputes.

20th – Criminal Sanctuary

Here is a 1477 document explaining the correct procedure for criminals hoping to claim sanctuary:

Let it be remembered that on the sixth day of October, William Rome and William Nicholson of the parish of Forsgate fled to the cathedral church of St Cuthbert at Durham where, on account of a felony, amongst other things, committed and publicly confessed by them, namely the murder by them some time before of William Aliand, they besought from the venerable and holy men, Thomas Haughton, sacristan of the said church, and William Cuthbert, master of the Galilee there, both brothers and monks of the same church, that the sanctuary of the church should be favourably extended to them in accordance with the liberties and privileges conceded to the most glorious confessor Saint Cuthbert of old; and by the ringing of a single bell, as is the custom, this boon was granted them.

As witnesses called and summoned specially for the occasion, two weeks past, there were present to see and hear those discreet men, William Heghyngton, Thomas Hudson, John Wrangham and Thomas Strynger.

Sanctuarium Dunelmense, V. Surtees Society

Thomas Haughton as sacristan was responsible for the sacristy, the room where church vestments, chalices and other valuables used during services were stored. William Cuthbert, master of the Galilee, would have been responsible for the chapel and/or porch at the entrance to the cathedral.

21st – Crab Apples

Gathered in October, crab apples grew wild in England. They were far too sour to eat raw but were often used in dishes made with sugar and spices; medieval folk loved to have sweet-and-sour on the menu. 'Crabs' were also used to make verjuice: the common people's vinegar for both pickling and cooking purposes.

In 1296, Simon de Monte of Wakefield was fined for failing to pick the lord of the manor's crab apples, amounting to the loss of two hogsheads of sour cooking cider.

T. McLean, *Medieval English Gardens*

Here is a recipe using verjuice for a medieval version of sweet-and-sour pork:

Take and boil pigs' feet in a pint of verjuice and sweet white wine. Take four dates, minced, with a few raisins. Take a little thyme and chop it small. Add to the dish and season with a little cinnamon and ginger and a quantity of verjuice.

T. Dawson, *The Good Housewife's Jewel*

22nd – A Known Troublemaker

In London, in 1488, Thomas Shelley, a wealthy mercer and one-time churchwarden, was accused not only of raping his neighbour's servant, but also committing adultery with his own maidservant. To make amends, Thomas gave the woman he had raped the huge sum of £40 for a dowry – otherwise, as 'used goods', she had little chance of finding a husband. As for his own servant, he paid a man, William Stevyns, 20 marks to marry her. Despite his monetary admission of guilt, no criminal proceedings were taken against Thomas, as was all too often the case in dealing with sexual crimes against women, even though his name crops up in the Mercers' Company's records as a troublemaker, from time to time.

For example, some strange things were going on in the company: In 1480, King Edward IV instructed the company to have words with two of its members. Thomas Wyndoute had done a deal with fellow mercer, John Llewellen, promising to pay him 540 Flemish pounds if he wed the wife of Thomas Shelley. Since we know Thomas was still alive and active at the time, the king described the deal as 'a sinister bargain', understanding that it involved a plan to murder Shelley.

S. McSheffrey, *Marriage, Sex and Civic Culture in Late Medieval London*

23rd – Priory Wages

Here are some examples of the wages paid at Miaxter Priory in 1425:

Fees with wages for servants –

For fee of John Langston, steward, holding the court per annum, 26s 8d. For fee of William Suleman, the prior's attorney in London, per annum, 6s 8d.

And for wages of John Baldwyn, the prior's groom of the chamber, this year 13s 4d. And for wages of William Puffe, baker, half-days, per annum 15s. And for wages of William Skynner, his assistant, 10s, and for his wife drying malt this year, 10s. And for wages of William Gulde, barber, this year, 6s, and for wages of Catherine Colyers making towels for the kitchen this year, 20d, and for wages of the laundress, per annum, 6s.

Wages for labourers –

For John Leseby, making fences at the sheepfolds of Wrechwyk and Crockwell, 13d, and to John Soler, cutting twenty-one cartloads of late-coming, for telling of tales, for chiding, for fighting (half-days), for breaking a shovel, for playing, for obstructing his fellows (whole days), for keeping of the whole underwood at Bernwood, 3s 2d, and to a certain stranger hired to drive the plough and harrow for twelve days, 12d.

A. F. Scott, *Everyone a Witness – The Plantagenet Age*

John Soler sounds as though he must have been the prior's fool, kept mostly for entertainment, or else a thorough nuisance. (N.B. I haven't been able to determine the location of Miaxter Priory.)

24th – The Treaty of Brétigny

The treaty of Brétigny, which had been drawn up by Edward the Black Prince, and Charles, the Dauphin of France, near Chartres on 8 May 1360, on behalf of their fathers, Edward III of England and John II of France, was signed on 24 October 1360 by both kings. It was ratified as the Treaty of Calais.

Under the terms, which were all in England's favour, there would henceforth be peace between the two countries for nine years. Although King Edward was to renounce his claim to the crown of France, he would receive Aquitaine, Poitou, Calais and other territories in exchange, as well as being paid three million gold crowns by the French. The French also renounced their alliance with Scotland. The treaty brought to a close twenty-three years of conflict, the first stage of what would become the Hundred Years War.

Historians have wondered why Edward III signed the treaty at a time when he had every advantage over the French, even holding their king to ransom. How would the war have played out if he had pressed on? Whatever the case, the treaty proved a significant point in the fortunes of medieval warfare.

http://digihum.mcgill.ca/~matthew.milner/teaching/classes/
hist214_f13/timeline/?show=events&id=69

25th – Agincourt

On this St Crispin's Day in 1415 the English won a victory over a French army of far superior numbers. The French plan for the battle was revealed to Henry V by a French prisoner who told the English king that they would utilise massed cavalry to charge through the ranks of the English archers. Henry ordered steps to be taken to counter the tactic: every archer was to drive a sharpened stake into the ground in front of him on the battlefield to stop a charging horse. The plan worked brilliantly but now we know it probably wasn't Henry's own idea. A French commander, Marshal Boucicaut, had once seen a cavalry charge stopped by sharpened stakes when he fought the Turks at Nicopolis. Boucicaut wrote about it in detail and it seems likely that King Henry or maybe his cousin and commander Edward, 2nd Duke of York, read it and remembered the tactic and its devastating effectiveness.

http://www.historyextra.com/article/military-history/
10-things-you-probably-didn%E2%80%99t-
know-about-henry-v-and-battle-agincourt

However, the Battle of Agincourt all did not go so well personally for the Duke of York: he became the highest-ranking English casualty – one of very few. The means of his death in battle isn't certain, being variously described as due to a head wound or to being 'smouldered to death by much heat and pressing'. Films of Shakespeare's *Henry V* show York falling from his horse and, weighed down by his armour and unable to rise and remount, he is trampled underfoot. Perhaps that was how it happened.

26th – Freight Charges

William Cely wrote a letter dated 26 October 1481 to his cousin, George Cely, in Calais, letting him know that the ship, the *Mary Grace* from London, captained by John Lokyngton, would be offloading various packs of sheep fleeces, or 'fells', when the ship reached Calais. He goes into great detail as to their positions in the ship's hold and how the packs were marked up, so that George could be certain he got the correct ones. Six packs lay at the lowest level, next to the mast; above those lay five packs belonging to Thomas Graunger. Some of the fleeces were 'winter fells', marked in ink with a 'C'; the 'summer' fells' were marked with an 'O'. William also reminded George that he must pay the 'ffrayte' (freight) charges on the cargo.

A. Hanham, *The Cely Letters 1472–88*

27th – Leeds Castle

When Queen Margaret, the second wife of King Edward I, died in 1318, her luxurious home at Leeds Castle in Kent became the property of the Crown once more. Her stepson, Edward II, made Bartholomew de Badlesmere governor of the castle. As lord steward of the royal household, Baldesmere had fought in both France and Scotland, alongside Edward I; but by 1321, the new king, Edward II, with his disastrous policies and hated favourites, had alienated many of his nobles, Badlesmere among them.

When Edward's queen, Isabella, was returning home after making a pilgrimage to Canterbury, Baldesmere's wife, Margaret de Clare, refused her access to the castle as overnight accommodation. Margaret, who loathed the queen, announced that she must go elsewhere. Isabella told her escort to force a way in, but Margaret instructed her archers to shoot back. Six of the queen's party were killed.

During the last week of October, to avenge the insult to Isabella Edward II besieged and took the castle. The siege lasted a week before the garrison surrendered. When the castle fell, the seneschal, Walter Colepepper, and twelve of the garrison were hanged from the battlements. Margaret was imprisoned, firstly in Dover Castle, and secondly in the Tower of London. Although she was released a year later, Bartholomew didn't fare so well. A few months later, he joined the Earl of Lancaster's rebellion against the king. He fought at the Battle of Boroughbridge on 16 March 1322 and was taken prisoner. Less than a month later, on 14 April 1322, Bartholomew was attainted and hanged, drawn and quartered at Blean, near Canterbury. His severed head was displayed on a pole on Canterbury's Burgate, a main entrance to the city.

http://www.englishmonarchs.co.uk/leeds%20castle.html

28th – Henry III's Coronation

On this day in 1216, little Henry III was crowned in Gloucester Cathedral.

*

In 1270, it was reported that at about midday in Bedfordshire, Gilbert, son of Richard the Reeve of Chalgrave, and William, son of John the Reeve of Tilsworth, came from Dunstable market to Houghton Regis field. A quarrel arose between them. William struck Gilbert on the top of his head with a Danish axe, giving him a wound four inches long and to the depth of the brain, so that his brain flowed forth. He (Gilbert) received the rites of the Church and died about midday on 31 October. The hue (and cry) was raised and followed. Richard the Reeve, in whose house he (Gilbert) was found slain, found pledges [men of good repute to bear witness to his exemplary character]: Richard le Blonde and Ralph of Leagrave of Chalgrave.

The inquest was held before Geoffrey Rodland, the coroner, by Chalgrave, Hockliffe, Milton Bryan and Battlesden. It was ordered that William be arrested. They also said he had no goods.

At the eyre (when a travelling justice heard the case) evidence was presented that Gilbert was struck in Chalgrave field, rather than in Houghton Regis, and that William immediately fled. He (William) was exacted [his property and possessions confiscated] and outlawed; his tithing in Tilsworth was amerced (taken as a fine).

R. F. Hunnisett (ed. and trans.), *Coroner's rolls for Bedfordshire from the National Archives* (Bedfordshire Historical Records Society, 1961), vol. 41, entry 83

29th – Buckingham's Indentures

Around this date in 1440, Henry, Earl of Buckingham was drawing up a series of indentures with his retainers. These were contracts of service in peacetime as well as war. Here are the indentures made between Buckingham and a squire, John Cursun, and Sir Richard Vernon:

This indenture made between the right worshipful lord Henry, Earl of Buckingham, etc. on the one party and John Cursun, esquire, on the other party, etc. of £10 annual fee for retinue, payable out of [i.e. from the rents and profits from] the manor of Naseby in the county of Northampton on this side of the sea with two yeomen, a page and four horses or as many persons and horses as etc. as before.

The like etc. to Sir Richard Vernon, knight, of an annual fee of £20 during [the] life of the said Sir Richard out of the manor of Rugby in Warwickshire etc. And the said Sir Richard to be ready at all times when he shall be sent for to come to the said earl upon reasonable warning, to do him service and with him to ride in all parts, countries and places on this side of the sea, with a gentleman, four yeomen, a page and seven horses, or as many persons and horses as the said earl pleases to assign or command reasonably, for the which he shall have such bouche of court [food?] and livery during the time of his demure as others of his degree [status] in the household of the said earl, with reasonable costs allowed to the said Sir Richard in his coming and returning again [i.e. travel expenses] as often as he is sent for by the earl aforesaid. In witness etc. given at London, October 1440.

Penarth MS.280D, ff.11–12

30th – The Yeomen of the Guard

On 30 October 1485, King Henry VII set up the Yeomen of the Guard – often called 'Beefeaters' at the Tower of London – as his personal royal bodyguard. No previous medieval king had felt so vulnerable as to need a bodyguard but Henry knew his seat upon the English throne was in doubt; his dubious claim was open to question (see 24 May, 16 June and 21 November).

31st – Hallowe'en

Known as Hallowe'en, or rather the e'en (evening) before the feast of All Hallows or All Saints, this night was long believed to be the time when witches, fairies, devils and hobgoblins roamed the world causing mischief. The Church did its best to play down these pagan fears, but medieval folk preferred to take no chances, lighting bonfires to scare away evil from their homes and villages and to protect their livestock.

NOVEMBER

1st – All Saints

The festival of All Saints – or All Hallows, as it was known in medieval times – was the day on which all Christian saints and martyrs were remembered, especially those who didn't have a dedicated feast day otherwise. The first day in November had been chosen and ordained for the purpose by Pope Gregory IV sometime before his death in 844. After the good fun and divertissement to allay the worries of the night before, perhaps All Saints brought safety once more.

2nd – 'Blank Maunger'

Here is a recipe for blancmange – in this case called 'blank maunger' – and as different from what we would make today as the name suggests. As with most medieval recipes, no amounts are given for the ingredients, nor cooking times. I have modernised the grammar and spelling because the original text uses many Middle English terms, such as 'mung it fynelich' (stir it very well) as well as the Old English letter thorn (Þ = th):

Put rice in water overnight, then rinse it until the water runs clear and set it on a high heat until the grains burst but not too much. Then take cooked capon or hen's meat and chop it small. Take almond milk, add it to the rice and bring to the boil. Add the meat. As the mixture thickens, stir it very well so it does not stick and burn. When it is thick enough, add a generous helping of sugar and almonds which have been fried in lard. Dress the dish and serve it forth.

S. Pegg, *The Forme of Cury*

3rd – Burned at the Stake

Petronilla de Meath was born around 1300 in Meath, Ireland. As far as we know, she was the first Irish woman to be burned at the stake for the crime of heresy.

Petronilla served as a maid to Lady Alice Kyteler in Kilkenny. In 1324, Lady Alice, along with her son and ten others, became one of the earliest targets of accusations of witchcraft, centuries before the more famous witch trials in the sixteenth and seventeenth centuries. Lady Alice was charged by the Bishop of Ossory with a list of crimes, ranging from sorcery and demonism to the murders of several husbands, and accused her of having acquired her wealth through magical and devilish means. It was said that an incubus visited her in the form of a large black cat.

K. Walker-Meikle, *The Medieval Pet*

To extract her confession, the bishop ordered the torture of Lady Alice's maid and confidante, Petronilla de Meath. Petronilla claimed that she and her mistress applied a magical ointment to a wooden beam which enabled them to fly. She was then forced to proclaim publicly that Lady Alice and her followers were guilty of witchcraft.

With the help of relatives, Lady Alice used her connections to flee to England, taking with her Petronilla's daughter, Basilia. Lady Alice's followers, including Petronilla, remained behind. Some were convicted and whipped but others, Petronilla included, were burned alive at the stake.

http://www.brooklynmuseum.org/eascfa/dinner_party/
place_settings/petronilla_de_meath.php

4th – Meat Carving

It was vital, as well as being courteous and good mannered, for a servant to know how to carve and serve meat, poultry, game and fish correctly and how to present it to his lord, looking beautiful on the dish. Each meat had a correct term for its carving and presentation. To 'slice brawn' or 'mince a plover' are fairly straightforward and say what they mean, but here are some more peculiar terms, to list just a few:

Lift a swan, spoil a hen, fruche a chicken, unlace a coney [rabbit], dismember a heron, disfigure a peacock, thigh a pigeon, break a deer, side a haddock, culpon a trout, undertranche a porpoise, tame a crab and [my personal favourite] splat a pike.

Wynkyn de Worde, *The Boke of Keruinge*

5th – Open Letter Dispute

In the year of 1489, Lawrence Swattock, an apothecary, was the mayor of Kingston upon Hull. On this date he wrote an open letter concerning a dispute between John Harper, the Lord Mayor of York, and a merchant, John Metcalf. Lawrence testified that Robert Prott of Kingston had come before him and three aldermen of the same and swore upon the gospels to the truth of the following incident:

Prott had been in York at the time of the dispute between Harper and Metcalf, concerning a pipe of red wine from Gascony. Mayor Harper claimed the wine belonged to him, but Prott was a witness to the fact that the wine was rightly Metcalf's and should be returned to him, not Mayor Harper.

H. Falvey, et al. (eds), *English Wills of York*

6th – The Menai Strait

The Welsh achieved a great victory over the English on this day in 1282, who had intended to surprise them by crossing the Menai Strait on the Welsh north coast. The Menai Strait is the narrow strip of water that separates the island of Anglesey from Gwynedd on the Welsh mainland. It can be a treacherous stretch of water, according to the tides. The rising tide approaches from the south-west, causing the water in the strait to flow north-eastwards as the level rises. It then flows anti-clockwise around Anglesey until, a few hours later, it shifts, and begins to flow the opposite way.

During King Edward I's wars against Prince Llewelyn ap Gruffydd and the Welsh, the English held Anglesey. On 6 November, the English commander, Luke de Tany, readied his troops at Llanfaes on the island, waiting to cross the strait to attack the unsuspecting Welsh in Bangor. At least, that was the plan. On the day of the attack, the English would cross as high tide approached, when the water was at its calmest.

http://www.sarahwoodbury.com/the-menai-straits/

After his successful capture of Anglesey, Luke de Tany had ordered his men to construct a bridge of boats across the Menai Strait to the mainland. King Edward planned to cross the River Conwy while de Tany crossed the strait on his bridge; together they would attack Llewelyn in Bangor. However, de Tany – having captured the island without the king's assistance – ignored the plan, thinking he could defeat the Welsh without Edward's aid. He had contacted some churchmen in Bangor who promised to give him a signal when the time was right to attack.

The bridge was finished and, on 6 November, the signal was given. But someone had betrayed the English. De Tany and his men crossed the bridge, but Llywelyn had been alerted and charged with a large army to meet the English as they crossed and landed on the beach on the mainland. The rising tide cut off de Tany's men from the bridge when they tried to retreat. Many of them drowned as their heavy armour dragged them under the water. The chronicler Walter of Guisborough wrote an account of the battle:

When they had reached the foot of the mountain and, after a time, came to a place at some distance from the bridge, the tide came in with a great flow, so that they were unable to get back to the bridge for the depth of water. The Welsh came from the high mountains and attacked them, and in fear and trepidation, for the great number of the enemy, our men preferred to face the sea than the enemy. They went into the sea but, heavily laden with arms, they were instantly drowned.

Luke de Tany, along with the noblemen Roger de Clifford, Phillip and William Burnell, sixteen English knights, along with their squires and 300 of de Tany's men were drowned while the Welsh suffered hardly any casualties. The remaining English limped back across the bridge when the tide ebbed, to Anglesey; but they had lost their commanders and too many men to launch a further attack. Llywelyn tried to capitalise on his victory, leaving his brother, Dafydd, in charge of Gwynedd while he went south to Powys to gather more support.

However, Menai was the last of Llewelyn's victories: he was lured into a trap at Cilmeri and killed a month later on 11 December 1282.

7th – A Gang of Glovers

On 7 November 1269 in the little hamlet of Roxton in Bedfordshire, a gang of thugs caused chaos. They broke into Ralph Bovetoun's house and carried off everything he had. Worse still, in the house next door, they killed Maud del Forde and mortally wounded Alice Pressade – it isn't stated whether they stole anything. The thugs then raided John Cobbler's house, killing John and his servant outright and badly injuring his wife Azeline and their daughter.

Azeline told the coroner that the gang consisted of four glovers from Bedford and was led by Richard of Neville, formerly a servant of the Prior of Newnham, who had supervised the collection of tithes earlier that autumn. The coroner had Neville and the glovers arrested and imprisoned, although he was uncertain whether or not it was the same Richard of Neville whom Azeline had described.

In the first recorded 'police line-up' in England; the coroner escorted Azeline to the prison in Bedford so she could personally confirm the identity of the villain. It was as well that the coroner did this because, sadly, Azeline later died of her wounds.

S. M. Butler, *Forensic Medicine and Death Investigation in Medieval England*

8th – Costiveness

Bearing in mind the forthcoming feast of Martinmas on 11 November, the traditional date for slaughtering livestock that couldn't be overwintered, and the salting, pickling, smoking and otherwise preserving of so much meat, today might be a good day to prepare a remedy for gastric upsets and another for costiveness (constipation):

A powder for the stomach. Take powder of ginger, galingale and mint, of each equally much and use them with a quantity of wine or ale at morn and in sage[water] at even.

For costiveness. Take the root of polypody [a fern] that groweth on an oak, and wash it and stamp it, and temper it with wine and let it stand all night; and on the morrow strain it and give him to drink and he shall soon make deliverance.

W. R. Dawson, *A Leechbook of the Fifteenth Century*

9th – The Conflict of Caister Castle

In 1468, the Paston family of Norfolk were in conflict with the Duke of Norfolk over who owned Caister Castle. The Pastons brought armed men to the castle, fearing the duke might lay siege to it. Here is Sir John Paston's letter to his brother about the men he has hired to defend Caister:

Right well beloved brother, I recommend me to you, letting you know that I have engaged four trustworthy and true men to help you and Daubeney to keep the place at Caister. They will do all manner of things ... they are proved men and cunning in war and in feats of arms: they can shoot both guns and crossbows well and mend and string them ... They are sad [serious] and sensible men, saving one of them, who is bald and called William Penny, who is as good a man as can be found on earth except that he is, as I understand, a little inclined to be cup-shotten [drunk], though he is no brawler but full of courtesy, much like James Halman. The other three are named Peryn Sale, John Chapman and Robert Jackson. As yet they have no harness [equipment] but when it comes it will be sent on to you and in the meanwhile I pray you and Daubeney to provide them with some ...

Remember to treat the men I have named as courteously as you can.

R. Virgoe (ed), *The Illustrated Letters of the Paston Family*

10th – A State of Chastity

Memorandum. On this day [10 November 1454] the reverend father in Christ and lord John, by God's grace, Lord Bishop of Lincoln, dressed in pontificals in the chapel within his house at Old Temple, London, during the service of mass, he received and acknowledged the oath of Isabel Maryone, read and made by her, and gave the veil and mantle of widowhood blessed by the reverend father and clothed her with them. [Before witnesses] the form of words of the vow that was uttered is:

In the name of the Father, the Son and the Holy Ghost, I, Isabel Maryone of your diocese, widow, promise and vow to God, Our Lady, St Mary and to all the saints, in your presence, reverend father in Christ, Sir John, by the grace of God, Bishop of Lincoln, to be chaste and I determine to keep myself chaste from this time forward as long as my life lasts. In witness of this I here subscribe with my own hand, and she made a cross.

P. J. P. Goldberg, *Women in England c. 1275–1525*

Making a formal promise to live in a state of chastity as a 'vowess' was a way for wealthy widows to ward off any would-be husbands who might hope to profit from their money and status. Widows could live independently, running their own or their deceased husbands' businesses and affairs. As the vow states, the chastity was meant to last for the rest of the widows' lives but that didn't always happen.

Eleanor, Countess of Leicester and sister to Henry III, had been a widow when she married Simon de Montfort and, although a very young widow, she had taken a vow of chastity, much like Isabel Maryone. The Church came down hard on the newly-weds for breaking her vow, making Eleanor and Simon do penance for their sins, but they were in love and came through the ordeal of papal displeasure.

A London widow, Joanna Large, had made her vow before Robert Gilbert, the Bishop of London, soon after April 1441 when her husband had died, swearing an oath 'to live in chastity and cleanness of my body from this time forward as long as my life lasteth, and never to take other spouse but only Christ Jesu'. Yet three years later she married John Gedney, twice Lord Mayor of London, a close friend of her late husband. A London chronicle of 1444 notes the scandal:

John Gedney, draper alderman of London [and she] which was Robert Large wife ... which was sworn chaste and had take the mantel and ring and should have kept her a godly widow time of her life. And anon after the marriage done they were troubled by holy church because of breaking of her oath and were put to penance both he and she.

Despite the restrained wording of the chronicle, the marriage of these two Londoners of high social standing was considered the scandal of the year and gave the gossip-mongers something they could get their teeth into. Both John and Joanna profited by their marriage, combining the estates each of them owned in Tottenham, Middlesex. By the time of her fourth widowhood, in 1449, Joanna was referred to as lady of the manor of Tottenham.

T. Mount, *Everyday Life in Medieval London*

11th – A Year and A Day

In York, John Fery took possession of three horses: one grey and white, another dun-coloured with a 'blaklist' and cut tail, and the third of the colour 'blackbay' with a star on the forehead and the near [left] ear cut off. Further, he was seised [in possession] of them during Martinmas [11 November] and they remain in his custody for a year and a day.

L. C. Attreed, *York House Books,* vol. 1

This entry in the York records of 1476 doesn't say how John Fery came to have the horses but it would seem to be by some dubious means. However, the fact that he had kept them for the legal timespan of 'a year and a day' meant they were now rightfully his. I have been unable to discover what a 'blaklist' was or quite what colour was described as 'blackbay'.

12th – Nearest Neighbours

It is rather unusual to find women mentioned in coroners' rolls by name unless they were the victim or perpetrator of the crime. However, one coroner, William Alisaundre of South Lynn in Norfolk, accepted and named women as 'nearest neighbours', i.e. witnesses, and even as 'pledges', i.e. those who swear on oath to tell the truth, in his records.

In November 1361, when enquiring into the death of seventy-year-old Margaret Ran of Cleye, Alisaundre recorded Agnes Barker and Alice of Brounfield as nearest neighbours to the event. Agnes Beverage was one of the pledges to their testimony.

In 1362, Alisaundre named Emma Julyon as nearest neighbour when Godfrey Skeppere died, and in November 1363 Annabil Hukester was called as one of the nearest neighbours when Sara, wife of William of Grimston, was attacked and killed by strangers to whom she had given a bed for the night.

S. M. Butler, *Forensic Medicine*

13th – Birth of Edward III

The future king, Edward III, was born at Windsor Castle on this day in 1312; he was often referred to as Edward of Windsor in his early years. To celebrate the birth, his father declared the day to be a national holiday and the conduits of London ran with wine.

The reign of his father, Edward II, was a time of great unrest in England for a number of reasons. Chief among them was Edward II's failures in the continuing war with Scotland. Secondly was the ill opinion of the king's exclusive patronage of a few royal favourites and his insulting treatment of his queen, Isabella, whom he called the 'She-Wolf of France'. The birth of a male heir in 1312 temporarily improved Edward II's position with the barons who opposed him and, to raise the prestige of the royal family further, the newborn prince was created Earl of Chester at only twelve days old.

14th – Livestock Led to Slaughter

Around this date in November, animals that weren't vital to next year's breeding or for work purposes were slaughtered; this usually meant the majority of male animals. In medieval times, it was difficult to keep enough fodder to feed the animals through the winter, so cattle and pigs were butchered – the official day for doing this was Martinmas, the feast of St Martin on 11 November, but the process was spread over the following weeks. The meat was salted, pickled or smoked to preserve it for as long as possible in the days before tinning and refrigeration.

This is what a thirteenth-century English bestiary book has to say about bulls and oxen:

The bulls in India are tawny gold in colour and as swift as birds. Their hair lies in opposite directions and they can open their mouths to the width of their heads. They can turn their horns at will and their backs are so hard that arrows bounce off. Elsewhere, bulls are the princes of this world, tossing the common people on the horns of their pride ... Bulls have both a good and evil significance; the good aspect is found in St Matthew's gospel [ch.22, v.4]: 'Behold, I have prepared my dinner, my bulls and fatlings are killed and all things are ready'. In Psalms [ch.22, v12], the evil aspect is reflected: 'The fat bulls have set about me'.

The ox treads on terra firma. If oxen are together they are very peaceful; they will seek out their partner under the yoke of the plough, and they show their affection for each other by frequent lowing [mooing] if they become tired. If it is about to rain they will return to their stables. If their natural senses tell them that the sky is clearing, they look out and stretch their necks out of the stable, as if to tell each other with one accord that they want to go out again ... Oxen in scripture can mean many things: the madness of those who lead sensual lives; the strength and labours of the preachers; the humility of the Israelites.

R. Barber, *Bestiary*

15th – Red Deer Pie

With so much fresh meat temporarily available, here is a Tudor dish called 'Red Deer'. Despite the name, it's actually a beef pie:

Take a leg of beef and cut out all the sinews clean. Then take a rolling pin and all to beat it; then parboil it. And when you have so done, lard it very thick. Then lay it in wine or vinegar for two or three hours, or a whole night. Then take it out and season it with pepper, salt, cloves and mace. Then put it into your paste [pastry] and so bake it.

T. Dawson, *The Good Housewife's Jewel*

16th – A Grand Inheritance

The will of John Isele of Sundridge in Kent was granted probate on 16 November 1494. John bequeathed a good many items to his son Thomas from his house in Sundridge, which must have been very grand. It seems there was even a private altar in the main bedchamber. Here are a few examples of the bequests made to Thomas:

To my son Thomas Isele all the hangings from the great parlour at Sundridge, tapestries of verdure [hunting scenes] and other and two cushions that belonged to Jesoppes. Also all the hangings in the chamber above the great parlour and the bed of silk cloth of baudekin [silken cloth embroidered with gold thread], three curtains of sarcenet [a fine silk] with a counterpane of the same, a featherbed and fustians [linen/cotton mix] and two pairs of sheets ... Also my little mass book covered with blue and the porteous [service book] and the *superaltare* [high altar?] and one of the gilt chalices and altar cloths such as it shall please my wife to give [to him] from the little closet in the said chamber above the parlour. Also to my said son Thomas my great chain of gold and my two silver gilt pots which I bought from Harding and the best silver basin and the best ewer and three gilt bowls with covers and two little gilt salts [salt-cellars] and a laver of silver [basin for hand-washing] which I got from Loring. Four great spits in the kitchen and the great brass pot, a little pot of brass and the great chaffer of brass [dish that went over hot charcoal to keep food warm] which was Nicholas Little's and the great cauldron and the furnace and all the brewing vessels and three pissing basins and a little flat chaffer.

L. L. Duncan (trans.), Vox 21,
PCC Wills, Canterbury

It is impossible to know whether the penultimate items were actually three basins to be used in an emergency when it was impossible to get to the privy, or whether John may have meant pots with a lip for pouring liquid, since he includes them with the kitchen cooking and brewing equipment.

17th – King Edward and Llewelyn

In 1272, Edward I succeeded to the throne of England. He would be a vigorous, forceful ruler and an able military leader, quite unlike his father, Henry III. During Henry's reign, there had been all sorts of trouble, not least the Barons War, led by Simon de Montfort from 1263 to 1265. The Welsh, too, had a free hand; in north Wales Llewelyn ap Gruffydd ruled, calling himself Prince of Wales. Simon de Montfort did a deal with Llewelyn as an ally, sealing it with a betrothal of marriage between the Welsh prince and de Montfort's daughter, Eleanor. But the marriage would be for the future; Eleanor was just a little child.

In 1274, tension between Llewelyn and King Edward increased when Llewelyn and his younger brother, Dafydd, quarrelled. Dafydd defected to the English, seeking protection from Edward. According to the Treaty of Shrewsbury, Llewelyn had to pay the English Crown a sum of money each year for the privilege of ruling the Welsh people and he was expected to pay homage and accept Edward as his overlord. Since the death of Edward's father, Henry III, the payments had stopped. Several times Edward sent for Llewelyn to come to Chester but the Welsh prince failed to come, insisting that an overlord was not permitted to harbour his vassal's enemies, i.e. Dafydd, so the treaty was null and void. Llewelyn then had the audacity to arrange for Eleanor de Montfort, his promised bride, who was now aged twelve and therefore considered old enough to marry, to come to Wales from France. She had lived there with her mother in exile since the death of her father in 1265, but she was still the king's cousin and needed his permission to wed.

For Edward, this was a step too far. On 16 November 1276, (another source says 12 November), Edward declared war on Llewelyn, his objective – so he said – simply to put down a recalcitrant vassal, not to begin a war of conquest. Edward's ships intercepted Eleanor de Montfort en route from France, and the bride-to-be was captured and brought to England as a hostage. Edward hoped Llewelyn would back down and pay homage and the money due in order to have Eleanor released, but the Welshman refused. In the south and central areas of Wales. The Welsh quickly abandoned their allegiance to Llewelyn as the Marcher lords, who had castles on the English–Welsh border areas, took control, leaving Llewelyn with little more than Snowdonia in North Wales. It was going to be all out war and conquest, whatever Edward planned at the outset.

Incidentally, in the best fairytale tradition, Llewellyn did get his bride, but their union wasn't a long one (see 6 November).

http://www.timeref.com/episodes/edward_i_and_wales.htm

18th – England's First Book

On this date in 1471, Edmund Paston wrote from Norwich to his brother John in London, sending him a long shopping list, wanting to look his fashionable best while job-hunting. Edmund had trained as a lawyer at Staple Inn, in London and, apparently, still owed money to people in the capital:

I send you now by the bringer of this some money, which I pray you bestow as I write to you: to Christopher Hanyngton 5s; to the Principal of Staple Inn 5s in part payment. Also I pray you to buy me 3 yards of purple camlet [like cashmere today], price 4s a yard; a bonnet of deep murrey [mulberry-colour], price 2s 4d; a hose-cloth of yellow kersey [a ribbed cloth], at 2s an ell [forty-five inches]; a girdle of plunket [blue-grey] ribbon, price 6d; 4 laces of silk, 2 of one colour and 2 of another [for lacing up doublets or gowns], price 8d; 3 dozen points [metal tips for laces which often got lost], price 6d; 3 pairs of pattens [wooden soled 'platform' shoes that slipped over your leather shoes to raise them out of the mud], at 2½d a pair but I pray you do not let them be left out ...

Also, sir, I send Parker his money by the bringer hereof and I have desired him to lend me a gown of puce and I have sent him a tippet [a streamer-like strip of fabric attached to a sleeve just above the elbow] of velvet to border it round about and I pray you be at the choosing thereof ...

R.Virgoe (ed.), *The Illustrated Letters
of the Paston Family*

'Puce' is a colour that causes debate among fashion historians. *Puce* is French for 'flea', but what colour is that? It has been variously described as purple-brown, pale red, terracotta and burnt rose, so take your pick.

*

Also on this date in 1477, William Caxton printed the first book in England at the sign of the Red Pale, in the Almonry at Westminster, where he had set up his press. The book was *The Dictes and Sayengis of the Phylosophers,* translated by Anthony Woodville, Earl Rivers, the queen's brother.

19th – Street Cleaning

The mayor and aldermen of Coventry passed an ordinance in 1421 to clean up the streets. It seems that those who ran cookshops were especially guilty of endangering public hygiene:

We command that no Cook cast no manner of filth under their stalls, nor in the High Street, nor to suffer [allow] it there to lie, that is to wit: feathers, hair, nor no entrails of pigs, nor of no other beasts.

B. Henisch, *The Medieval Cook*

20th – An Unrightful Death

The London Coroners' rolls for 20 November 1301 recorded the following:

On Monday the morrow of St Edmund the King in the twenty-ninth year of King Edward [I], information given to John the Clerk, coroner, and the sheriffs of London that a certain Christina de Menstre lay dead of a death other than her rightful death in the churchyard of St Mary of Woolchurch Haw in the ward of Walbrook. Thereupon they proceeded there and having summoned good men of the ward and of the three nearest wards ... they diligently enquired how it happened.

They say on their oath that when on the preceding Sunday in the twilight of evening a certain William le Sawiere of Carshalton met the said Christina at the eastern corner of the said churchyard and asked her to spend the night with him, and she refused and endeavoured to escape from his hands. The said William, moved with anger, drew a certain Irish knife and struck the said Christina under the right shoulder blade, causing a wound an inch broad and six inches deep, of which wound she then and there died.

P. J. P. Goldberg, *Women in England c. 1275–1525*

21st – The Trial of the Pretender

In a letter to his benefactor, Sir Robert Plumpton, John Pullan wrote from London in 1499 telling of the trials that had taken place at Westminster of Perkin Warbeck, a pretender to Henry VII's throne, and also of Edward Plantagenet, the young Earl of Warwick:

Sir, so yt was that Parkin Warbek [*sic*] and other iij [three men] were arreyned on Satterday ... in the Whitehall at Westminster for ther offences afore Sir John Sygly, knight marshall, and Sir John Trobifeild; and ther they were attended, and judgement given that they shold be drawn on hirdills from the Tower, throwout London, to the Tyburne and ther to be hanged, and cut down quicke, and ther bowells to be taken out and burned: ther heads to be stricke of, and quartered, ther heads and quarters to be disposed at the Kyngs pleasure ...

Sir, this present day, in Westminster hall, was brought Therle of Warwek and arrened afore Therle of Oxford, being the Kyngs grace comyssioner, and afore other Lords, bycause he is a pere of the Realme. [Pullan lists all the nobles who sat in judgement.] And Therle of Warweke confessed thenditments that were laid to his charge, and like Judgement was given of him, as is afore rehersed. When thes persones shalbe put in execution I intend to shew to your mastership right shortly; and give credence unto this berrer [the person who delivers this letter].

From Lyncolns Inne at London, this xxi day of November. By your servant and bedman ['bedesman' – someone who prays for you],

John Pullan

T. Stapleton (ed.), *The Plumpton Correspondence*

The trial of Perkin Warbeck – the lowly son of a Tournai boatman, a 'feigned' boy, as Henry VII referred to him – was the outcome of years of turmoil since 1491 for the Tudor king. Perkin claimed to be Prince Richard, Duke of York, younger of the two little Princes in the Tower (see 26 June), and now, since his elder brother was dead, rightful King of England as Richard IV. This wasn't just wishful thinking on the young man's part either. He had gathered a sizeable following: some were Yorkist dissidents, eager to cause trouble for the hated Tudor, but King

Charles VIII of France accepted him at court, gave him a royal bodyguard and openly supported him, whereupon Henry VII declared war on France. Henry demanded that Perkin be declared *persona non grata* in France as part of the treaty to prevent war. Would he have gone to such trouble if Perkin was a man of no importance?

Perkin simply removed himself to the Low Countries, welcomed to the court of Margaret of York, dowager Duchess of Burgundy, who declared upon close questioning that he was her undoubted nephew. When the Emperor Frederick III died in 1493, the young man was invited as King Richard of England to attend the funeral in Vienna; Henry Tudor didn't get an invitation. In England, churchmen, knights and gentry rallied to Perkin's cause. It was said that 'such private marks as he had been known from his cradle', i.e. birthmarks, determined his identity as the prince.

He attempted an invasion of England, landing at Deal in Kent in the summer of 1495, but was betrayed by a Tudor spy, Sir Robert Clifford. His men were rounded up on the beach, tried and executed. Fleeing to Scotland, Perkin was treated as a royal brother by James IV, King of Scots, who provided him with an allowance and a noble bride. The two then organised a combined invasion of England from the north, setting out with high hopes of success. However, James intended to conduct the war in the normal Scottish fashion – by burning, looting and pillaging – but Perkin realised this was no way for a would-be king to treat his future subjects if he wanted their support. The enterprise was called off, to the huge disappointment of both parties.

Perkin's final attempt was made in 1497, when he landed in Cornwall. Cornishmen flocked to his banner but he was soon faced with the royal army itself. Tin-miners, farmers and fishermen were no match for trained soldiers; Perkin's army melted away and the Perkin himself disappeared, and was later found in Beaulieu Abbey in Hampshire, where he had sought sanctuary. Henry Tudor had him brought to London, humiliating this would-be king by every means for the next two years. After a final session in the stocks, being pelted with rubbish, he was imprisoned in the Tower of London, close to his supposed cousin, Edward Plantagenet, Earl of Warwick, son of the late Duke of Clarence (see 18 February). In Warwick's case there was no doubt as to his possible threat to Henry's throne. The poor lad had been incarcerated ever since the Battle of Bosworth (see 22 August) and 'could not tell a goose from a capon', so it was said, but Henry had had no legitimate excuse to dispose of Warwick ... until now.

Their gaolers encouraged the young cousins to write to each other, sending cheerful notes about what they would do when they escaped from the Tower. Of course the gaolers took this treasonous correspondence straight to the king. Henry now had his excuse their fates were sealed.

T. Mount, *Richard III – King of Controversy*

22th – Birth of a Kingmaker

Richard Neville, Earl of Warwick, later known as the 'Kingmaker', was the eldest son of the Earl of Salisbury. He was born on 22 November 1428 in Norwich and was betrothed to Anne, daughter of Richard Beauchamp, Earl of Warwick, while just a boy. When her brother died, Anne brought her husband the title and the Warwick estates, making him the premier earl in England.

Richard, Duke of York was his uncle; when York became Lord Protector in 1453, after King Henry VI lost his reason, Warwick consequently became a royal counsellor. The king recovered in 1455, undoing all York's good government, so Warwick and his father took up arms in York's support. After their victory at St Albans on 22 May, Warwick was rewarded with the office of Captain of Calais.

In 1460, Warwick, Salisbury and Edward of York, Earl of March – the duke's eldest son – crossed from Calais to Sandwich on 26 June. A few days later they entered London. Then Warwick marched north, routing the Lancastrian army at Northampton on 10 July, taking King Henry prisoner. Warwick was virtually ruling the country in the king's name and was in London when Richard, Duke of York and the Earl of Salisbury (Warwick's father) were defeated and slain at Wakefield (see 30 December). Although the Lancastrians won the second battle that took place at St Albans on 17 February 1461, possibly due to Warwick's mistakes, the earl escaped and met up with Edward of York. Young Edward was fresh from a victory at Mortimer's Cross; Warwick brought him to London in triumph and proclaimed him king, as Edward IV. Within a month of his defeat at St Albans, Warwick was marching north again, the new king beside him, in pursuit of the Lancastrians. The victory of Towton (see 29 March) may have been due to Edward rather than to Warwick, but the earl had his reward.

For four years, Warwick was at the centre of government. His brother John, Lord Montague, elevated to the earldom of Northumberland, kept the Lancastrians at bay in the north while Warwick was playing politics, determined that England should have an alliance with France. The Nevilles' power reached its peak when George, the third brother, became Archbishop of York; Warwick truly was the 'Kingmaker' – for now.

The first hitch came when King Edward announced in September 1464 that he had secretly married Elizabeth Woodville the previous May, even as Warwick was in France arranging a French bride for the king. Warwick felt insulted. Further trouble began in 1466, when Edward made Earl Rivers, the queen's father, treasurer, and then refused permission for a marriage between Warwick's daughter, Isabel, and George, Duke of Clarence. Clarence was the king's younger brother who, at the time, was still heir to the throne – the queen had yet to provide a son for Edward. Greater insult followed when, in May 1467, Warwick again went to France with the king's agreement to conclude a treaty with the French, only to find, when he returned, that in his absence Edward had confirmed an alliance and trading agreement with the Duke of Burgundy, an enemy of France.

This was too much; Warwick began to plot his revenge. In the summer of 1469, the Neville family sailed to Calais, where Isabel and Clarence were married by the Archbishop of York without the king's knowledge. Warwick's next move was to arrange for his allies to raise a rebellion in Yorkshire and, when King Edward hastened north to deal with it, Warwick seized the opportunity to invade England. Warwick mustered his numerous supporters and the king, finding he was outnumbered, had to surrender, becoming Warwick's prisoner. The queen's father and her brother John were swiftly executed as Warwick took his revenge on the loathed Woodvilles. Matters soon turned: although Warwick promised Clarence that he would play kingmaker again and put George and Isabel on the throne, in March 1470 a rebellion in Lincolnshire gave Edward the chance to gather an army of his own and, taking Warwick by surprise, forced him and George to flee to France. There, with the connivance of King Louis XI, Warwick was reconciled to his old enemy, the Lancastrian queen, Margaret of Anjou. To seal the deal he agreed to marry his second daughter, Anne, to her son, the Lancastrian Prince of Wales.

In September 1470, Warwick and George, along with the Lancastrian lords, landed at Dartmouth. It was now Edward's turn to flee to Burgundy, and for six months Warwick ruled England as regent for the Lancastrian king, Henry VI – restored to the throne in name only. But the Lancastrian restoration held no advantages for George, who began to intrigue with his brother. In March 1471, when Edward landed at Ravenspur near the Humber estuary with Burgundian troops, weapons and money, George changed sides to join him. At Barnet on 14 April, Edward and both his brothers, George and Richard, faced Warwick and his brother, John, through the fog. Warwick and John were defeated, both slain in the field. The once mighty Kingmaker was no more.

Encyclopaedia Britannica, 11th edition, vol. XVIII.

23rd – The Pretender's Punishment

Perkin Warbeck, pretender to the throne of Henry VII, was hanged and quartered at Tyburn, on the Oxford Road (now Oxford Street), just west of the City of London on 23 November 1499 (see 21 November).

24th – Rotten Pigeons

In London *c*. 1380, William Fot, a poulterer in Fleet Street, was accused of attempting to sell eighteen rotten pigeons, 'putrid and stinking', to the citizens, not only endangering their health but trying to deceive them. The mayor and aldermen summoned four local cooks to examine the meat. The cooks determined that the pigeons were definitely unfit for sale and not to be eaten. Fot was sentenced to be put in the pillory and his pigeons to be burned beneath his nose.

B. Holsinger, 'Sin City' in *Medieval Life*

25th – Maritime Disaster

The most devastating maritime disaster of the medieval period not only cost 300 lives, but changed the course of English history. On the clear, calm night of 25 November 1120, a beautiful, state-of-the-art vessel, the *White Ship,* sank just off Barfleur, in the English Channel.

King Henry I was at the peak of his power, having crushed all his opponents in Normandy, and was about to return to England. He had even managed to convince the King of France to acknowledge that his son, William the Atheling, would succeed him as Duke of Normandy.

Henry had at least a dozen children, but only two were born of his wife, Matilda of Scotland: a daughter, also named Matilda, and a son named William. The rest of his children were illegitimate, although he treated them all very well, giving the boys important positions in his government and arranging excellent marriages for the girls. But it was William, as his only legitimate son, who would inherit his kingdom. With the recent agreement between Henry and the French king, and the marriage of William to the daughter of Fulk, Count of Anjou a year earlier, all was set fair for the young prince to inherit the Anglo-Norman empire.

King Henry and his party, including his son, often crossed the English Channel, although such a trip wasn't always easy or safe. The fleet was assembled and the wind perfect to sail for England. A shipowner, Thomas FitzStephen, offered the king the use of his new vessel, called the *White Ship*, which was well fitted out and ready for royal service. Henry approved but had already had his baggage stowed on another ship. He suggested his children and other young noble men and ladies might use the *White Ship* instead.

As the king set sail, his son William, along with two of William's half-siblings – Richard and Matilda – and others began to board the *White Ship*. A report by the contemporary chronicler, Oderic Vitalis, suggests that almost 300 people were on board, including fifty crew to man the sails and oars. The passengers were soon passing the wine around, including the crew. Perhaps concerned to see the crewmen getting drunk and thinking the ship was overcrowded with riotous youngsters, some had second thoughts and disembarked. This included Stephen of Blois, who said he was too sick from diarrhoea to make the trip. Orderic Vitalis noted that when, as was the custom, 'priests came there with other ministers carrying holy water to bless them, they laughed and drove them away with abuse and guffaws'. Instead, William and the other passengers called upon the ship's captain to set sail in haste, to test whether they could overtake the king's ship which had already departed. It was just before midnight. Orderic Vitalis explains what happens next:

At length he gave the signal to put to sea. Then the rowers made haste to take up their oars and, in high spirits because they knew nothing of what lay ahead, put the rest of the equipment ready and made the ship lean forward and race through the sea. As the drunken oarsmen were rowing with all their might, and the luckless helmsman paid scant attention to steering the ship though the sea, the port side of the *White Ship* struck violently against a huge rock, which was uncovered each day as the tide ebbed and covered once more at high tide. Two planks were shattered and, terrible to relate, the ship capsised without warning. Everyone cried out at once in their great peril, but the water pouring into the boat soon drowned their cries and all alike perished.

Hundreds of people were flung into the water and very few could swim. Although the sea was calm, it was dark, a night with little moon. On shore and on King Henry's own ship, the screams could be heard but no one could see what was happening. According to one report, William the Atheling was urged to climb aboard a small boat, but as they rowed away William heard his half-sister Matilda crying out and ordered the oarsmen to go back. As desperate people tried to clamber into the little boat, it was swamped and sank. A butcher from Rouen named Berold would be the only survivor; he alone could tell what had happened on the *White Ship*.

Over the next few days many bodies were washed ashore, but William the Atheling's was never found. King Henry was overcome and wept for his children and the others who had died.

Chroniclers explained that the sinking of the *White Ship* was an accident, or God's punishment for the sinful behaviour of those aboard. Henry had his barons swear homage to his only remaining legitimate child as the future ruler of England and Normandy, but the world just wasn't ready for a queen regnant and Matilda would lose out to her cousin, Stephen of Blois – he who had felt too unwell to sail on the doomed ship – heralding years of strife and anarchy as they fought for the Crown.

http://www.medievalists.net/2013/05/21/
was-the-white-ship-disaster-mass-murder/

26th – Irreconciliable Differences

In London on 26 November 1476, John Lewys testified that he, together with a fellow neighbour, Gilbert Horne, and Sir John, the parson of Lambeth parish, had managed to persuade Katherine Bachelere, *née* Burwell, and William Bacheler, her estranged husband, to meet at the Saracen's Head tavern, by St Paul's Cathedral. They had hoped to reconcile Katherine and William, who had lived apart for five years. However, it didn't work out: William said he would slit Katherine's throat if he was forced to live with her. So Lewys and Horne appeared as witnesses on Katherine's behalf when she sued William for divorce on the grounds of his cruelty to her.

S. McSheffrey, *Marriage, Sex and Civic Culture in Late Medieval London*

27th – Margaret Tudor

On this day in 1489 – although one source gives 28 November – Henry VII's eldest daughter, Margaret Tudor, was born to his wife, Elizabeth of York. The couple already had a son and heir, Arthur, Prince of Wales, who had been born three years before. Margaret Tudor would marry James IV, King of Scots, in 1503 and, after his death in 1513, would wed the Earl of Angus. Margaret was the grandmother of both Mary, Queen of Scots and her husband, Henry, Lord Darnley, the parents of James VI/James I, King of England.

Margaret's next brother, Henry, Duke of York, was born on 28 June 1491. He would become King Henry VIII. Margaret's younger sister, Mary, was born 18 March 1496. She would become Queen of France, briefly, as the wife of Louis XII. After Louis's death, Mary married Charles Brandon, Duke of Suffolk, the man Henry VIII had sent to escort the young widow home. It was a romantic match and they had to suffer Henry's anger when they wed without his consent. By this marriage, Mary became a grandmother to Lady Jane Grey – the 'nine-days queen'.

Two other sisters, Elizabeth and Katherine, and a brother, Edmund, died very young.

28th – A Yorkshire Widow's Will

Isabel Grymston, widow of Thomas Grymston of Flinton, a Yorkshire gentleman, wrote her will on 28 November 1479. She bequeathed her considerable wardrobe to her daughters, both called Elis (Alice), so it seems likely that Elis Grymston was her daughter-in-law, married to her son, William, while Elis Colynson was Isabel's own daughter, wed to a Mr Colynson:

I witt [will] to my doughter Elis Grymston my furd gown, a rede girdill harnest [decorated] with silver and gilted, my blak girdill silver harnest and the half of corall bedis [a rosary], a gold ryng and a purs[e] of cloth of gold. I wyt to my doughter Elis Colynson my grene gown, a musterdevelis gown with a velwyt [velvet] collar, my cremesyn [crimson] kirtle, half of my corall bedis, a pair of get [gilt?] bedes gawded with silver, my blew girdill and my rede girdill, a gold ryng and a purs of Royn[?]. And it is my will that my silver spo[o]nes be skist [shared] betwix my daughters Elis Grymston and Elis Colynson.

H. Falvey, et al. (eds) *English Wills proved in the Prerogative Court of York, 1477–99*

29th – Holly Berries

At this time of year, medieval foresters would be checking out the holly trees for those with the best crop of berries, suitable for Christmas decorations in homes and churches.

'Holm' was the medieval name for holly. Its prickly leaves symbolised Christ's crown of thorns and the red berries the droplets of His blood. Its pale wood was used for table-boards – at a time when tables were simply boards resting on trestles – and also for carving chess pieces.

T. McLean, *Medieval English Gardens*

30th – The Feast of St Andrew

This day was celebrated as the feast day of St Andrew. He was the elder brother of St Peter and, like him, a fisherman. Andrew had been a follower of John the Baptist before becoming one of Christ's apostles. He was later crucified in Greece, still preaching to the spectators there as he hung for two days before he died. However, the story that he insisted that he should be impaled upon a saltire or X-shaped cross, so as not to imitate and devalue Christ's death, seems to have originated much later, in the fourteenth century. Legend tells that St Regulus brought Andrew's relics to Kilrymont in Scotland, the town being renamed St Andrews and the saint adopted as patron of his new country.

L. W. Cowi and J. S. Gummer, *The Christian Calendar*

So let's celebrate St Andrew's day with a unique dish – a cockintrice. Medieval people loved jokes at mealtimes and this impossible creature came in two forms. This recipe comes from Harleian MS.279, *c.* 1430 (I have modernised the spelling):

Cokyntryce. Take a capon and scald him and draw him clean [remove the innards] & smite him in two in the waist overthwart; take a pig and scald him & draw him in the same manner & smite him also in the waist. Take a needle & a thread & sew the fore part of the capon to the after part of the pig; & the fore part of the pig to the hind part of the capon & then stuff them as thou stuffest a pig. Put them on a spit & roast them & when he is [cooked] enough, dore [adorn] him with yolks of eyroun [eggs] & powder[ed] ginger & saffron, then with the juice of parsley without & then serve it forth as a royal mete [dish].

T. Austin (ed.), *Two Fifteenth-Century Cookery-Books*
c. 1430–1450

'Eyroun' was a Kentish dialect word for 'eggs'. William Caxton in the foreword to his book *Aeneidos* complains that, as a printer, he had problems knowing which words to use when dialects could be so different. He tells how a merchant from the Midlands sailing to the Low Countries was stranded in north-east Kent by bad weather. The ship put passengers ashore and the hungry merchant asked a local housewife if he could have some eggs for his breakfast. She shrugged and said sorry, she couldn't understand French. The bewildered merchant said he couldn't speak French either. Then another passenger, presumably from Kent, asked the woman for some eyroun and was served with eggs for his breakfast. Presumably, the penny dropped for the merchant: he asked for eyroun and was given a good breakfast after all. 'So what word should *I* use?' asks Caxton.

The cockintrice would have been brightly coloured when served, with parsley juice dyeing it green and saffron golden-yellow. A medieval meal was as much a feast for the eyes as for the taste buds and stomach.

DECEMBER

1st – A Surfeit of Lampreys

King Henry I of England died on 1 December 1135, of, so it was said at the time, 'a surfeit of lampreys'. Here is a medieval dish using these primitive eel-like sucker fish:

For to make lamprey fresch in galentyne:

[The lamprey] schal be latyn blod atte Navel and schald yt and rost yt and ley yt al hole up on a Plater and zyf hym forth wyth Galentyn that be mad of Galyngale gyngener and canel and dresse yt forth.

S. Pegge, *The Forme of Cury*

A galantine is a French dish of deboned stuffed meat, most commonly poultry or fish (as in this case) that is poached and served cold, coated with aspic. Lampreys have very few bones, so deboning wouldn't be a problem. Galingale can be bought fresh from supermarkets these days, along with ginger and cinnamon (canel).

2nd – The Beautiful Disport

Then, as now, football was a popular winter 'disport', despite a number of kings trying to ban the game by law. This is how a late fifteenth-century monk in Surrey, Alexander Barclay, described the game on a chilly winter day:

> Each one contendeth and hath great delight
> With foot and with hand the bladder for to smite:
> If it fall to ground they lift it up again,
> This wise [way] to labour they count it for no pain,
> Running and leaping they drive away the cold,
> The sturdy ploughmen lusty, strong and bold,
> Overcometh the winter with driving the foot ball,
> Forgetting labour and many a grievous fall.

M. Collins and V. Davis, *A Medieval Book of Seasons*

Perhaps it was played more like rugby, since players could handle the ball. The ball wouldn't have bounced either, being a stuffed pig's bladder.

William FitzStephen made the first mention of football in 1170 when he was visiting London: 'after dinner all the youths of the city go out into the fields for the very popular game of ball.' He also mentioned that every trade had its own football team. The name 'football' referred to the game being played on foot, rather than on horseback, and not to using only your feet. Any part of the body was allowed to be used to propel the ball. The game often took place in the open country but sometimes in towns and villages, which caused quite a commotion and property damage.

The 'goals' were sometimes miles apart and there were no rules. The teams may have consisted of 300 to 500 people each. Wrestling, punching and kicking were allowed and injuries to the players were quite usual. In some cases, the injuries were so bad that they led to the death of the participants. As in one case:

Henry, son of William de Ellington, while playing at ball at Ulkhamon on Trinity Sunday with David le Ken and many others, ran against David and received an accidental wound from David's knife of which he died on the following Friday.

In another:

During the game at ball as he kicked the ball, a lay friend of his, also called William, ran against him and wounded himself on a sheath knife carried by the canon, so severely that he died within six days.

Despite the rowdiness of the game, there were versions of football played by women. Often the two teams would be the married women against the unmarried ones. In 1314, King Edward II became concerned that football was a waste of energy and time for men who should be practising their skills with the bow and tried to ban it. In 1331, his son, Edward III, was focused on war so he reintroduced the ban. In 1477, Edward IV passed a law that ordered:

No person shall practise any unlawful games such as dice, quoits, football and such games, but that every strong and able-bodied person shall practise with bow for the reason that the national defence depends upon such bowmen.

However, plenty of records show that young men who loved the game refused to accept the bans. Many people were fined or arrested for playing 'unlawful games of football'. Despite this, some believed that football had its benefits as well, especially to the health of its participants. Richard Mulcaster, the headmaster of the Merchant Taylors' School, claimed that football:

Great helps, both to health and strength. It strengtheneth and brawneth the whole body and by provoking superfluities downward, it dischargeth the head and upper parts, it is good for the bowels and to drive the stone and gravel from both the bladder and kidneys.

http://bleacherreport.com/articles/122315-history-of-football-medieval-football-part-1

3rd – Spree of Violence

The Coroner's Rolls of Bedfordshire in 1270 recorded that:

Emma, daughter of Richard Toky of Southill went to Houleden in Southill to gather wood. Walter Garglof of Stanford came carrying a bow and a small sheaf of arrows. He seized Emma and tried to throw her to the ground and deflower her but she immediately shouted and her father came. Walter shot an arrow at him, striking him on the right side of the forehead and mortally wounding him. He shot him again with an arrow under the right side and so into the stomach. Seman of Southill came and asked why he wanted to kill Richard. Walter immediately shot an arrow at him and struck him in the back so that his life was despaired of. Walter then fled. Later, Emma, wife to Richard, came and found her husband wounded to the point of death and shouted. Neighbours came and carried him to his home. He had the rites of the Church, made his will and died at twilight.

P. J. P. Goldberg, *Women in England c. 1250–1525*

4th – Pope Adrian IV

The only Englishman ever to be Pope, Nicholas Breakspear, was elected as pontiff by the cardinals in conclave on this day in 1154, taking the name Adrian IV. Nicholas had been born to humble parents at Abbots Langley in Hertfordshire around 1100, but spent most of his life away from England. He studied in Paris and became a canon at St Rufus, near Avignon, eventually being chosen as abbot. His skills and abilities were quickly recognised; Pope Eugenius III, who sent him to reorganise the church in Scandinavia, made him a cardinal. Here, Nicholas was so successful that when the intervening Pope, Anastasius IV, died in 1154, he was chosen to succeed him.

The new Pope had plenty of trouble to deal with: there was revolt in Rome and problems with the Holy Roman Emperor, Frederick Barbarossa. Although Adrian crowned him in 1155, Frederick made it clear that, as Emperor of Rome, *he* intended to control the city. As regards England and Ireland, Adrian issued a papal bull, known as *Laudabiliter* (its opening word), which gave Henry II of England papal approval for the conquest of Ireland. In 1155, in response to a request from the Archbishop of Canterbury, the Pope 'granted and donated Ireland to the illustrious King of England, Henry, to be held by him and his successors and sent the king a gold ring, set with a magnificent emerald, as a sign that he had invested the king with the right to rule Ireland'. This is the relevant text in translation from the Latin of the papal bull, *Laudabiliter*:

Laudably and profitably does your magnificence contemplate extending your glorious name on earth ... to enlarge the boundaries of the Church and to expound the truth of the Christian faith to ignorant and barbarous peoples ... [The Pope] is pleased to agree that you may enter that island [Ireland] and perform therein the things that have regard to the honour of God and the salvation of that land ...

http://www.historytoday.com/richard-cavendish/
election-Pope-adrianiv

Henry's conquest of Ireland didn't happen until the 1170s. It is also disputed whether the document was genuine or a forgery, but most authorities now accept that the Pope *did* issue it or something very similar. Meanwhile, Adrian – the one and only ever English Pope – had died in 1159.

5th – Winter Chills

What with winter chills and feverish colds, this remedy might be helpful:

For the fever of a man's head that maketh the head to ache so that he cannot sleep.

Take everfern that groweth upon an oak, and seethe the root thereof, and mint, of each equally much; and stamp them [pound them in a mortar] and make a plaster to thy forehead. And over the eyes anoint with wild thyme.

W. R. Dawson, *A Leechbook*

6th – The Feast of St Nicholas

No one really knows how Nicholas, a fourth-century Bishop of Myra (in Turkey), came to be transformed into our modern-day Santa Claus. One possible source is the story that he saved three young girls from prostitution by throwing three bags of gold into their house one night, so they had dowries and could marry. Those bags have been turned into the pawnbrokers' sign of three golden balls, and Saint Nicholas became the patron saint of moneylenders as well as children, maidens, sailors and numerous other disparate groups far removed from any Christmas celebration.

However, we have already seen how the medieval Christmas season could extend until 6 January, or even 2 February, for those with wealth and leisure enough to enjoy it and, for those same fortunate folk, Christmastide could begin with the exchange of small gifts on St Nicholas' Day. In England, it was traditional for parishes to choose a Boy-Bishop, a lad to perform the functions of the priest and command the elders – just for fun and only for one day.

7th – Continental Imports

On this day in 1479, William Cely wrote to his cousin, George Cely, about the great market that should have been happening in Bergen-op-Zoom in Holland; it seems to have been a big disappointment. As merchants, the Celys attended these trade markets to stock up on goods to sell back home in England, but on this occasion there was very little to buy:

Informing you that the Saturday after I departed from your mastership I came to Bergen in safety with all my things, thanked be God. As for Hollanders [Dutchmen], there be but few come to the mart [market] yet. There is none come that I have to do [business] with but Peter Johnson and his fellows but now, this week, they say there will come as many as will come [to] this mart. As for money, I have received none yet off no man, nor none of our fellowship that I can hear [of] since they came to the mart. As for giving over of money, I can not tell how it will be yet, for I hear of none exchange-making yet. Men fear it will be nought for there is little ware here for men to bestow their money upon: they think the ships shall go home half unladen, etc. Sir, as shortly as I can receive my things I shall make me ready and come unto you, with the grace of God it shall not be long until, who has you in His keeping.

A. Hanham, *The Cely Letters 1472–1488*

8th – Winter Court

The manor court of Lushot (Ludshott, Hampshire) was convened again on 8 December 1458:

[It is said] that tenants of the Lord Bishop of Winchester at Headley have appropriated a piece of the Lord's land at Lightwood, 2 furlongs long by half a furlong wide. Writ to be taken out.

John Bugenell [Bicknell], Thomas Benifold and John Farlee have let their houses fall into disrepair. Ordered to repair them adequately and to mend them in *sine dilato* [without delay]. The homage assesses damages for mending the house of Thomas at —; Richard Vallor is his surety that he will do the work before Pentecost.

John Andrew of Bramshott has cut a bough in the Lord's woodland and carried it away, without permission. John Langford of Graveshut [Grayshott] cut and carried away one cart-load of wood and one of bracken from the common pasture of the Lord's tenants without permission, fined 3d. And whereas Thomas Benifold seized 7 young cattle belonging to John Hownesham which were doing damage in the said Thomas's oats and put them in the Lord's pound, the said John broke the aforesaid pound and recovered the said young cattle without permission, so he is fined 6d. The same John grazed, trampled and consumed with his pigs the Lord's grass and corn in the Gardenfeild, fined 2d.

No reaper fines [fines for failing to do field-work for the lord at harvest time] at this Court.

http://www.johnowensmith.co.uk/headley/ludshott2rolls.htm

9th – Commercial Lease

[In 1476] Agnes Scauceby, wife of the late Robert Scauceby of York, glover, and Thomas Bene of York, capmaker, came into the council chamber on Ouse Bridge, in the presence of the mayor and chamberlains, and leased from them a shop on Ouse Bridge formerly in the tenure of Robert Scauceby. They are to have and to hold the shop from Martinmas [11 November] last past for a term of seven years, rendering annually to the keepers of Ouse Bridge 8s in equal portions at Pentecost and Martinmas. And if it should happen that the aforesaid rent is in arrears in part or whole after any of the feasts by one month, then let it be well lawful for the aforesaid mayor, chamberlains and keepers of Ouse Bridge to enter the shop, retain it and repossess it, this lease notwithstanding.

L. C. Attreed, *York House Books*

On 20 February 1478, Agnes Scauceby and Thomas Bene came to the council chamber and returned the shop to the mayor and commonality.

10th – Lionheart's Return Home

Richard the Lionheart had left the Holy Land in the second week of October 1192. The Third Crusade was only a partial success and, after three years of fighting the Saracens, the Christian warriors were exhausted and their numbers much depleted by disease, desertion and death in battle. Richard finally agreed a three-year truce with Saladin, the great Muslim general. Unfortunately, the Lionheart's domineering character meant that he had made powerful enemies during the Crusade. He had insulted Duke Leopold of Austria, the leader of the German contingent, and upset Henry VI, the Holy Roman Emperor, who controlled most of Germany.

The story of Richard's return home is confused, but the weather was stormy and he landed on the northern Adriatic coast near Trieste in north-eastern Italy. Possibly, he was shipwrecked there. Whatever happened, the king found himself hundreds of miles from friendly lands, on 10 December 1192, with only a few companions. Disguised as either a Templar knight or a merchant, Richard headed north, making for the safety of the lands of his brother-in-law, Henry the Lion, Duke of Saxony.

In terrible winter weather, Richard took shelter in a 'disreputable house' or brothel in the outskirts of Vienna. Some stories suggested it was his demand for a roast chicken dinner, rather than humbler food, that led to his discovery; or that it was his companions calling him 'Sire' that gave him away. Another story told is that he lent his gloves to his squire – gloves embroidered with the royal arms of England – and gave the lad a ruby ring to buy dinner; all a bit of a *faux pas* when trying to travel incognito. Whatever the truth, upon realising who he was, the king was captured by Duke Leopold of Austria's men. Duke Leopold must have been delighted to have the King of England in his clutches and he promptly locked Richard in Durnstein Castle, fifty miles west of Vienna. The duke also informed his overlord, Henry VI, the Holy Roman Emperor; a letter still exists, written by Henry to Philip Augustus of France, gloating over the capture of the royal pilgrim. Seizing King Richard was illegal as Pope Celestine III had decreed that knights who took part in the Crusade were not to be molested as they travelled to and from the Holy Land. Both Emperor Henry and Duke Leopold were subsequently excommunicated for Richard's detention.

Richard was moved from castle to castle in the German lands controlled by Henry and Leopold until he arrived at Ochsenfurt in March 1193. There the English emissaries, the Abbots of Boxley and Robertsbridge, caught up with their king and began negotiations for his ransom and release, which took almost a year. After strenuous diplomatic efforts by Richard's mother, Eleanor of Aquitaine, the payment of 100,000 marks – an enormous sum mostly collected from his English subjects, especially the Londoners – and the handing over of hostages, the king was released in early February 1194.

http://www.angus-donald.com/history/
king-richards-return-imprisonment-and-ransom/

11th – An Entertainer's Reward

On this date in 1483, the mayor of York and the aldermen decided it was time to reward those who had planned the entertainments when King Richard III had visited the city the previous September:

It was agreed by all that Sir Henry Hudson shall have for his labour about the site of the show made to our sovereign lord the king, 40*s*. And it was agreed that for their great labour Master Wrangwysh, Richard Marston and William White have had in their recent journey to meet with our sovereign lord the king, that the said Master Wrangwysh have for his labour 40*s* and each of the said Richard and William [have] 30*s*.

L. C. Attreed, *York House Books 1461–1490*, vol. I

12th – The First Day of Winter

According to a fifteenth-century translation of the *Secretum Secretorum* or 'Secret of Secrets', this day was the first day of winter:

Winter begins when the sun enters the sign of Capricorn and contains eighty-eight days, fifteen hours and fourteen minutes, that is to say, from the twelfth day of December until the eleventh day of March. At this time the night is longest and the days are shortest.

M. Collins and V. Davis, *A Medieval Book of Seasons*

13th – Death by Misadventure

In Bedfordshire in 1271 Lady Christine de Fornival's servant, Alexander le Gardiner of Potton, was digging under the walls of an old dovecote in the garden in Lady Christine's courtyard in Sutton to demolish them. As he dug the wall, by misadventure, [it] fell upon him and broke his head so that he died there at once. His wife Alice came with his breakfast, looked for him, saw his surcoat and cap and the spade with which he dug and so found him dead.

Bedfordshire Coroners' Rolls

14th – A Servant Answers Back

At the Borough Court at Nottingham, the following case was recorded as having happened on this day in 1404:

Joan Potter of Nottingham, through her guardian Geoffrey Baker, complains of John Lorymer in a plea of trespass in that he, here at Nottingham, on Sunday after the feast of the conception of the Blessed Mary last, assaulted the said Joan, beat her there, wounded and ill treated her, and did other injuries to her to the serious damage of this plaintiff, 100s ... He [John Lorymer] comes and defends ... saying that Joan is and was [his] servant and the said Joan gave him a contrary reply [answered back cheekily] and consequently [he] took an 'elenwand' and struck her on the head and elsewhere, as is just. And the aforesaid Joan, through the said Geoffrey [her guardian] and John Braydale her attorney, seeks judgement in respect of his answer, and John Lorymer likewise, and so judgement is respited until the next court.

P. J. P. Goldberg, *Women in England c. 1275–1525*

Unfortunately, it was lawful for a master to beat his servant and, as is so often the case, we don't know the outcome of this suit. Joan was probably under twenty-one years old as she has a guardian, Geoffrey Baker, who has also employed an attorney. However, whatever her age, a woman almost always required a man to represent her in court. The exception was in the case of her husband being murdered, then she could take the felon to court, or if she ran her own business as a *femme sole* (literally, a woman alone, responsible for her business deals even if she was married), she could sue in her own name for debts owed to her.

15th – A New Apprentice

On this day in 1451, a contract was drawn up between a master in the Merchant-Taylors Guild of London and a new apprentice from Harrietsham in Kent:

John Harrietsham contracts with Robert Lucy to serve the said Robert as well in the craft and in all his other works and doings ... from Christmas day next ensuing for the term of 7 years.

He is to receive 9s 4d at the end of the term, and he shall work one year after the seven at wages of 20s. Robert is to find his apprentice all necessaries, food, clothing, shoes and bed and to teach him his craft in all its particulars ... During the term the apprentice is to keep his master's secrets, to do him no injury and commit no excessive waste of his goods. He is not to frequent taverns, not to commit fornication in or out of his master's house, nor make any contract of matrimony nor affiance himself without his master's permission. He is not to play at dice, tables [backgammon] or checkers or any other unlawful games but is to conduct himself soberly, justly, piously, well and honourably, and to be a faithful servant according to the custom of London. For all his obligations Robert binds himself, his heir and his executors, his goods and chattels, present and future, wherever found.

T. Mount, *Everyday Life in Medieval London*

The two parties signed and delivered the contract to the guild for safe keeping. These indentures were always written out twice on the same piece of parchment, which was then cut in two with a jagged cut, like pointed teeth – 'indentured' – so the two halves fitted together like jig-saw pieces. The copies were identical and neither party could change the wording of one without the other.

Sometimes contracts contained clauses about the education that was to be provided as well as the teaching of the craft. Apart from dealing with money matters, the emphasis was on the behaviour expected of both master and apprentice. The master had to act *in loco parentis* and mustn't ask the apprentice to carry out menial jobs, such as fetching water. He must treat the youngster as a member of his family and had a father's duty to chastise him for wrongdoing, but he couldn't be abusive. Most important, he was to instruct the apprentice without concealing any trade secrets that would hinder the youngster from becoming a master. On his part, the apprentice was to accept his master's discipline, including corporal punishment, provided it wasn't too severe, to agree not to leave to serve another master nor to run away. If he did, his sponsors would be liable and he could be barred from the craft.

16th – Henry VI, King of France

In December 1431, at the age of just ten, King Henry VI of England made a majestic entry into Paris for his coronation as King of France – the only monarch ever to wear both crowns. By tradition kings of France were always crowned in Reims, but that city had been under the control of the French Dauphin since 1429 and Paris had to do as its replacement. On the great day, 16 December, Henry was not even crowned by the Bishop of Paris, but by his great-uncle, the Cardinal-Bishop of Winchester. The cardinal insisted on singing the Mass, much to the annoyance of the French bishop whose cathedral, Notre Dame, was being used for the occasion. Not only was the celebrant English but the ceremony itself was more in the English tradition than the French. The singing, however, in the opinion of critical witnesses was at least of a good standard.

After the ceremony, a great feast was held but the organisation was unsatisfactory. The food was awful, having been cooked three days before. The celebrations that followed the feast were also criticised as inadequate since they failed to bring to the trades-people the profits that they had a right to expect. In spite of the great welcome given to the king on his arrival, despite being at a time of poverty and an unfavourable season, when he departed nobody had a good word to say for him as neither he nor the English had given much in return. Perhaps not surprisingly Henry stayed little more than a week in Paris before setting out on the journey home. By early February 1432 he was back in England. He had left his French kingdom for the first and last time.

http://www.historytoday.com/ct-allmand/
coronations-henry-vi#sthash.E2ac7ref.dpuf

*

Also on this day in 1484, probate was granted on the will of Joanne Mudeford, a widow of Glastonbury in Somerset. She left most of her belongings to her son, Thomas, and daughter, Joanne:

I leave all the utensils of my house, namely pots, plates, cooking pots, mortars, beds, bed furniture, vessels of pewter and the like, with basins and ewers, except those of silver or gilt, which are to be shared equally between my son Thomas Mudeford and my daughter Joanne Mudeford. Also, I leave to my servant Joanne Edmunds a whole measure of cloth and to Alice Newman my former servant a whole measure of cloth ...

Also I leave to Joanne Hygyns the wife of William Hygyns a coral rosary. Also I leave to Joanne Mudeford my daughter my best gown, a tunic called a kirtle, my best studded belt and my best rosary. Also I leave the best veil I have to be made into a cloth for the altar of St Erasmus when it is erected in the church of St John the Baptist [in Glastonbury, where she wishes to be buried]. Also I leave another veil to make a canopy above the host over the high altar of the same church. Also to Sir Peter at this time parish chaplain of the said church, 6s 8d. Also I leave the rest of my veils not bequeathed to my daughter Joanne Mudeford.

The remainder of all my goods I give and leave to my son Thomas Mudeford whom I make my executor.

L. Boatwright, et al. (eds), *The Logge Register of PCC Wills, 1479–1486*

An awful lot of cloth must have gone into making each of those veils for them to be large enough to use as Joanne instructs. Incidentally 'Sir Peter', the chaplain wasn't a knight – 'sir' was a courtesy title and the correct form of address for a priest.

17th – The Traitors' Execution

On 17 December 1489, four men were executed as traitors to King Henry VII: Edward Frank, Henry Davy, John Mayne and Christopher Swan. Edward Plumpton wrote of the event to Sir Robert Plumpton:

Pleaseth your mastership, after all due recommendacion, to wyte that this day was hanged at the tower hill iiij [four] servants of the Kings; wherfore, the brynger herof can shew to you by mouth [i.e. tell you the details].

Using a priest, Thomas Rothwell of London, as a go-between, the four men had been in communication with John, the Abbot of Abingdon, near Oxford, who was to supply the quartet with money. This was to finance a plot to release the young Edward, Earl of Warwick, from his long confinement in the Tower of London, planned for 20 December. Warwick was the teenaged son of George, Duke of Clarence – he who had been drowned in that infamous butt of malmsey wine (see 18 February). If not for his father being attainted for treason back in 1477, with the 'Princes in the Tower' having disappeared from the scene Warwick could claim to be the rightful Yorkist heir to the English throne. Without a doubt, his claim was better than that of Henry VII – hence his imprisonment in the Tower ever since the death of his uncle Richard III at the battle of Bosworth in 1485 (see 22 August).

Edward Frank and his fellow conspirators were discovered, accused of high treason and, as Edward Plumpton said, hanged on Tower Hill – although a herald's chronicle said 'beheded'. This would be unusual unless the men were of high social status; Henry Davy was described as a tailor of London. The Abbot of Abingdon had been an ardent Yorkist supporter and thorn in King Henry Tudor's side since he seized the throne and would continue to be so.

T. Stapleton (ed.), *The Plumpton Correspondence*

18th – Three Days of Peril

According to medical advice:

In the month of December, hot meats use [eat] and blood, for need, thou mayest let. Three days of peril there be, the fifteenth, the sixteenth and the eighteenth. Forebear then [on those days] cold worts [vegetables] for they be venomous and melancholic.

Whoso this regimen holdeth [keeps to], of his health he may be secure.

W. R. Dawson, *A Leechbook of the Fifteenth Century*

On the days when vegetables didn't have to be avoided, here is how to cook cabbage:

Take fair caboges and cut them and pick them clean and wash them. Parboil them in fair water and then press them on a fair board; and then chop them and cast them in a fair pot with good fresh broth and with marrowbones and let it boil. Then take fair grated bread and cast thereto saffron and salt, or else take good gruel made of fresh flesh, draw through a strainer and cast thereto. And when thou servest it in, knock out the marrow of the bones and lay the marrow, two pieces or three in a dish, as seemeth best, and serve forth.

T. Austin, *Two Fifteenth-Century Cookery-Books c. 1430–50*

19th – King Henry II's Coronation

The coronation of Henry II, the first of the Plantagenet kings of England, took place in Westminster Abbey on 19 December 1154. He has been described as a 'reddish haired, quick-tempered and hyper-active young man'. Henry put his seal to this Coronation Charter – the first of its kind. English monarchs still make an oath based on these words during the coronation ceremony:

Henry, by the grace of God, king of England, duke of Normandy and Aquitaine and count of Anjou, to all the earls, barons, and his faithful, French and English, greeting ...

Know that, to the honour of God and of the holy church and for the advantage of my whole kingdom, I have conceded and granted, and by my present charter confirmed to God and to the holy church, and to all the earls and barons, and to all my men all the concessions and grants and liberties and free customs which King

Henry [I], my grandfather, gave and conceded to them. Similarly also, all the evil customs which he abolished and remitted, I remit and allow to be abolished for myself and my heirs. Therefore, I will and strictly require that the holy church and all the earls and barons, and all my men should have and hold all those customs and grants and liberties and free customs, freely and quietly, well and in peace, and completely, from me and my heirs to them and their heirs, as freely and quietly and fully in all things as King Henry, my grandfather, granted and conceded to them and by his charter confirmed them.

http://conclarendon.blogspot.co.uk/2012/09/
coronation-charter-of-king-henry-ii.html

20th – The Most Marvellous Blazing Star

Beginning on this day in 1471:

Two or three hours before sunrise, four days before Christmas, there appeared the most marvellous blazing star ... It arose in the southeast and so continued twelve nights, rising more and more easterly. When it arose in the east, it rose at ten of the clock in the night, and kept its course flaming westwards over England. And it had a white flame of fire fervently burning, the flame endlongs from east to west, and so endured fourteen nights, full little changing, and some time it would seem quenched out and suddenly it burnt fervently again. And then it was at one time plain [due] north and then it compassed about the lodestar [Polaris, the North Star] ... And so the star continued four weeks until the twentieth day of February. Twelve days before the vanishing thereof, it appeared in the evening and was down within two hours and ever of a colour pale steadfast ... and so every night it appeared less and less till it was as little as a hazel stick; and so it vanished away the twentieth day of February.

K. Dockray, *Three Chronicles of the
Reign of Edward IV*

This spectacular comet wasn't the famous Halley's comet which had appeared in 1454. This comet is designated C/1471 Y1 – such a boring name for the brightest and closest comet known in recorded history.

R. Stoyan, *Atlas of Great Comets*

21st – An Earthquake in England

In Advent ... the fourth day before Christmas [1248], there was an earthquake in England, as was told to the writer by the Bishop of Bath in whose diocese it happened, the walls of buildings were burst asunder, the stones were torn from their places and gaps appeared in the ruined walls. The vaulted roof which had been set up on the top of the cathedral church of Wells through the great efforts of the builders, a mass of great size and weight, was hurled from its place and fell on the church, causing considerable damage and, as it fell from on high, making a dreadful noise so as to strike great terror into all who heard it ... This earthquake was the third which had occurred in three years this side of the Alps; one in the region of Savoy and two in England; a circumstance unheard of since the beginning of the world and therefore the more terrible.

Revd J. A. Giles (trans.),
Matthew Paris (1853) vol. 2

22nd – Offending Horsebread

On this date in 1438, the city council in York recorded:

At this day it was agreed ... that in as much as the baxters [female bakers] of this city have offended in the weight of their horsebread, it is agreed for the said offence ... that from henceforth the baxters of this city shall, as long as the price of beans be at 4s or under, sell four horseloaves for 1d and that every horseloaf shall weigh 3lbs; and if the price of beans be above 4s then they shall sell three horseloaves for 1*d* and that every horseloaf shall weigh 3lbs. This ordinance to endure for a year... and for the said offence the said baxters shall pay to the [mayor's] chamber 40*s*.

L. C. Attreed, *York House Books*, vol. I

Horsebread was, literally, the very cheapest sort of bread intended to feed horses. It isn't the city bakers who are guilty of making underweight loaves or overcharging for them; it's the women baxters. I suspect the men didn't demean themselves by baking horsebread, rather than that they were too honest to cheat the customers. Horsebread, in this case, was being made from ground beans but, during food shortages, it could be made from acorns or beechnuts instead. In the worst times of famine or poverty, the poor might be reduced to buying and eating horsebread themselves.

23rd – Dragons

With magic in the air as Christmas drew near, this is what a thirteenth-century bestiary, or book of beasts, has to say about dragons:

The dragon is larger than all the rest of the serpents and than all other animals in the world. It is often tempted to come out of caves and the air is shaken by it. It has a crest, a small mouth and narrow nostrils and it puts out its tongue. Its strength is not in its teeth but its tail and it harms by blows. It has no harmful poison in order to kill because it slays anything which it embraces. Not even the elephant is safe from it. It lies concealed near the paths which elephants use, entangles their feet with its coils and suffocates them to death. Its homes are Ethiopia and India where there is always heat.

R. Barber, *Bestiary*

24th – John Lackland

On Christmas Eve 1166/67 – sources vary as to the year – at Beaumont Castle in Oxford, Eleanor of Aquitaine, queen to Henry II and now into her forties, gave birth to her youngest child, a son whom they called John.

John was her fifth son. William had died in infancy; Henry became known as the 'Young King'; Richard became his mother's heir as Duke of Aquitaine and Geoffrey married the heiress of Brittany to become Duke of Brittany. Since Henry the Young King would also have the dukedom of Normandy and various earldoms to go with his crown, there was nothing left for John to inherit – except for the nickname 'Lackland'.

Despite being his father's favourite, when John was a teenager he still had no titles and no estates to bring him an income. When his eldest brother Henry died and Richard became heir to the throne instead, Henry II tried to persuade Richard to give Aquitaine to John. Richard and his mother, the feisty Eleanor, were having none of it: Richard was her favourite son and Aquitaine was his.

Henry II then promised John he could be Lord of Ireland – he just had to go and take it, subduing the assorted kings and warlords who ruled there. John certainly took the title but failed to take the country. He hoped, at least, to gather the Irish taxes due to the English Crown – money his father said he could keep – and sailed to Dublin, full of expectation. The story goes that he insisted that Irish lords appearing before him had to wear underpants beneath their tunics – an unheard-of novelty in Ireland, apparently – and improve their barbaric table manners. Shortly after these noble achievements, he argued with his new subjects and fled back to England without having collected a pennyworth of taxes. It was not a good beginning to the career of England's future monarch, King John, and it didn't improve over the years.

25th – Christmas Day

William the Conqueror was crowned King of England in Westminster Abbey on Christmas Day in 1066. This was such a momentous occasion that the cheering inside the abbey made the guards outside think the king was being attacked. They ran to his assistance and the coronation ended in a riot, with people killed and houses burned.

Twenty-one years later, on Christmas Day 1087, William announced that he wanted to be certain all his English subjects were paying him the correct amount of tax. To that end, he commanded that a thorough survey be made of everyone's lands and possessions, ploughs, mills, meadows, woodland – everything – county by county. His clerks made an excellent job of it over the next year or so, by which time the Conqueror was dead, although his son, Rufus had the benefit, as do historians to this day. The survey was known as the 'Domesday' by those required to answer it, because it seemed more like the reckoning of the biblical Day of Judgement.

*

For a celebration feast, here is a recipe for roast pork or wild boar with spiced wine:

Take coriander, caraway seeds ground small, powder of pepper and ground garlic in red wine. Meddle all these together and salt it. Take loins of pork (raw) and fle of the skin [remove the skin] and prick it well with a knife and lay it in the sauce [i.e. marinade it]. Roast it when you will and keep all that falleth therfro in the roasting and seethe it in a possynet [pot] with fair broth and serve it forth with the roast anon.

M. Black, *The Medieval Cookbook*

26th – Boxing Day

On the day after Christmas, in late-twelfth-century Bury, St Edmunds, there were gatherings in the cemetery, wrestling bouts and matches between the abbot's servants and the burgesses of the town: and from words they came to blows, and from buffets to wounds and bloodshed. But the abbot when he heard of it, after calling to him ... persons who had watched the show ... ordered the names of the evil-doers to be written down and ... caused all of them to be brought before him on 30 December.

In the meantime he abstained from inviting a single burgess to his table, as he used formerly to do during the first five days of Christmas.

On the appointed day, having sworn sixteen law-worthy men and heard their testimony, the abbot said, 'Because they are laymen and do not understand how great a crime it is to commit such sacrilege, I will, that others may be more afraid, excommunicate these by name and in public and ... I will begin with my own household and servants'. And so it was done when we had put on stoles and lighted candles.

Then all of them [the miscreants] went out of the church ... they stripped themselves and, naked save for their drawers [underpants with a drawstring] they prostrated themselves before the door of the church. And when they ... told him that more than a hundred men were lying thus naked, the abbot wept. Therefore, after they had all been smartly scourged and then absolved, they all swore they would stand by the judgement of the Church concerning the commission of sacrilege. And on the morrow they were given penance ... and the abbot recalled them all to unity and concord, uttering terrible threats against all those who by word or deed should give cause for dissension. But he publicly forbade all gatherings or shows in the cemetery.

So all having been brought back to the blessing of peace, the burgesses feasted with their lord [the abbot] during the days that followed with much rejoicing.

The Chronicles of Jocelin of Brakelond concerning the Acts of Samson, Abbot of the Monastery of St Edmund

On Boxing Day, rich lords often gave their tenants a small gift containing a moral lesson. The poor received money from their masters in hollow clay pots with a slit in the top. They had to break them to get the money out. Nicknamed 'piggies', these offerings were the earliest version of a piggy bank, although it is doubtful whether they encouraged much saving.

27th – Manor Treats

Some manors dished out Christmas treats depending on status. In the thirteenth century, one manor near Wells Cathedral in the south of England invited two common folk – one a large landholder and the other a small one. The first got a feast for himself and two friends, including beer, beef and bacon, chicken stew, cheese and even candles to light the feast with. The poorer man did not fare so well. He had to bring his own cup and plate but at least he got to take home the leftovers, and he was even given a loaf of bread to share with his neighbours.

28th – Festive Gifts

If you were higher on the social scale, a member of a knight's household, or even the king's, you would be treated to a fabulous feast and gifts of jewels and robes. In 1482, the famously generous King Edward IV gave a spectacular Christmas gift to his people when he held a feast that fed over 2,000 people each day. Even then the pressures to give at Christmas were immense. Edward's brother, Richard III, presented the City of London with a gold cup encrusted with jewels. He and his wife Anne spent a staggering £1,200 on new clothes and gifts for the court. In 1484, he licensed a merchant to bring jewels to England so he could give his wife impressive gifts during the Christmas season. Perhaps he already knew it might be her last – she died the following March.

29th – The Murder of Thomas Becket

On 29 December 1170, Thomas Becket, Archbishop of Canterbury, was murdered before the high altar in his cathedral.

Thomas Becket was born around 1120, the son of a wealthy London wine merchant. He was well educated in the household of Theobald, Archbishop of Canterbury, and became a clerk. Theobald sent his young protégé on several missions to Rome. Theobald wasn't alone in recognising the Londoner's talents and ambition: when King Henry II was in need of a new Chancellor of England, Becket got the job. The two men became close friends, hunting and dealing with matters of state together. At the time, the king was in conflict with the Church; when Theobald died in 1161, thinking to solve these problems, Henry made Becket archbishop. For the king, the result was completely unexpected: his pleasure-loving friend was transformed overnight into a serious, austere cleric and staunch upholder of Church rights. Their friendship collapsed as Becket supported the Church in all its disagreements with the king.

In 1164, realising the extent of Henry's displeasure, Becket fled to France, remaining in exile for several years while the quarrels continued between himself, the king and the Pope. When a compromise of sorts was reached, Becket returned to England, just before Christmas 1170. On the 29 December, four knights, wrongly thinking that King Henry wanted to see the end of the troublesome archbishop, confronted and murdered Becket in Canterbury Cathedral.

Almost at once, the monks of Canterbury began recording miracles performed by the blood spilt at the site of Becket's murder, building up a large dossier that was presented to the Pope as evidence of his saintliness. So convincing was the case they made that Thomas Becket was canonised in record time, achieving sainthood in February 1173, just two years after his martyrdom. His shrine in Canterbury Cathedral quickly became the most important pilgrimage destination in England.

30th – The Battle of Wakefield

On this fateful Tuesday in 1460, during the holiday of the Twelve Days of Christmas and the customary time of peace and goodwill, there occurred the culmination of almost a decade of sporadic violent unrest between the supporters of the Lancastrian king, Henry VI, and his cousin Richard, Duke of York.

The Duke of York and his supporters were enjoying the Christmas festivities at Sandal Castle, near Wakefield in Yorkshire; but the Lancastrians had other matters in mind. They marched to Wakefield and deployed on a low hill just south of the town, separated from Sandal Castle by a mile of farmland and common land. Seeing the enemy on his doorstep, York ordered his army of around 5,000 or 6,000 men to go out and meet them. Perhaps they were over confident, having had a little too much Christmas cheer, but the Yorkists' hopes of a quick victory before dinnertime were soon dashed.

The Lancastrians fielded perhaps twice that number of men, with a reserve nine miles away at Pontefract Castle. Little is recorded of how the armies were deployed or the course of the battle itself. If it was conducted in the usual way for fifteenth-century engagements, the armies were probably organised into three 'wards': the main (centre), van (right) and rear (left). The Yorkist wards were most likely commanded by the duke himself, his brother-in-law Richard Neville, Earl of Salisbury, and possibly York's second son Edmund, Earl of Rutland, although he was only seventeen and would have had a more experienced captain to advise him.

Henry Beaufort, Duke of Somerset, James Butler, Earl of Wiltshire, and John, Lord Clifford of Craven, led the opposing Lancastrians. In support were Henry Percy, Earl of Northumberland, and Henry Holland, Duke of Exeter, York's own son-in-law. As the engagement began, Anthony Trollope, supposedly a Yorkist ally, attacked his own side, causing panic in the duke's ranks. York was suddenly horribly outnumbered. In under an hour, his army faced defeat. He attempted to retreat, fighting a rearguard action, only to be overwhelmed and killed not far from Sandal Castle. Other desperate Yorkists tried to flee northwards into the town of Wakefield but they were pursued and became trapped where the River Calder made a loop in the fields. Among those attempting to escape was young Edmund. He was overtaken and killed beside the chapel on Wakefield Bridge by Lord Clifford – an act the Yorkists never forgave. Up to 2,000 Yorkists died on the field – ten times the Lancastrian losses – while others were taken alive, including the Earl of Salisbury who was beheaded at Pontefract the following day.

As the ultimate insult to the Duke of York, his body was taken from the field, decapitated, and his head displayed on a spike on top of Micklegate Bar, the gateway to his city of York, wearing a crown of straw to mock his delusions of kingship. This was another insult the family wouldn't forget nor forgive. When York's heir, Edward, Earl of March, became King Edward IV just a few months later (see 28 June), retribution would follow.

http://www.military-history.org/articles/the-battle-of-wakefield.htm

31st – New Year's Gifts

The medieval chronicler, Matthew Paris, recorded that, on this day in 1249, King Henry III received from the London citizens 'the first gifts which the people are accustomed superstitiously to call New Year's gifts, as portents of success for the coming year'.

This seems like a good way and a happy note on which to end our *Year in the Life of Medieval England*.

Happy New Year!

ACKNOWLEDGEMENTS

I should like to thank the staff at Amberley Publishing who suggested I write this book and have supported my efforts.

My greatest debt is to my husband, Glenn, whose support was unstinting. His endless patience in finding, identifying and researching all the illustrations showed his stalwart commitment to the project.

I must thank Gale Horn of the Medieval Combat Society for her kind permission to use the photographs that she took in Cyprus of the sugar cane and the remains of the fourteenth-century sugar refinery at Kouklia-Stavros.

BIBLIOGRAPHY

Ashdown-Hill, J, *Richard III's 'Beloved Cousyn': John Howard and the House of York* (History Press, 2012)

Attreed, L. C., *York House Books 1461–1490*, 2 vols (Stroud, 1991)

Aungier, G. J., *Croniques de London* (London: Camden Society, 1844)

Austin, T. (ed.), *Two Fifteenth-Century Cookery-Books c.1430–1450* (London: EETS, 1888)

Baildon, W. P., *Selected Cases in Chancery AD 1364 to 1471* (Seldon Society, X, 1896)

Barber, R., *Bestiary* (Suffolk: Boydell Press, 1999)

Bennett, H. S., *The Pastons and their England* (Cambridge: Canto, 1990)

Biddle, M. and S. Badham, *King Arthur's Round Table: An Archaeological Investigation* (Boydell and Brewer, 2000)

Black, M., *The Medieval Cookbook* (British Museum Press, 1992)

Boatwright, L., M. Habberjam and P. Hammond (eds), *The Logge Register of PCC Wills, 1479–86*, 2 vols (Richard III Society, 2008)

Brears, P. (ed.), Wynkyn de Worde's *The Boke of Keruinge, 1508* (Sussex: Southover Press, 2003)

Brewer, C., *The Death of Kings – A Medical History of the Kings and Queens of England* (London: Abson Books, 2000)

Butler, S. M., *Forensic Medicine and Death Investigation in Medieval England* (New York and London: Routledge, 2015)

Collier, Mrs, 'Saint Christopher and Some Representations of Him in English Churches', *Journal of the British Archaeological Association* (1904), pp.130–45

Collins, M. and V. Davis, *A Medieval Book of Seasons* (New York: Harper Collins, 1992)

Cowie, L. W. and J. S. Gummer, *The Christian Calendar* (London: Weidenfeld and Nicolson, 1974)

Darby, H. C., *The Medieval Fenland* (Cambridge: University Press, 1940)

Davis, M. and A. Prescott, (eds), *London and the Kingdom, Essays in Honour of Caroline M. Barron* (Donington: Shaun Tyas, 2008)

Dawson, W. R., *A Leechbook… of Medical Recipes of the Fifteenth Century* (London: MacMillan and Co. Ltd. 1934)

Dawson, Thomas, *The Good Housewife's Jewel* (reprinted from the sixteenth-century original by Southover Press, 1996)

Derby, H. C., *The Medieval Fenland* (Cambridge: University Press, 1940)

Dockray, K. (intro), *Three Chronicles of the Reign of Edward VI* (Gloucester: Alan Sutton Publishing, 1988)

Falvey, H., L. Boatwright and P. Hammond, (eds), *English Wills proved in the Prerogative Court of York, 1477–99* (Richard III Society, 2013)

Fryde, E. B. et al. (eds), *Handbook of British Chronology* (London: Boydell and Brewer, 1986)

Giles, Rev J. A. (trans.), *Matthew Paris* (1853)

Goldberg, P. J. P., *Women in England c. 1275–1525* (Manchester: University Press, 1995)

Hamilton, J. S., *The Plantagenets: History of a Dynasty* (London and New York: Continuum, 2010)

Hanham, A. (ed.), *The Cely Letters 1472–1488* (EETS: 1975)

Henisch, B., *The Medieval Cook* (Suffolk: The Boydell Press, 2008)

Hodgett, G. A. J., *Stere htt Well – Medieval recipes from Samuel Pepys's Library* (Cambridge: Magdalene College, 1972)

Holsinger, B., 'Sin City' in *Medieval Life, Collectors' Edition* (BBC History Magazine, 2015)

Horrox, R. and P. W. Hammond (eds), *British Library Harleian Manuscript 433*, 4 vols (Richard III Society, 1979)

Kennedy, M. and L. Foxhall, *The Bones of a King – Richard III Rediscovered* (University of Leicester, 2015)

Labarge, M. W., *Mistress, Maids and Men* (London: Orion Books Ltd, 1980)

McLean, T., *Medieval English Gardens* (New York: Dover Publications, 2014)

McSheffrey, S., *Marriage, Sex and Civic Culture in Late Medieval London* (Philadelphia: University of Pennsylvania Press, 2006)

Mortimer, I., *The Time Travellers' Guide to Medieval England* (London: Bodley Head, 2008)

Mount, T., *Dragon's Blood and Willow Bark* (Stroud: Amberley Publishing, 2014)

Mount, T., *Everyday Life in Medieval London* (Stroud: Amberley Publishing, 2014)

Mount, T., *Richard III – King of Controversy* (Echoes from History, 2013)

Orme, N. (trans.), *Table Manners for Children 1476,* John Lydgate (London: Wynkyn de Worde Society, 1990)

Pegg, S., *The Forme of Cury* (Forgotten Books, 2008)

Prestwich, M. et al. (eds), *Thirteenth-Century England VII: Proceedings of the Durham Conference, 1997* (Boydell Press, 1999)

Ravi, Z. and R. Smith, (eds), *Medieval Society and the Manor Court* (Oxford: Clarendon Press, 1996)

Rickert, E., C. C. Olson and M. M. Crow, (eds), *Chaucer's World* (Oxford University Press, 1948).

Sass, L. J., *To the King's Taste – Richard II's book of feasts and recipes* (Metropolitan Museum of Art, 1975)

Scott, A. F., *Everyone a Witness – The Plantagenet Age* (Book Club Edition, 1975)

Stapleton, T. (ed.), *The Plumpton Correspondence,* (Glos: Alan Sutton, 1990)

Stoyan, R., *Atlas of Great Comets* (Cambridge: University Press, 2015)

Thrupp, S. L., *The Merchant Class of Medieval London, 1300–1500* (Michigan: University Press, 1962)

Virgoe, R. (ed.), *The Illustrated Letters of the Paston Family* (London, Macmillan, 1989)

LIST OF ILLUSTRATIONS

13. May – Henry II and Eleanor of Aquitaine holding court, *Aliénor et Henri II écoutent, l'histoire de Lancelot du Lac*; c. 1100s. (Courtesy of Bib Paris, ms. fr. 123 fol. 229)

14. 23 May – Manorial Records. (Courtesy Warks County Records Office)

15. 14 June – Peasants' revolt, Blackheath. (Courtesy of British Library, Royal 18 E I f. 165v)

16. 1 June – 'Sumer is icumen in'; c. 1275–1300, England. (Courtesy of British Library, Harley 978 f. 11v)

17. 29 June – Edward IV coronation roll. (Courtesy of Philadelphia Free Library)

18. 15 June – Death of Wat Tyler. (Courtesy of British Library, Royal 18 E I f. 175)

19. 8 July – License to Export to Calais, Master of the London Wavrin; England. (Courtesy of British Library Royal 15 E IV f. 24v)

20. 16 July – Coronation of Richard II. (Courtesy of British Library, Royal 20 C VII f. 192v)

21. 16 July 16 – Fourteenth-century sugar cane factory; Cyprus (© G. Horne)

22. 25 July – St Christopher, Westminster psalter. (Courtesy of British Library, Royal 2 A XXII)

23. August – Harvesting, Calendar Page. (Courtesy of British Library, Add 21114 f. 4v)

24. August – Threshing, Calendar Page; c. 1500, Bruges. (Courtesy of British Library, King's 9 ff. 9v-10)

25. September – Calendar Page, *(the Golf Book) Book of Hours, Use of Rome*; workshop of Simon Bening, c. 1540, Bruges. (Courtesy of British Library, Add 24098, f20v)

26. 4 September – Fifteenth-century will from prerogative court Canterbury.

27. 19 October – King John poisoned. (Courtesy of British Library, Cotton Vitellius A XIII, f. 5v)

28. 28 October – Coronation of Kings Henry II, Richard I, John and Henry II, inset centre shows Henry the Young King; Matthew Paris, *Chronica Majora*. (Courtesy of British Library, Royal C vii f. 9r)

29. 11 November – Martinmas. (Courtesy of British Library, Add 21114 f. 6)

INDEX